Step by Step

Microsoft
Outlook
Version 2002
 Microsoft® Office XP Application

Kristen Crupi

PUBLISHED BY
Microsoft Press
A Division of Microsoft Corporation
One Microsoft Way
Redmond, Washington 98052-6399

Library of Congress Cataloging-in-Publication Data
Microsoft Outlook Version 2002 Step by Step / Kristen Crupi
        p. cm.
    Includes index.
    ISBN 0-7356-1298-6
    1. Microsoft Outlook.   2. Time management--Computer programs.   3. Personal
information management--Computer programs.   I. Perspection, Inc.

    HD69.T54 M62   2001
    005.369--dc21   2001030475

Printed and bound in the United States of America.

1 2 3 4 5 6 7 8 9   QWT   6 5 4 3 2 1

Distributed in Canada by Penguin Books Canada Limited.

A CIP catalogue record for this book is available from the British Library.

Microsoft Press books are available through booksellers and distributors worldwide. For further information about international editions, contact your local Microsoft Corporation office or contact Microsoft Press International directly at fax (425) 936-7329. Visit our Web site at mspress.microsoft.com. Send comments to *mspinput@microsoft.com*.

Acquisitions Editor: Kong Cheung
Project Editor: Jenny Moss Benson

Body Part No. X08-06217

Contents

1   Working with E-mail   1

2   Managing E-mail Messages   28

Contents

12 Sending Newsgroup and Instant Messages 256

13 Configuring and Customizing Outlook 270

Quick Reference 295

Glossary 315
Index 321

What's New in Microsoft Outlook 2002

You'll notice some changes as soon as you start Microsoft Outlook 2002. The toolbars and menu bar have a new look, but the features that are new or greatly improved in this version of Outlook go beyond just changes in appearance. Some changes won't be apparent to you until you start using the program.

New feature
new for
OfficeXP

To help you quickly identify features that are new or greatly enhanced with this version, this book uses the **new** icon in the margin whenever those features are discussed or shown. If you want to learn about only the new features of the program, you can skim through the book, completing only those topics that show the **new** icon.

The following table lists the new features that you might be interested in, as well as the chapters in which those features are discussed.

To learn how to	Using this new feature	See
Access Internet e-mail from within Outlook	Outlook Hotmail support	Chapter 1, page 2
Follow hyperlinks, open attachments, and respond to meeting requests without opening the message	Enhanced preview pane	Chapter 1, page 6
Edit e-mail messages using Microsoft Word	Word as the default e-mail editor	Chapter 1, page 11
Address e-mail messages	AutoComplete addressing	Chapter 1, page 12
Display a contact's name instead of his or her e-mail address in the To field of messages to that contact	Friendly names instead of e-mail addresses	Chapter 1, page 15
Choose from which account an e-mail message is sent	Accounts button	Chapter 1, page 25
Search for messages, appointments, or tasks	Find	Chapter 2, page 41
Specify archive settings for all folders	Global AutoArchive settings	Chapter 2, page 45
Delete, move, or archive files	Mailbox Cleanup	Chapter 2, page 48
Change between different e-mail formats	Word as the default e-mail editor	Chapter 3, page 54
Color-code your Calendar	Calendar coloring	Chapter 4, page 93

(continued)

(continued)

To learn how to	Using this new feature	See
Propose a new time in response to a meeting request	Propose new time	Chapter 5, page 118
Save multiple group calendars	Group schedules	Chapter 5, page 128
Share free/busy information on the Internet	Outlook free/busy sharing	Chapter 5, page 130; Chapter 11, page 244
Use Outlook in offline mode	Synchronization improvements	Chapter 11, page 247
Know if the sender of an e-mail message is online at the time you receive that message	MSN Messenger integration	Chapter 12, page 266

For more information about the Outlook product, see *www.microsoft.com/Outlook.*

Getting Help

Every effort has been made to ensure the accuracy of this book and the contents of its CD-ROM. If you do run into problems, please contact the appropriate source for help and assistance.

Getting Help with This Book and Its CD-ROM

If your question or issue concerns the content of this book or its companion CD-ROM, please first search the online Microsoft Knowledge Base, which provides support information for known errors in or corrections to this book, at the following Web site:

http://mspress.microsoft.com/support/search.htm

If you do not find your answer at the online Knowledge Base, send your comments or questions to Microsoft Press Technical Support at:

mspinput@microsoft.com

Getting Help with Microsoft Outlook 2002

If your question is about a Microsoft software product, including Outlook 2002, and not about the content of this Microsoft Press book, please search the Microsoft Knowledge Base at:

http://support.microsoft.com/directory

In the United States, Microsoft software product support issues not covered by the Microsoft Knowledge Base are addressed by Microsoft Product Support Services. The Microsoft software support options available from Microsoft Product Support Services are listed at:

http://support.microsoft.com/directory

Outside the United States, for support information specific to your location, please refer to the Worldwide Support menu on the Microsoft Product Support Services Web site for the site specific to your country:

http://support.microsoft.com/directory

Using the Book's CD-ROM

The CD-ROM inside the back cover of this book contains all the practice files you'll use as you work through the exercises in this book. By using practice files, you won't waste time creating sample content with which to experiment—instead, you can jump right in and concentrate on learning how to use Microsoft Outlook 2002.

Important

The CD-ROM for this book does not contain the Outlook 2002 software. You should purchase and install the program before using this book.

Minimum System Requirements

To use this book, your computer should meet the following requirements:

Computer/Processor

Computer with a Pentium 133-megahertz (MHz) or higher processor

Memory

RAM requirements depend on the operating system used.

- Microsoft Windows 98, or Windows 98 Second Edition

    24 MB of RAM plus an additional 8 MB of RAM for each Microsoft Office program (such as Microsoft Word) running simultaneously

- Microsoft Windows Millennium Edition (Windows Me), or Microsoft Windows NT

    32 MB of RAM plus an additional 8 MB of RAM for each Office program (such as Microsoft Word) running simultaneously

- Microsoft Windows 2000 Professional

    64 MB of RAM plus an additional 8 MB of RAM for each Office program (such as Microsoft Word) running simultaneously

Hard Disk

Hard disk space requirements will vary depending on configuration; custom installation choices may require more or less hard disk space.

- 245 MB of available hard disk space with 115 MB on the hard disk where the operating system is installed. (Users without Windows 2000, Windows Me, or Office 2000 Service Release 1 require an extra 50 MB of hard disk space for System Files Update.)

- An additional 2 MB of hard disk space is required for installing the practice files.

Operating System

Windows 98, Windows 98 Second Edition, Windows Me, Windows NT 4.0 with Service Pack 6 or later, or Windows 2000 or later. (On systems running Windows NT 4.0 with Service Pack 6, the version of Microsoft Internet Explorer must be upgraded to at least version 4.01 with Service Pack 1.)

Important

> The exercises in the book were created on a computer running Windows 98. Other operating systems might display different results than those shown in this book.

Drive

CD-ROM drive

Display

Super VGA (800 × 600) or higher-resolution monitor with 256 colors

Peripherals

Microsoft Mouse, Microsoft IntelliMouse, or compatible pointing device

Applications

Microsoft Outlook 2002
Microsoft Word 2002
Microsoft Excel 2002

Installing the Practice Files

You need to install the practice files on your hard disk before you use them in the chapters' exercises. Follow these steps to prepare the CD-ROM's files for your use:

1   Insert the CD-ROM into the CD-ROM drive of your computer.

A menu screen appears.

Important

> If the menu screen does not appear, start Windows Explorer. In the left pane, locate the icon for your CD-ROM drive, and click this icon. In the right pane, double-click the file named *StartCd*.

2   Click **Install Practice Files**.

3   Click **OK** in the initial message box.

4   If you want to install the practice files to a location other than the default folder (*C:\SBS\Outlook*), click the **Change Folder** button, select the new drive and path, and then click **OK**.

Important

If you install the practice files to a location other than the default folder, the file location listed in some of the book's exercises will be incorrect.

5   Click the **Continue** button to install the selected practice files.

6   After the practice files have been installed, click **OK**.

Within the installation folder are subfolders for each chapter in the book that requires practice files.

7   Remove the CD-ROM from the CD-ROM drive, and return it to its envelope.

Making the Practice Files Available to Outlook

Throughout this book, you will be working with e-mail messages, calendar appointments, and contact and task information. To follow along with the exercises in this book, you need to copy the installed practice files from your hard disk to the correct Outlook folders.

Important

Before you can copy the files, you first need to set up Outlook on your computer. (The process for setting up Outlook is described in "Starting Outlook for the First Time" in Chapter 1 of this book.)

Microsoft Outlook

1   Start Outlook by double-clicking its icon on the desktop.

2   On the **Start** menu, point to **Programs** and then click **Windows Explorer** to open Windows Explorer. If you're using Windows 2000, on the **Start** menu, point to **Programs**, point to **Accessories**, and then click **Windows Explorer**.

3   If the Explorer window obscures the bar on the left side of the Outlook window, drag the Explorer window to the right side of the screen so that the **Inbox** icon on the **Outlook Bar** is visible.

4   In the left pane of the Explorer window, browse to the Practice Files subfolder of the SBS\Outlook folder, which is probably located on drive C.

The contents of the folder are displayed in the right pane.

Inbox

5   Drag the following messages from SBS\Outlook\PracticeFiles to the **Inbox** icon on the **Outlook Bar**: NextShow, OrderStatus, NewSupplier, ReNextShow, Schedule, Kick-off, Status, and TeamMeet.

The items are added to your Inbox.

Calendar

6   Drag the following Calendar items from SBS\Outlook\PracticeFiles to the **Calendar** icon on the **Outlook Bar**: DayCareVisit and TeamMeeting.

The items are added to your Calendar.

Tasks

7 Drag the following task item to the **Task** icon on the **Outlook Bar**: Invoices.

The item is added to your Tasks folder.

Notes

8 Drag the following note to the **Notes** icon on the **Outlook Bar:** PhoneCall.

The note is added to your Notes folder.

Journal

9 On the **Outlook Bar**, click **My Shortcuts**, and then drag the following Journal item to the **Journal** icon on the **Outlook Bar**: Package.

The item is added to your Journal.

Close

10 On the **Outlook Bar**, click **Outlook Shortcuts**, and then close Windows Explorer by clicking its **Close** button.

If you have upgraded to Outlook 2002 from an earlier version of the program, the practice files will now be mixed with your real messages, appointments, contacts, and tasks.

Using the Practice Files

Each chapter's introduction lists the folders where you will find the files that are needed for that chapter. Each topic in the chapter explains how and when to use any practice files. The majority of the files deal with a fictitious garden and plant store called The Garden Company. However, the type of file varies from topic to topic, so be sure to use the files specified for the particular topic you are working on. The file or files that you'll need are indicated in the margin at the beginning of the procedure above the CD icon, like this:

GardenCo

The following table lists the practice files you must have to complete each chapter:

Chapter	Files	Location
Chapter 1: Working with E-mail Messages	NextShow	SBS\Outlook\PracticeFiles
	Attachment.doc	SBS\Outlook\Attach
Chapter 2: Managing E-mail Messages	OrderStatus	SBS\Outlook\PracticeFiles
	New Supplier	SBS\Outlook\PracticeFiles
	NextShow	SBS\Outlook\PracticeFiles
	ReNextShow	SBS\Outlook\PracticeFiles
	Schedule	SBS\Outlook\PracticeFiles

Chapter	Files	Location
Chapter 3: Customizing and Organizing E-mail Messages	OrderStatus	SBS\Outlook\PracticeFiles
	NextShow	SBS\Outlook\PracticeFiles
	ReNextShow	SBS\Outlook\PracticeFiles
	Schedule	SBS\Outlook\PracticeFiles
	Travel.pst	SBS\Outlook\Address
	GardenCo.pab	SBS\Outlook\Personal
Chapter 4: Managing Your Calendar	DayCareVisit	SBS\Outlook\PracticeFiles
	TeamMeeting	SBS\Outlook\PracticeFiles
Chapter 5: Scheduling and Managing Meetings	Kickoff	SBS\Outlook\PracticeFiles
	Status	SBS\Outlook\PracticeFiles
	TeamMeet	SBS\Outlook\PracticeFiles
	CatherineT	SBS\Outlook\Contacts
	KimY	SBS\Outlook\Contacts
	HomeShow	SBS\Outlook\Meeting
Chapter 6: Creating and Organizing a List of Contacts	CatherineT	SBS\Outlook\PracticeFiles
	KimY	SBS\Outlook\Contacts
	CatherineT	SBS\Outlook\Contacts
	KimY	SBS\Outlook\Organize
	BrittaS	SBS\Outlook\Organize
	PeterP	SBS\Outlook\Organize
	Package	SBS\Outlook\Organize
	CatherineT	SBS\Outlook\Tracking
	CatherineT	SBS\Outlook\Sending
	KimY	SBS\Outlook\Sending
	CatherineT	SBS\Outlook\Printing
	BrittaS	SBS\Outlook\Printing
Chapter 7: Creating and Organizing Tasks	Invoices	SBS\Outlook\PracticeFiles
	Timesheet	SBS\Outlook\Tasks
	Brochures	SBS\Outlook\Tasks
	TaskPayments	SBS\Outlook\Tasks
	TaskLayout	SBS\Outlook\Tasks
Chapter 8: Creating and Organizing Notes	PhoneCall	SBS\Outlook\PracticeFiles
	Agenda	SBS\Outlook\Notes
Chapter 9: Using the Journal	CatherineT	SBS\Outlook\Journal
	KimY	SBS\Outlook\Journal
	OfferLetter.doc	SBS\Outlook\Journal
	JournalSent	SBS\Outlook\Journal
	RequestStatus	SBS\Outlook\Journal
Chapter 10: Using Outlook with Other Programs	SeanC.vcf	SBS\Outlook\Import
	Calendar.xls	SBS\Outlook\Import
	Contacts.pst	SBS\Outlook\Import
	KimY	SBS\Outlook\OutlookData
	ProfLetter.doc	SBS\Outlook\FormLetter

(continued)

Chapter	Files	Location
Chapter 11: Sharing Information and Working Offline	NewSupplier OrderStatus Schedule NextShow To Do.pst	SBS\Outlook\Sharing SBS\Outlook\Sharing SBS\Outlook\Sharing SBS\Outlook\Sharing SBS\Outlook\Offline
Chapter 12: Sending Newsgroup and Instant Messages	NONE	
Chapter 13: Configuring and Customizing Outlook	NONE	

Uninstalling the Practice Files

After you finish working through this book, you should uninstall the practice files to free up hard disk space.

1   On the Windows taskbar, click the **Start** button, point to **Settings**, and then click **Control Panel**.

2   Double-click the **Add/Remove Programs** icon.

3   Click **Microsoft Outlook 2002 SBS Files**, and click **Add/Remove**. (If you're using Windows 2000 Professional, click the **Remove** or **Change/Remove** button.)

4   Click **Yes** when the confirmation dialog box appears.

If you've worked through the Outlook exercises, you've probably created some additional files (files with .msg, .cal, and .pst extensions, for example) that will not be deleted by the uninstall procedure shown above. To help you find and delete these files, you can follow these additional, optional steps:

1   On the **Tools** menu on Outlook's toolbar, click **Advanced Find**.

2   In the **Look for** list, click **Any type of Outlook item**, and when a message tells you that your search will be cleared, click **OK**.

3   Click the **More Choices** tab, and click the **Categories** button.

4   In the **Available categories** list, select the **Practice Files** check box, and click **OK**.

5   Click **Find Now**.

Outlook searches all your Outlook folders for items assigned to the **Practice Files** category.

6   When the search is complete, select all the found items, and on the **Edit** menu, click **Delete**.

7 If prompted to send any meeting responses, select the **Delete without sending a response** option, and click **OK**.

The items remain in the list but are moved to the Deleted Items folder.

8 Delete the following items, which you created during this book's exercises:

Where	Files
Inbox	Approve invoice payments FW: Catherine Turner FW: Kim Yoshida New Supplier Order Status? Project Kick-off Quarterly Status Review brochure layout Sending and Receiving Test This is a message of high importance This is a message of low importance Today's Schedule Travel Schedule Upcoming Show FW: Upcoming Show Re: Upcoming Show *Any undeliverable messages or messages sent to yourself*
Drafts	This is a message of low importance
Calendar	Budget Meeting (the day and week after you completed the exercise and 6/18/02) Collaborate on Sales Report (the business day after you completed the exercise or 6/20/02) Day Care Visit (6/18/02) Plan for Home Show Exhibition (6/18/02) Out for Holidays (12/23/02) Quarterly Status (6/17/02) Project Kick-off (6/18/02) Team Meeting (6/18/02)
Tasks	Approve invoice payments Order new brochures Process supply invoices Review brochure layout Submit report Submit timesheet

(continued)

(continued)

Where	Files
Contacts	Britta Simon
	Catherine Turner
	Garden Co
	Kim Yoshida
	Mike Galos
	Peter Porzuczek
	Team
	Sean Chai
Notes	Meeting Agenda
Folders in the Folder List	MikeG
	To Do
	Travel
My Documents (folder on hard disk)	Order Status.htm
	Travel Schedule.txt
Address Books	Garden Co (Personal Address Book)
	To delete this file, on the **Tools** menu, click **E-mail Accounts**, select **View or change existing directories or address books**, click **Next**, click **GardenCo**, and then click **Remove**.
Journal	Journal Test, on the date you completed the exercise
	Request Status Report, on the date you completed the exercise.

Deleted Items **9** If you want to empty your Deleted Items folder, on the **Outlook Bar**, right-click the **Deleted Items** icon, and click **Empty Deleted Items Folder** on the short-cut menu. When prompted to confirm that you want to permanently delete the items, click **Yes**.

Important

If you need additional help installing or uninstalling the practice files, please see the "Getting Help" section earlier in this book.

Conventions and Features

You can save time when you use this book by understanding how the *Step by Step* series shows special instructions, keys to press, buttons to click, and so on.

Convention	Meaning
1 **2**	Numbered steps guide you through hands-on exercises in each topic.
(CD icon)	This icon at the beginning of a chapter indicates the files that the lesson will use.
FileName (CD icon)	At the beginning of an exercise, this icon often appears, preceded by a list of the practice files required to complete the exercise.
OL2002-3-5 (MOUS icon)	This icon indicates a section that covers a Microsoft Office User Specialist (MOUS) exam objective. The specific MOUS objective number is listed above the icon. Multiple objectives may be covered in each exercise.
new for **Office**XP	This icon indicates a new or greatly improved feature in this version of Microsoft Outlook.
Tip	This section provides useful background information or a helpful hint or shortcut that makes working through a task easier.
Important	This section points out information that you need to know to complete the procedure.
Troubleshooting	This section shows you how to fix a common problem.
Save (button icon)	When a button is referenced in a topic, a picture of the button appears in the margin area, preceded by the name of the button.
Alt + Tab	A plus sign (+) between two key names means that you must press those keys at the same time. For example, "Press Alt + Tab" means that you hold down the Alt key while you press Tab.
Black boldface type	Program features that you click are shown in black boldface type.
Blue boldface type	Terms explained in the glossary are shown in blue boldface type.
Red boldface type	Text that you are supposed to type appears in red boldface type in the procedures.
Italic type	Folder paths, URLs, and emphasized words appear in italic type.

MOUS Objectives

Each Microsoft Office User Specialist (MOUS) certification level (core and expert) has a set of objectives. To prepare for the MOUS certification exam, you should confirm that you can meet its respective objectives.

This book will prepare you fully for the MOUS exam at either the core or the expert level because it addresses all the objectives for both exams. Throughout this book, topics that pertain to MOUS objectives are identified with the MOUS logo and objective number in the margin, like this:

OL2002-3-5

Multiple MOUS objectives may be covered within one topic.

Core Microsoft Outlook 2002 MOUS Objectives

Objective	Skill	On Page(s)
OL2002-1	**Creating and Viewing Messages**	
OL2002-1-1	Display and print messages	4, 26
OL2002-1-2	Compose and send messages to corporate/workgroup and Internet addresses	10, 13, 23
OL2002-1-3	Insert signatures and attachments	18, 20
OL2002-1-4	Customize views	29
OL2002-2	**Scheduling**	
OL2002-2-1	Add appointments, meetings, and events to the Outlook Calendar	83, 109
OL2002-2-2	Apply conditional formats to the Outlook Calendar	93
OL2002-2-3	Respond to meeting requests	116
OL2002-2-4	Use categories to manage appointments	89
OL2002-2-5	Print Calendars	103
OL2002-3	**Managing Messages**	
OL2002-3-1	Move messages between folders	35
OL2002-3-2	Search for messages	41

(continued)

Expert Microsoft Outlook 2002 MOUS Objectives

Taking a MOUS Exam

As desktop computing technology advances, more employers rely on the objectivity and consistency of technology certification when screening, hiring, and training employees to ensure the competence of these professionals. As an employee, you can use technology certification to prove that you meet the standards set by your current or potential employer. The Microsoft Office User Specialist (MOUS) program is the only Microsoft-approved certification program designed to assist employees in validating their competence using Microsoft Office applications.

About the MOUS Program

A Microsoft Office User Specialist is an individual who has certified his or her skills in one or more of the Microsoft Office desktop applications of Microsoft Word, Microsoft Excel, Microsoft PowerPoint, Microsoft Outlook, Microsoft Access, Microsoft FrontPage, or Microsoft Project. The Microsoft Office User Specialist Program typically offers certification exams at the "core" and "expert" skill levels. (The availability of Microsoft Office User Specialist certification exams varies by application, application version, and language. Visit *http://www.mous.net* for exam availability.) The Microsoft Office User Specialist Program is the only Microsoft-approved program in the world for certifying proficiency in Microsoft Office desktop applications and Microsoft Project. This certification can be a valuable asset in any job search or career advancement.

What Does This Logo Mean?

APPROVED COURSEWARE

It means this courseware has been approved by the Microsoft Office User Specialist Program to be among the finest available for learning Outlook 2002. It also means that upon completion of this courseware, you may be prepared to become a Microsoft Office User Specialist.

Selecting a MOUS Certification Level

In selecting the MOUS certification(s) level that you would like to pursue, you should assess the following:

■ The Office application and version(s) of the application with which you are familiar

■ The length of time you have used the application

■ Whether you have had formal or informal training

Candidates for the core-level MOUS certification exams are expected to successfully complete a wide range of standard business tasks, such as formatting a document. Successful candidates generally have six or more months of experience with the application, including either formal instructor-led training with a MOUS Authorized Instructor or self-study using MOUS-approved books, guides, or interactive computer-based materials.

Candidates for expert-level certification, by comparison, are expected to complete more complex business-oriented assignments utilizing the application's advanced functionality, such as importing data and recording macros. Successful candidates generally have two or more years of experience with the application, again including formal instructor-led training with a MOUS Authorized Instructor or self-study using MOUS-approved materials.

MOUS Exam Objectives

Every MOUS certification exam is developed from a list of exam objectives, which are derived from studies of how the Office application is actually used in the workplace. Because these objectives dictate the scope of each exam, they provide you with critical information on how to prepare for MOUS certification.

Tip

See the previous section, "MOUS Objectives," for a complete list of objectives for Outlook.

MOUS Approved Courseware, including Microsoft Press's Step by Step series, is reviewed and approved on the basis of its coverage of the MOUS exam objectives.

The Exam Experience

The MOUS certification exams are unique in that they are performance-based examinations that allow you to interact with a "live" version of the Office application as you complete a series of assigned tasks. All the standard menus, toolbars, and keyboard shortcuts are available—even the Help menu. MOUS exams for Office XP applications consist of 25 to 35 questions, each of which requires you to complete one or more tasks using the Office application for which you are seeking certification. For example:

Prepare the document for publication as a Web page by completing the following three tasks:

1   Convert the memo to a Web page.
2   Title the page **Revised Company Policy**.
3   Name the memo **Policy Memo.htm**.

The duration of MOUS exams ranges from 45 to 60 minutes, depending on the application. Passing percentages range from 70 to 80 percent correct.

The Exam Interface and Controls

After you fill out a series of information screens, the testing software starts the exam and the respective Office application. You will see the exam interface and controls, including the test question, in the dialog box in the lower right corner of the screen.

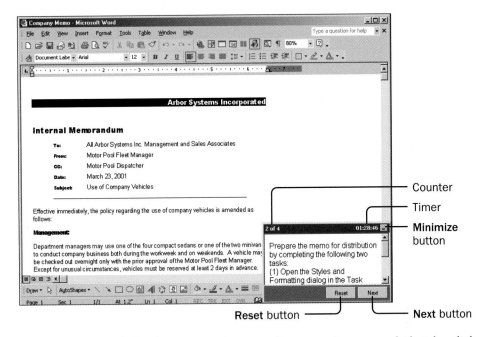

- If the exam dialog box gets in the way of your work, you can hide it by clicking the **Minimize** button in the upper right corner, or you can drag it to another position on the screen.

- The timer starts when the first question appears on your screen and displays the remaining exam time. If the timer and the counter are distracting, click the timer to remove the display.

Important

> The timer will not count the time required for the exam to be loaded between questions. It keeps track only of the time you spend answering questions.

- The counter tracks how many questions you have completed and how many remain.

- The **Reset** button allows you to restart work on a question if you think you have made an error. The **Reset** button will *not* restart the entire exam or extend the exam time limit.

- When you complete a question, click the **Next** button to move to the next question.

Important

It is not possible to move back to a previous question on the exam.

Test-Taking Tips

- Follow all instructions provided in each question completely and accurately.

- Enter requested information as it appears in the instructions but without duplicating the formatting. For example, all text and values that you will be asked to enter will appear in the instructions as **bold** and **underlined**; however, you should enter the information without applying this formatting unless you are specifically instructed to do otherwise.

- Close all dialog boxes before proceeding to the next exam question unless you are specifically instructed otherwise.

- There is no need to save your work before moving on to the next question unless you are specifically instructed to do so.

- Do not cut and paste information from the exam interface into the application.

- For questions that ask you to print a document, spreadsheet, chart, report, slide, and so forth, nothing will actually be printed.

- Responses are scored based on the result of your work, not the method you use to achieve that result (unless a specific method is explicitly required), and not the time you take to complete the question. Extra keystrokes or mouse clicks do not count against your score.

- If your computer becomes unstable during the exam (for example, if the application's toolbars or the mouse no longer functions) or if a power outage occurs, contact a testing center administrator immediately. The administrator will then restart the computer, and the exam will return to the point before the interruption occurred.

Certification

At the conclusion of the exam, you will receive a score report, which you can print with the assistance of the testing center administrator. If your score meets or exceeds the minimum required score, you will also be mailed a printed certificate within approximately 14 days.

For More Information

To learn more about becoming a Microsoft Office User Specialist, visit *http://www.mous.net*.

To purchase a Microsoft Office User Specialist certification exam, visit *http://www.DesktopIQ.com*.

To learn about other Microsoft Office User Specialist approved courseware from Microsoft Press, visit *http://mspress.microsoft.com/certification/mous*.

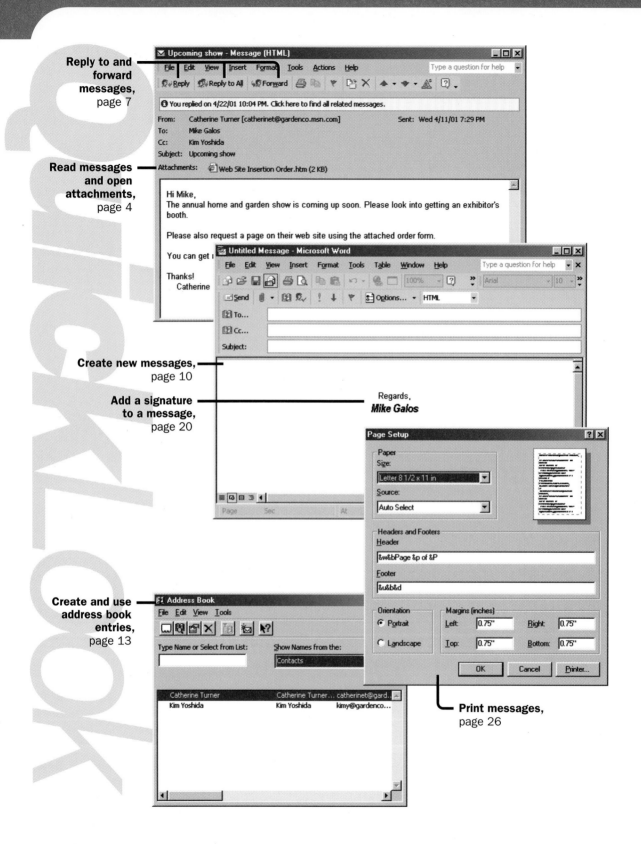

Reply to and forward messages, page 7

Read messages and open attachments, page 4

Create new messages, page 10

Add a signature to a message, page 20

Create and use address book entries, page 13

Print messages, page 26

Chapter 1
Working with E-mail

After completing this chapter, you will be able to:

✔ **Read messages and open attachments**
✔ **Reply to and forward messages**
✔ **Create new messages and attach files and signatures**
✔ **Create and use address book entries**
✔ **Print messages**

Microsoft Outlook 2002 is a desktop communications program that helps you manage your time and information more effectively and enables you to share information and collaborate with others more easily.

Electronic mail, or **e-mail**, is an essential form of communication in today's workplace. Outlook gives you all the tools you need to use e-mail effectively and to manage your electronic messages. With Outlook, you can:

■ Send and receive e-mail messages.

■ Attach files to your messages.

■ Create and manage an address book.

■ Organize and archive your messages.

■ Personalize your messages.

This chapter first discusses the ways Outlook can be set up and what to expect when you first start the program. Then you'll learn how to read and write messages, send and receive messages, attach files to messages, and create and use an address book.

This chapter uses the practice files that you installed from this book's CD-ROM onto your hard disk and copied into Outlook. For details about installing and copying the practice files, see "Using the Book's CD-ROM" at the beginning of this book.

Starting Outlook for the First Time

Outlook 2002 supports e-mail accounts that work with a computer running Microsoft Exchange Server or a computer set up as an Internet mail server. This section discusses these two types of accounts and explains what you might expect to see the first time you start Outlook.

If you are connected to a **local area network (LAN)** that includes a computer running **Microsoft Exchange Server**, you send and receive e-mail both internally (within your organization) and externally (over the Internet) using that server. Your network or system administrator will supply the information you need to set up an Exchange e-mail account.

If you are working on a stand-alone computer or on a network that does not have its own mail server, using Internet mail requires that you have an e-mail account with an **Internet service provider (ISP)**. You connect to the ISP using a modem and a phone line, DSL line, cable, or through a LAN.

- If you are using a modem, you can manually establish a connection when you need it, or you can set up dial-up networking to automatically connect whenever you start Outlook. Your ISP can provide the phone number, modem settings, and any other special information you need for both types of connection.

- If you are connected to a LAN, it must be configured to provide access to your ISP from your computer. Your network or system administrator can provide you with the appropriate information to gain access to Internet mail via the LAN.

- Regardless of how you connect to your ISP, in order to send and receive Internet mail, you will need to know the names of your incoming and outgoing e-mail servers, your account name, and your password.

Different Types of Internet Mail Accounts

Microsoft Outlook 2002 supports more types of Internet e-mail accounts than ever—POP3, IMAP, and HTTP (including Hotmail).

- **Post Office Protocol 3 (POP3)** is a very common type of e-mail account provided by ISPs. With a POP3 account, you connect to an e-mail server and download your messages to your local computer.

- **Internet Message Access Protocol (IMAP)** is similar to POP3 except that your messages are stored on the e-mail server. You connect to the server to read message headers and select which messages you want to download to your local computer.

Hotmail
support
new for
OfficeXP

- **Hypertext Transfer Protocol (HTTP)** is used whenever you access Web pages from the Internet. When HTTP is used as an e-mail protocol, messages are stored, retrieved, and displayed as individual Web pages. Hotmail is an example of an HTTP e-mail account.

When you start Outlook for the first time, what you see depends on whether you have upgraded Outlook or are using it on this computer for the first time.

Upgrading to Outlook 2002

If you have used a previous version of Outlook on your computer, you already have an Outlook **profile**. This profile is a collection of all the data necessary to access one or more e-mail accounts and address books. In this case, Outlook 2002 picks up your existing profile settings, and you don't have to enter them again to start using the new version of Outlook.

Using Outlook for the First Time

If this is the first time you have used Outlook on this computer, you will be asked to create a profile. To complete this step, you will need specific information about your e-mail account, including your account name, your password, and the names of the incoming and outgoing e-mail servers that handle your account. Your system administrator or ISP can provide you with this information.

Here are the general steps for setting up Outlook:

Microsoft
Outlook

1 On the desktop, double-click the **Microsoft Outlook** icon.

When Outlook starts, you see the **New Profile** dialog box.

2 Type a name for your profile (typically your full name), and click **OK**.

The **E-mail Accounts** dialog box appears.

3 Click **Add a new e-mail account**, and then click **Next**.

The **Server Type** dialog box appears.

4 Select the type of your e-mail account, and click **Next**.

An account settings dialog box appears. The content of this dialog box is determined by the type of e-mail account you selected in the **Server Type** dialog box.

5 From here on, you will need to enter the information and follow the instructions provided by your system administrator or ISP.

When you complete the process, the Outlook window appears.

Important

If you upgraded to Outlook 2002 from an earlier version, any custom settings you made for your old version of the program carry over to the new version. As a result, as you work your way through the exercises in this book, some of the instructions might not work quite the same way for you, and your screen might not look the same as the book's graphics. The instructions and graphics are based on a default installation of Outlook on a networked computer with an Exchange e-mail account. If you are not working on a network or you have changed the default settings, don't worry. You will still be able to follow along with the exercises, but you might occasionally have to reverse a setting or skip a step. (For example, if AutoPreview is already active on your screen, you would skip the step to turn on AutoPreview.)

Reading Messages and Opening Attachments

OL2002-1-1

When you start Outlook, any new messages are moved from your e-mail server, or **downloaded**, to your Inbox. With Outlook, you can view and read your messages in several ways:

■ You can scan for your most important messages by using AutoPreview, which displays the first few lines of messages in your Inbox.

■ You can read a message without opening it by looking at the preview pane.

■ You can open the message in its own window for easier reading.

E-mail messages can contain many types of files as attachments. For example, a colleague might send a Microsoft Word document to you by attaching it to an e-mail message. You can open these files from the preview pane or from an open message.

For the exercises in this book, you'll act as Mike Galos, the administrative assistant for The Garden Company, a plant and garden accessories store. The practice files used in this book will reflect this assumed identity. In this exercise, you will preview a message, open a message, and open an attachment.

Important

NextShow

If you haven't installed and copied the practice files for this book, please do so now. For details about installing the practice files on your hard disk and copying them into Outlook, see "Using the Book's CD-ROM" at the beginning of this book. If you want to complete only this exercise, follow the instructions in the "Using the Book's CD-ROM" section to copy just the practice file shown above the CD icon in the margin.

Inbox

1 If your Outlook window shows a summary of the appointments, tasks, and messages you need to attend to today, click the **Inbox** icon on the **Outlook Bar** on the left side of the window. Then if necessary, maximize the window.

You now see the **Inbox**, where you store and manage your e-mail messages.

Toolbar —

Outlook Bar

Inbox icon —

Inbox —

Preview pane —

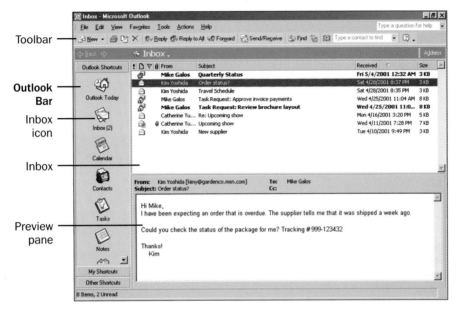

2 Turn on AutoPreview by clicking **AutoPreview** on the **View** menu.

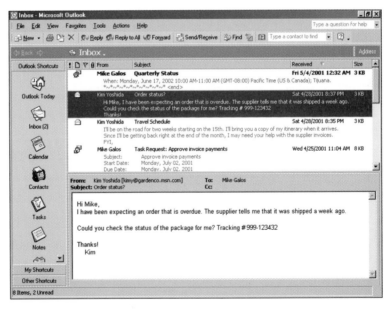

You can now see up to three lines of each of the messages in your Inbox.

3 If necessary, scroll up or down in your Inbox to locate the **Upcoming show** message from Catherine Turner, the owner of The Garden Company. Then click the message to display it in the preview pane.

Attached file ——

Message header

Scroll bar

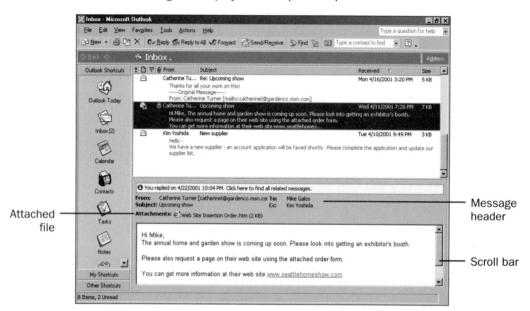

Enhanced
preview pane
new for
OfficeXP

Using the scroll bar in the preview pane, you can see the full content of the message. Note that the preview pane shows the full **message header** (the information that appears at the top of the e-mail message, including the sender, recipient, and date) and the names of any attached files.

4 To open the attachment, double-click **Web Site Insertion Order.htm**.

5 If you see a message warning you about opening attachments, select the **Open it** option, and then click **OK**.

The Web Site Insertion Order form appears in your Web browser.

6 Return to the Inbox by clicking its name on the Windows taskbar.

7 Close the preview pane by clicking **Preview Pane** on the **View** menu.

If your Inbox contains many messages, you can now see more of them at a glance.

8 Open the **Upcoming show** message by double-clicking it in the Inbox.

The message appears in its own Message window.

Message header

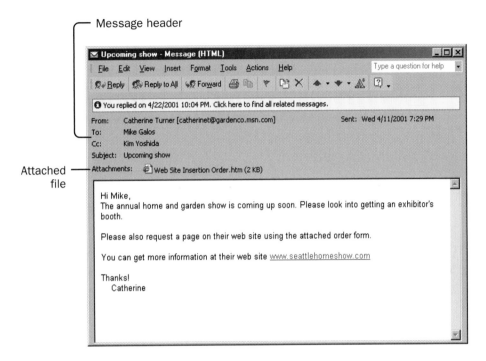

Attached file

Note the message header and the names of any attached files at the top.

Tip

Maximize & Restore

Don't worry if your window is not the same size as this one. As with other windows, you can size Outlook windows to suit the way you work by using the **Maximize** and **Restore** buttons or by dragging the window's frame.

Close

9 Click the **Close** button to close the Message window.

Responding to Messages

OL2002-1-2

You can respond to messages in several ways. You can reply only to the person who sent the message, or you can reply to the person who sent the message and all the people whose addresses were on the original **To** and **Cc** lines. Whether you reply to only the sender or to everyone, your reply will not include any files that were attached to the original message.

You can forward a message you have received to anyone, not just the person who originally sent the message or any of the other recipients. A forwarded message will include any files that were attached to the original message.

As Mike Galos, the administrative assistant for The Garden Company, your first task of the day is to read and respond to your e-mail messages. In this exercise, you will reply to and forward messages.

Important

NextShow

If you haven't installed and copied the practice files for this book, please do so now. For details about installing the practice files on your hard disk and copying them into Outlook, see "Using the Book's CD-ROM" at the beginning of this book. If you want to complete only this exercise, follow the instructions in the "Using the Book's CD-ROM" section to copy just the practice file shown above the CD icon in the margin.

1 With your Inbox displayed, double-click the **Upcoming show** message from Catherine Turner.

The message appears in the Message window.

Note that this message was sent to you, Mike Galos, and was copied to Kim Yoshida, the head buyer for The Garden Company. The message also includes an attachment.

2 On the toolbar, click the **Reply** button.

The Reply form is displayed on your screen.

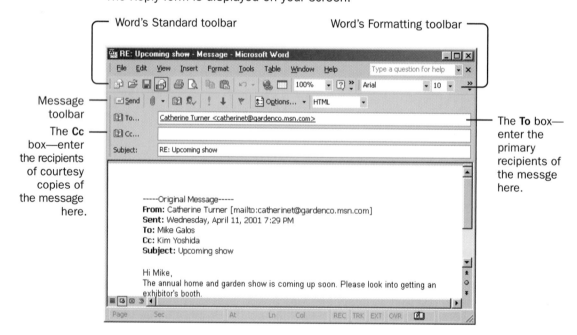

Note that the reply will be sent only to Catherine Turner and that the attachment is not included. Note also that a prefix, *RE:*, has been added to the subject line. This prefix indicates that this is a response to an earlier message.

Tip

If Microsoft Word is your default e-mail editor, the Reply form displays Word's Standard and Formatting toolbars in addition to the regular toolbar. If you don't use the buttons on Word's toolbars, you can turn the toolbars off to save space. On the form's **View** menu, point to **Toolbars**, and then click **Standard** or **Formatting**.

3 The insertion point is already in the message box, so type What size booth would you like?

 4 Click the **Send** button.

Important

Because the e-mail addresses in these exercises are fictitious, any messages you send to these addresses will be returned to your Inbox because the messages are undeliverable. Simply delete any returned message by clicking it and then clicking the **Delete** button.

5 If sending the message closes the Message window, double-click the message to open the window again.

6 On the toolbar, click the **Reply to All** button.

The Reply form appears. You can see from the message header that this reply will be sent to both Catherine Turner and Kim Yoshida. Again, the attachment is not included.

Important

Because this practice message was copied into your Inbox rather than sent to you, your address (*mikeg@gardenco.msn.com*) also appears in the **To** box. When you reply to a message that someone else sent to you, your address will not appear in the **To** box and your reply will not be sent back to you.

7 Type I have faxed the form to the show organizers, and then click the **Send** button.

The Reply form closes.

8 If necessary, reopen the Message window, and then on the toolbar, click the **Forward** button.

The Forward Message form appears.

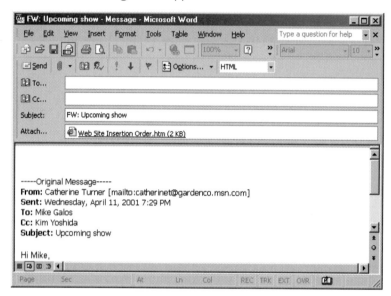

Note that the address lines are blank and that the attachment is included. Note also that a prefix, *FW:*, has been added to the subject line. This prefix indicates that this is a forwarded message.

9 In the **To** box, type your own e-mail address (not that of Mike Galos).

10 Press the [Tab] key until you get to the message body, type **Thought you might be interested in this**, and click the **Send** button.

The message closes, and it will now be forwarded back to you. If the message arrives quickly, look at it in your Inbox, and then open it and examine the message header. Note how the subject line and attachment appear. If your message doesn't arrive quickly, you can examine it later.

Close

11 If necessary, close the open Message window by clicking its **Close** button.

Creating New Messages

OL2002-1-2

With Outlook, communicating by e-mail is quick and easy. You can send messages to people in your office and at other locations. And, in addition to using Outlook's many formatting options, you can embed hyperlinks and attach files to your messages.

Word as the
default e-mail
editor
new for
OfficeXP

If you installed Word 2002 when you installed Outlook, Outlook 2002 will use Word as its default e-mail editor. Many of Word's powerful text editing capabilities, including styles, tables, and themes, are available to you as you create messages in Outlook. Also, Word will check your spelling as you type, correcting many errors automatically. You can also have Word check the spelling of your message when you send it.

Tip

If Word is not your default e-mail editor and you would like it to be, click **Options** on the **Tools** menu. Click the **Mail Format** tab, and select the **Use Microsoft Word to edit e-mail messages** check box. To turn off Word as your default e-mail editor, make sure the check box is cleared.

Important

The exercises in this book assume that you are using Word as your default e-mail editor.

In this exercise, you will compose a new e-mail message. You don't need any practice files for this exercise.

New Mail
Message

New

1   On the toolbar, click the **New Mail Message** button.

A new, blank message appears in the Message form.

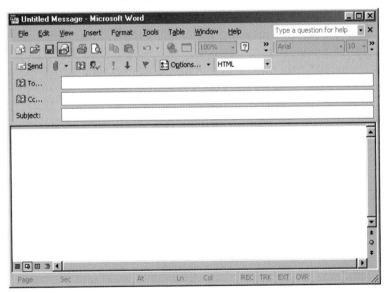

Take a few minutes to investigate the menus and menu options. If you are familiar with Word, you will recognize many of them.

Tip

By clicking the down arrow to the right of the **New Mail Message** button, you can create something other than a new e-mail message. You can create new appointments, contacts, tasks, and Office documents as well.

2 In the **To** box, type catherinet@gardenco.msn.com. Then type ; (a semicolon) and a space, and type kimy@gardenco.msn.com.

Note that you use semicolons to separate multiple addresses.

Tip

If you are working on a network that uses Exchange Server, when you send messages to other people on your network, you can type just the part of the address that is to the left of the @ sign. The remaining part of the address identifies the server that handles the e-mail account, so within an organization, the server name is not needed.

AutoComplete addressing
new for
OfficeXP

When your recipient's address is in your **address book** or you've typed it in a message header before, Outlook automatically completes the address for you, and pressing the ⎚Tab⎚ key inserts the entry. If there are multiple matches, Outlook presents a list of items that match what you've typed so far. Use the arrow keys to select the item you want, and press the ⎚Enter⎚ key.

3 Press the ⎚Tab⎚ key, and in the **Cc** box, type your own e-mail address.

Tip

If you want to send a copy of a message to a person without the other recipients' being aware of it, you can send a "blind" copy. Display the **Bcc** box by clicking the arrow to the right of the **Options** button, and then clicking **Bcc**. Then type the person's e-mail address in the **Bcc** box.

4 Press the ⎚Tab⎚ key to move to the **Subject** box, and type Today's schedule.

5 Press the ⎚Tab⎚ key again, and type Here are the people who will be working today. Then press the ⎚Enter⎚ key twice.

Important

After your message has been open for a period of time, Outlook saves a **draft** of it in the Drafts folder so that any work you have done is saved if you are somehow disconnected from Outlook before you send the message. If you close a message without sending it, Outlook asks you if you want to save the message in the Drafts folder. To find these messages later, click the **Drafts** folder in the **Folder List**. If the **Folder List** is not visible, click **Folder List** on the **View** menu to display it.

6   On the **Table** menu, point to **Insert**, and then click **Table**.

Word's **Insert Table** dialog box appears.

7   Change the number of columns to **4**, and click **OK**.

A table appears in your message.

8   Fill in the cells of the table as shown here, pressing the ⊞ key to move from cell to cell:

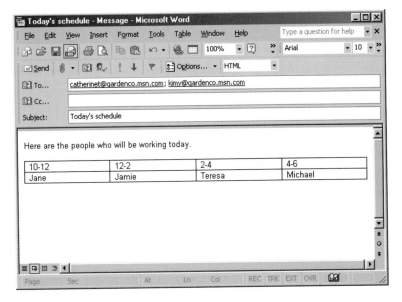

9   Click the **Send** button.

The Message form closes, and the message is sent on its way.

Using an Address Book

OL2002-1-2

You can store cumbersome e-mail addresses in an address book so that you can avoid having to type them each time you send a message. With an address book, you can click the **To** button in the Message form and then select recipients by name.

If you are using Outlook with Exchange Server, an Exchange address book, which is called **Global Address List** and contains the e-mail addresses of all the people on your network, might already be available to you. If a Global Address List is available to you, Outlook will use this as your default address book. Because the Global Address List is maintained by your system administrator, you cannot add to it; you must use another address book to create any entries not included in that list. By default, entries you created are stored in your Contacts folder, which is a type of address book.

Address book entries can be for an individual contact or for a **distribution list**— a group of individual addresses stored under a single name. For example, to facilitate communication with a team, you might create a distribution list including the addresses for all the people working on a particular project.

Tip

With or without an address book, you can address messages by typing the full address into the **To**, **Cc**, or **Bcc** boxes in the Message form.

In this exercise, you will add address book entries, create a distribution list, and address a message using your address book. You don't need any practice files for this exercise.

1 On the **Tools** menu, click **Address Book**.

The **Address Book** window appears. If you are working on a network, the **Show Names from the** setting is **Global Address List**. Otherwise, it is **Contacts**.

2 If necessary, click the down arrow to the right of the **Show Names from the** box, and click **Contacts** in the drop-down list.

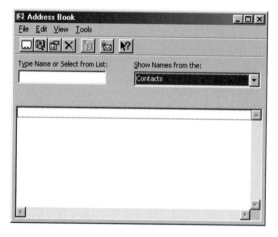

New Entry

3 On the toolbar, click the **New Entry** button.

The **New Entry** dialog box appears.

4 In the **Select the entry type** box, click **New Contact**, and then click **OK**.

The Contact form appears.

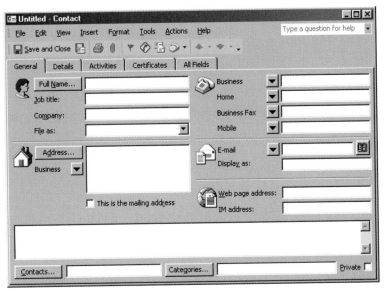

5 In the **Full Name** box, type your boss's name, Catherine Turner.

6 In the **E-mail** box, type your boss's e-mail address, catherinet@ gardenco.msn.com.

7 Click the **Save and Close** button.

The Contact form closes, and the contact appears in the **Address Book** window.

8 Now you'll add another entry. On the toolbar, click the **New Entry** button.

The **New Entry** dialog box appears.

9 In the **Select the entry type** box, click **New Contact**, and then click **OK**.

The Contact form appears.

10 In the **Full Name** box, type the name of The Garden Company's head buyer, Kim Yoshida.

11 In the **E-mail** box, type the head buyer's e-mail address, kimy@ gardenco.msn.com.

12 Press the Tab key, and in the **Display as** box, delete the e-mail address and parentheses so that the box contains only the name *Kim Yoshida*.

13 Click the **Save and Close** button.

The Contact form closes, and the contact appears in the **Address Book** window. Your address book should look as shown on the next page.

Friendly names
instead of
e-mail
addresses
new for
OfficeXP

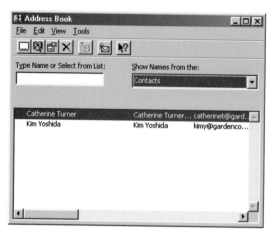

14 Now you'll create a distribution list. On the toolbar, click the **New Entry** button.

The **New Entry** dialog box appears.

15 In the **Select the entry type** box, click **New Distribution List**, and then click **OK**.

The Distribution List form appears.

Tip

Maximize

If a form window is too small to work with easily, you can click the **Maximize** button or resize it by dragging its frame.

16 In the **Name** box, type Garden Co, and then click the **Select Members** button.

The **Select Members** dialog box appears.

17 If necessary, click the down arrow to the right of the **Show Names from the** box, and click **Contacts** in the drop-down list.

18 In the **Name** list, click **Kim Yoshida**, and click the **Members** button.

Kim Yoshida is added to the distribution list.

19 In the **Name** list, click **Catherine Turner**, and click the **Members** button.

Catherine Turner is added to the distribution list.

Tip

To add multiple names to the distribution list simultaneously, click a name in the **Name** list, hold down the [Ctrl] key, click any additional names you want to add, and then click the **Members** button.

20 Click **OK** to close the **Select Members** dialog box.

You return to the Distribution List form.

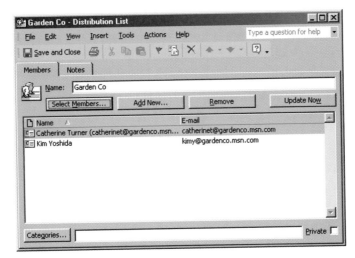

21 Click the **Save and Close** button.

The Distribution List form closes, and the **Address Book** window appears.

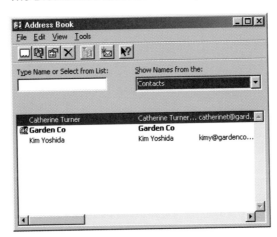

Close

22 Click the **Close** button.

The **Address Book** window closes.

New Mail
Message

New

23 On the toolbar, click the **New Mail Message** button.

A new, blank message opens in the Message form.

24 Click the **To** button to the left of the **To** box.

The **Select Names** dialog box appears.

25 If necessary, change the **Show Names from the** setting to **Contacts**.

26 In the **Name** list, click **Kim Yoshida**, and then click the **To** button.

Kim's name is added to the list of recipients in the **To** box.

27 In the **Name** list, click **Garden Co**, and then click the **Cc** button.

The distribution list's name is added to the list of recipients in the **Cc** box.

28 Click **OK**.

The **Select Names** dialog box closes, and the recipient names are added to the **To** and **Cc** boxes on the Message form.

Tip

You can type distribution list names in the **To** and **Cc** boxes just like any other e-mail address. Outlook will then match what you type with the name in your address book and will display the name as bold and underlined, which indicates that the name represents a distribution list rather than an individual address.

29 Click in the **Subject** box, and type **Test**.

30 Close the message without sending it. When prompted to save it, click **No**.

Attaching Files to Messages

OL2002-1-3

A convenient way to share files with others or send files such as Word documents or Excel spreadsheets across an intranet or the Internet is to attach them to an e-mail message. Outlook makes it easy to attach files to your messages.

As the assistant for The Garden Company, you have been asked to craft a standard form for a company letter. You want to send your first draft to the company's owner for review. In this exercise, you will attach the draft Word document to an e-mail message.

Important

Attachment

If you haven't installed and copied the practice files for this book, please do so now. For details about installing the practice files on your hard disk and copying them into Outlook, see "Using the Book's CD-ROM" at the beginning of this book. If you want to complete only this exercise, follow the instructions in the "Using the Book's CD-ROM" section to copy just the practice file shown above the CD icon in the margin. The document you will use is located in the SBS\Outlook\Attach folder on your hard disk.

New Mail
Message

📧 New

1 On the toolbar, click the **New Mail Message** button.

A new, blank message appears in the Message form.

2 In the **To** box, type **catherinet@gardenco.msn.com;** and then type your own address.

3   Click in the **Subject** box, and type The First Draft.

4   Press the `Tab` key, type Here it is – let me know what you think in the message body, and press `Enter`.

Insert File

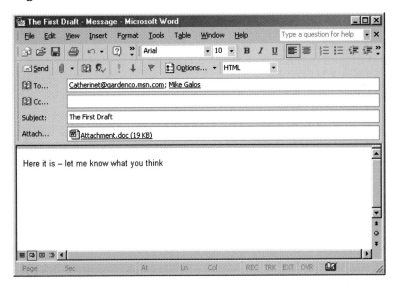

5   On the form's toolbar, click the **Insert File** button.

The **Insert File** dialog box appears.

6   Browse to the SBS\Outlook\Attach folder (which is probably located on drive C), and double-click the folder name.

The contents of the folder are displayed.

7   Click the **Attachment** document, and then click the **Insert** button.

The document appears in the **Attach** box in the message header. Your message now looks similar to this one:

Important

You can attach any type of file to an e-mail message, but when sending attachments, be sure that your recipients have the software required to open your file. For example, if you are attaching a Word document, your recipients must have Word installed on their computers to open your attachment.

8   Close the message without sending it. If prompted to save it, click **No**.

Tip

You can embed a hyperlink to a Web site in an e-mail message simply by including the site's **universal resource locator (URL)**. To embed a hyperlink, simply type the URL (for example, *www.microsoft.com*) followed by a space. Outlook formats the URL to appear as a link. Your recipients can simply click the link in the message to open the Web page.

Adding Signatures to Messages

OL2002-1-3

By using a **signature**, you can personalize your messages and save time. A signature is a predefined block of text that can be inserted, manually or automatically, at the end of your messages. Your signature can include any text you like but typically includes your name, title, and company name. Signatures can also be formatted in the same ways that message text can be formatted. You can define several different signatures to choose from, perhaps one for professional use and one for personal use.

In this exercise, you will create a signature and then set Outlook to insert it in all new messages. You don't need any practice files for this exercise.

1   On the **Tools** menu, click **Options**.

The **Options** dialog box appears.

2   Click the **Mail Format** tab.

These options are shown:

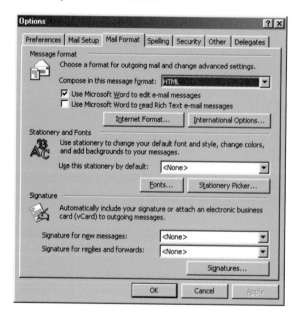

3 Click the **Signatures** button, and then click the **New** button.

The **Create New Signature** dialog box appears.

4 Type Professional as the name of your signature, and click the **Next** button.

The **Edit Signature** dialog box appears.

5 In the **Signature text** box, type Regards and a comma, press the [Enter] key, and then type Mike Galos.

6 Select the words *Mike Galos*, and then click the **Font** button.

The **Font** dialog box appears.

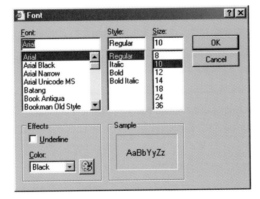

7 Change the font to **Arial Narrow**, the style to **Bold Italic**, and the size to **14**. Then click **OK**.

The name changes to reflect the new font, style, and size.

8 Select both lines of the signature, and click the **Paragraph** button.

The **Paragraph** dialog box appears, as shown on the next page.

9   Click **Center**, and click **OK**.

Your professional signature looks like this:

10   When you are satisfied with your signature, click **Finish**.

The **Create Signature** dialog box appears.

11   Click **OK**.

The **Options** dialog box appears. Note that the signature you just created is selected in the **Signature for new messages** list. Outlook will insert your signature into all new e-mail messages.

12   Click **OK**.

The **Options** dialog box closes.

New Mail
Message

13   On the toolbar, click the **New Mail Message** button.

A new message, containing your new signature, appears in the Message form.

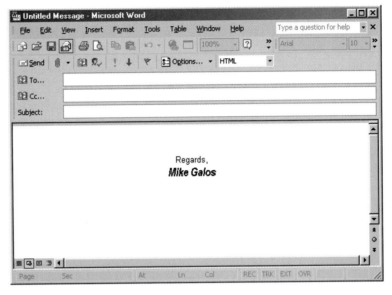

14 Close the message.

Tip

To have your signature automatically inserted into replies or forwarded messages, too, click **Options** on the **Tools** menu, and click the **Mail Format** tab. Click the signature you want in the **Signature for replies or forwards** list, and click **OK**.

15 On the **Tools** menu, click **Options**.

The **Options** dialog box appears.

16 Click the **Mail Format** tab.

17 In the **Signature for new messages** list, click **<None>**.

New messages will appear without a signature.

18 In the **Options** dialog box, click **OK**.

The **Options** dialog box closes.

Sending and Receiving Messages

OL2002-1-2

Depending on your e-mail account and network configuration, messages you send could go out instantaneously or be kept in your Outbox until you choose to send them. If you are connected to a LAN, your messages will usually go out instantaneously. If you are not connected to a LAN (for example, if you connect to an ISP via phone line, DSL line, or cable), your messages will typically be kept in your Outbox.

How you receive messages also depends on your type of e-mail account and your Outlook configuration. Outlook might check for new messages periodically and download them automatically. Or, you might need to check for new messages.

Copies of messages you send are kept in the **Sent Items** folder by default. To see these messages, click **Sent Items** in the **Folder List**. If you do not want to keep copies of your sent messages, click **Options** on the **Tools** menu, click the **E-mail Options** button, clear the **Save copies of messages in Sent Items folder** check box, and click **OK**.

In this exercise, you will send a message, check for new messages, and delete a message. You don't need any practice files for this exercise.

New Mail
Message

1   On the toolbar, click the **New Mail Message** button.

A new message appears in the Message form.

2   In the **To** box, type your own e-mail address.

3   Click in the **Subject** box, and type the subject of the message: Sending and Receiving Test.

4   Press the Tab key, and in the message body, type **This is a test**. Then click the **Send** button.

The message closes.

5   On the **View** menu, click **Folder List**.

The Outlook window now looks like this:

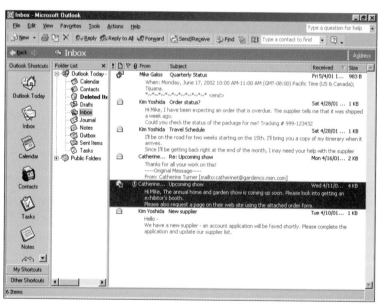

6   In the **Folder List**, click **Outbox**.

The contents of the Outbox are displayed. If the message you sent appears in the Outbox, you must send the message manually. If the Outbox is empty, your message was sent automatically.

When a message is waiting to be sent, your Outbox looks similar to this one:

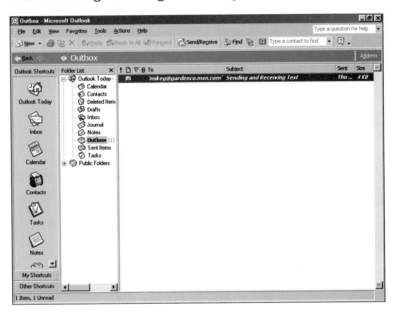

Multiple E-mail Accounts

Accounts button
new for
OfficeXP

With Outlook, you can get all your e-mail in one place by configuring more than one account in your profile. To add an e-mail account to your profile:

1   On the **Tools** menu, click **E-mail Accounts** to start the **E-mail Accounts Wizard**.

2   Select the **Add a new e-mail account** option, and click **Next**.

3   Select the option for the appropriate server type, and click **Next**.

4   Enter the required server and account settings, and click **Next**.

5   Click **Finish** to close the **E-mail Accounts Wizard**.

If you have more than one e-mail account in your profile, you can send your mail from any of your accounts. In the Message form, on the toolbar, click the down arrow to the right of the **Accounts** button, and then click the account you want in the drop-down list.

7 To send any messages in your Outbox and download any new messages from your e-mail server, click the **Send/Receive** button on the toolbar.

Outlook connects to your e-mail server to send and receive messages. Depending on your setup, it might access your modem and connection line. When your message is sent, it disappears from the Outbox. When it is received, the message appears in your Inbox, along with any other new messages.

8 In the **Folder List**, click **Inbox** to see your new message(s).

The contents of the Inbox are displayed.

Printing Messages

OL2002-1-1

Occasionally, you might need a hard copy, or printout, of an e-mail message. For example, you might need to print the directions to an afternoon appointment or distribute copies of a message at a meeting. With Outlook, you can print your e-mail messages in much the same way you would any other document.

Depending on the format (HTML, Rich Text, or Plain Text) of the message you want to print, you can set a number of page setup options, including paper size, margins, and orientation. You can also use Print Preview to see how a message will appear when printed. (Print Preview is not available for messages in HTML format.)

Important

The exercises in this book assume that you are using Word as your default e-mail editor.

In this exercise, you will change the page setup for a message and then print it.

Important

NextShow

If you haven't installed and copied the practice files for this book, please do so now. For details about installing the practice files on your hard disk and copying them into Outlook, see "Using the Book's CD-ROM" at the beginning of this book. If you want to complete only this exercise, follow the instructions in the "Using the Book's CD-ROM" section to copy just the practice file shown above the CD icon in the margin.

1 In the Inbox, double-click the **Upcoming show** message from Catherine Turner to open it.

The message appears in the Message window.

2 On the **File** menu, point to **Page Setup**, and click **Memo Style**.

The **Page Setup** dialog box appears.

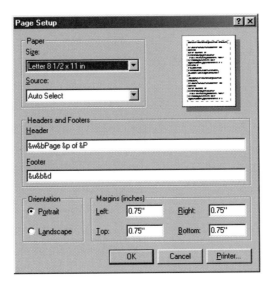

Tip

To display the **Page Setup** dialog box, you must have at least one printer installed. If you are working on a network, your administrator can provide the information you need to install a printer. If you are working on a stand-alone computer, click the **Start** button, point to **Settings**, and click **Printers**. Then click the **Add Printer** icon, and follow the wizard's instructions.

3   In the **Left** box, type **1.0** to set the left margin to **1** inch, and click **OK**.

The **Page Setup** dialog box closes, and your new settings are now in effect for this message.

Print

4   On the toolbar, click the **Print** button.

The message is printed with the default print options.

Tip

You can change print options in the **Print** dialog box. On the **File** menu, click **Print** to display the **Print** dialog box.

5   Click **AutoPreview** on the **View** menu to turn off AutoPreview.

Close

6   On the **View** menu click **Preview Pane** to turn on the preview pane. Then click the **Close** button at the right end of the **Folder List** title bar to close the **Folder List**.

7   If you are not continuing on with the next chapter, on the **File** menu, click **Exit** to quit Outlook.

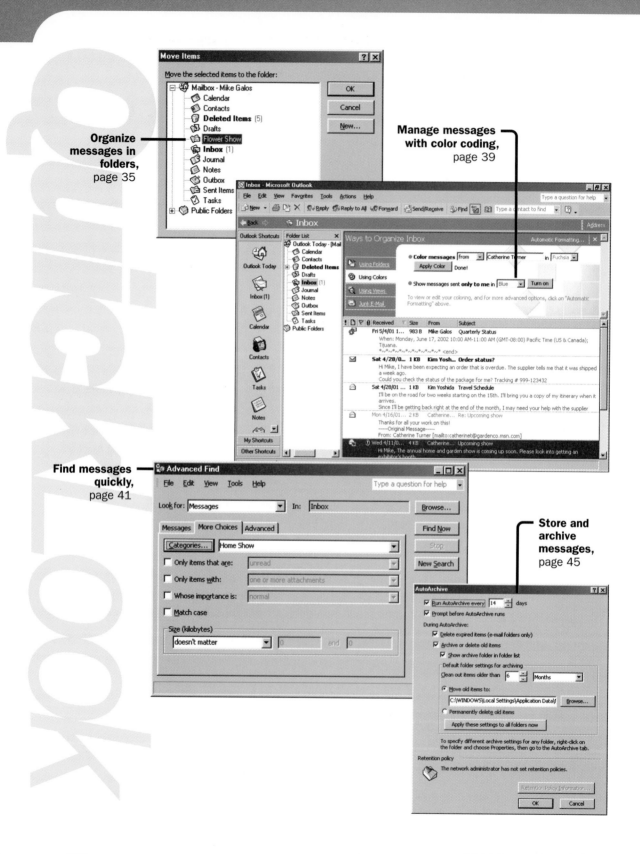

Organize messages in folders, page 35

Manage messages with color coding, page 39

Find messages quickly, page 41

Store and archive messages, page 45

Chapter 2
Managing E-mail Messages

After completing this chapter, you will be able to:

✔ **Customize how you view messages**
✔ **Organize messages**
✔ **Find messages**
✔ **Store and archive messages**

In today's business world, e-mail is an essential method of communication. But when you use your e-mail regularly and receive a large volume of messages, it can be difficult to manage them all. Microsoft Outlook 2002 has many features to help you read, organize, find, and store e-mail messages quickly.

You can choose to view your messages in a way that makes it easier for you to scan, read, and respond to them. You can organize your messages in folders, search for messages by category and other criteria, and archive your messages in Outlook and on your hard disk.

In this chapter, you will work specifically with the files that came on this book's CD-ROM. If you have not already installed these files onto your hard disk and copied them into Outlook, see "Using the Book's CD-ROM" at the beginning of the book.

Customizing How You View Messages

OL2002-1-4

As your Inbox gathers messages, it can be challenging to prioritize them. You can use Outlook to customize how you view, group, and sort messages. You can then quickly determine which are the most important, decide which can be deleted, and locate that message from your boss that you haven't responded to yet.

Regardless of the **view** you choose, you can sort your messages by any column simply by clicking the column heading. By default, messages in your Inbox are sorted by the received date in descending order—the most recent messages appear at the top of the list. But you can sort columns in either ascending or descending order. You can also group your messages by the contents of any column—by the sender of the message, for instance, or by the subject.

In this exercise, you will sort and group messages, select a defined message view, and customize your message view.

Important

If you haven't installed and copied the practice files for this book, please do so now. For details about installing and copying the practice files, see "Using the Book's CD-ROM" at the beginning of this book.

1 If it is not already open, start Outlook. Then if necessary, maximize the Outlook window.

2 In the Inbox, click the heading of the **From** column.

Outlook sorts the messages by the name in the **From** column, in ascending order.

3 Click the heading of the **From** column again.

Outlook sorts the messages in descending order.

4 Click the heading of the **Received** column.

Outlook sorts the messages by the date received in descending order.

5 Right-click the heading of the **Subject** column, and click **Group By This Field** on the shortcut menu.

Outlook groups your messages by subject and sorts the subjects in ascending order.

Note that the total number of items and the number of unread items in each group is indicated in parentheses following the subject line.

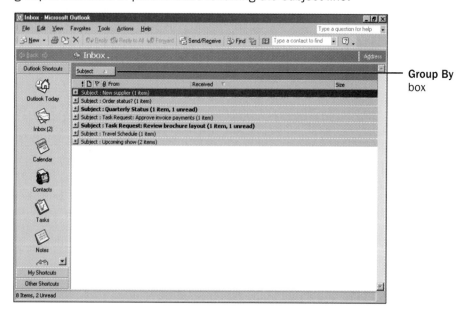

Group By box

Tip

Unread items are distinguished from read ones by their bold type and closed-envelope icons. If you do not have any unread messages in your Inbox, for purposes of this exercise, right-click a message, and click **Mark as Unread** on the shortcut menu. The message header in the Inbox will then change to bold, and its message icon will change from an open to a closed envelope.

6 Click the plus sign (+) to the left of the **Subject: Upcoming show** line.

The messages in that subject group are displayed.

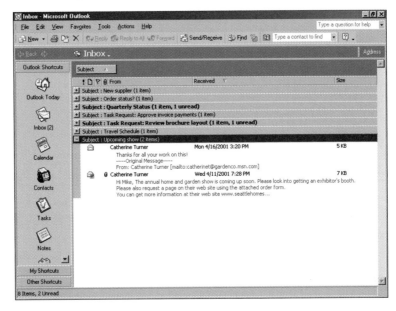

7 In the **Group By** box, click the **Subject** button.

The subjects are sorted in descending order.

8 In the **Group By** box, right-click the **Subject** button, and click **Don't Group By This Field** on the shortcut menu.

Messages are no longer grouped by subject.

9 Right-click any column heading, and click **Group By Box** on the shortcut menu.

The **Group By** box disappears.

10 If none of the messages in your Inbox appears in bold type, which indicates that you have not yet read them, right-click the **Order Status** message from Kim Yoshida, and click **Mark as Unread** on the shortcut menu.

11 On the **View** menu, point to **Current View**, and click **Unread Messages**.

Outlook filters the messages to show only unread messages.

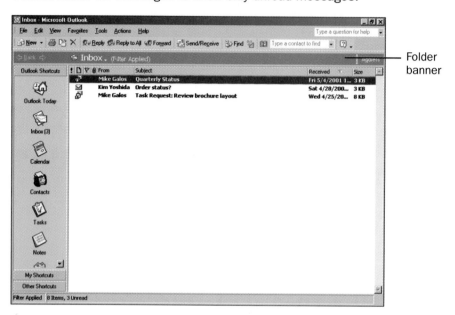

Folder
banner

The **Folder banner** indicates that a **filter** has been applied. (If you have no unread messages in your Inbox, it will appear to be empty.)

12 On the **View** menu, point to **Current View**, and click **Messages**.

The messages are no longer filtered.

Tip

The **Ways to Organize Inbox** pane provides an alternative method for selecting a view for your messages. On the **Tools** menu, click **Organize** to open the pane. Then click **Using Views**, and click a view in the list.

13 On the **View** menu, point to **Current View**, and click **Customize Current View**.

The **View Summary** dialog box appears.

14 Click the **Fields** button.

The **Show Fields** dialog box appears.

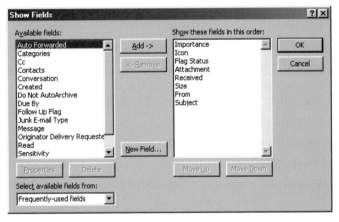

15 In the **Available fields** list, click **Sensitivity**, and then click the **Add** button.

The **Sensitivity** field is added to the list of columns to be shown in this view.

16 In the **Show these fields in this order** list, drag **Sensitivity** to appear just after **Importance**, and click **OK**.

The **Show Fields** dialog box closes, and you return to the **View Summary** dialog box.

Tip

To change the order of columns in any view, simply drag the column headings to the locations you prefer. While you are dragging a column heading, red arrows indicate where the column will appear if you release the mouse button.

17 Click the **Other Settings** button.

The **Other Settings** dialog box appears, as shown on the next page.

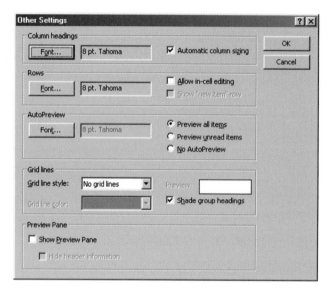

18 Click the down arrow to the right of the **Grid line style** box, click **Small dots**, and then click **OK**.

The **Other Settings** dialog box closes, and you return to the **View Summary** dialog box.

19 In the **View Summary** dialog box, click **OK**.

The **View Summary** dialog box closes, and the Inbox is displayed with the new view settings.

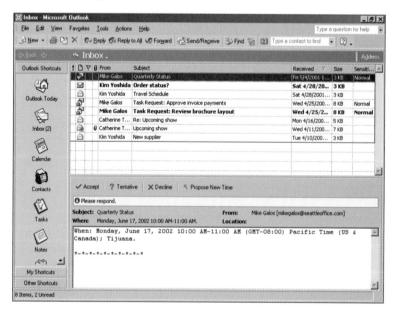

20 Drag the **Sensitivity** column heading downward, and release the mouse button when a large black X appears over the heading.

The **Sensitivity** column is removed from the view.

21 To return to the default settings, on the **View** menu, click **Current View**, and then click **Define Views**.

The **Define Views** dialog box appears.

22 Click the **Reset** button, click **OK**, and then click **Close**.

The Inbox is displayed with the default view settings.

Organizing Messages in Folders

OL2002-3-1

After you've read and responded to messages, you might want to keep some for future reference. With Outlook, you can organize your messages in a variety of ways.

Creating folders to organize your messages helps you avoid an accumulation of unrelated messages in your Inbox. For example, you can create a folder for each project you're working on and store all messages regarding a particular project in its own folder. Or, you can create a folder to store all messages from your boss. You can move messages to the folders manually or have Outlook move them for you.

Tip

If you are using a Microsoft Exchange Server account, the **Out of Office Assistant** can help you manage messages while you are away from the office. When you have more experience with Outlook, you might want to explore this handy helper. On the **Tools** menu, click **Out of Office Assistant** to see what options are available.

In this exercise, you will create a new folder, move messages to that folder, move and rename the folder, and then delete a message and delete the folder.

Important

NextShow
NewSupplier

If you haven't installed and copied the practice files for this book, please do so now. For details about installing and copying the practice files, see "Using the Book's CD-ROM" at the beginning of this book. If you want to complete only this exercise, follow the instructions in the "Using the Book's CD-ROM" section to copy just the practice files shown above the CD icon in the margin.

1 With the Inbox displayed in Outlook, on the **Tools** menu, click **Organize**.

The **Ways to Organize Inbox** pane appears, as shown on the next page.

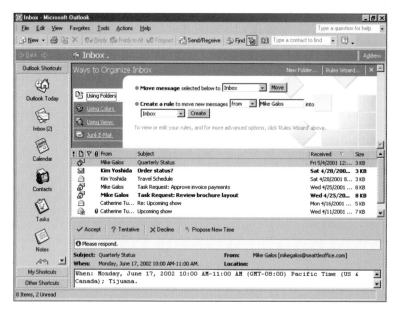

2 At the top of the **Ways to Organize Inbox** pane, click the **New Folder** button. The **Create New Folder** dialog box appears.

Tip

If you are not working on a networked computer, the first item in the **Select where to place the folder** box is **Personal Folders** because your Outlook information is stored on your hard disk, not on a server.

3   In the **Name** box, type Home Show as the name of your new folder, and click **OK**.

The **Create New Folder** dialog box closes.

4   If Outlook asks whether you want to put a shortcut for this folder on the **Outlook Bar**, click **No**.

The new Home Show folder appears in the **Folder List** as a subfolder of the Inbox folder. (You can scroll down the **Folder List** to see the folder.)

5   To display the **Folder List**, click **Folder List** on the **View** menu.

The **Folder List** is displayed.

New folder ————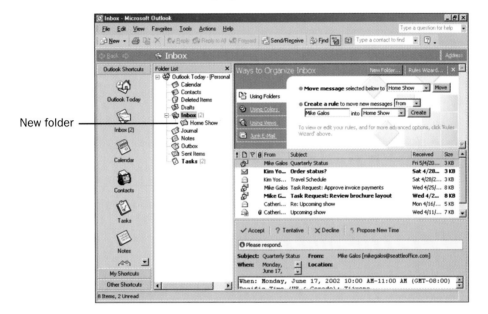

6   In the Inbox, click the **Upcoming show** message from Catherine Turner, and in the **Ways to Organize Inbox** pane, click the **Move** button.

The message is moved to the new folder.

7   Repeat step 6 to move the **New Supplier** message to the new folder.

Tip

You can move messages to another folder automatically by creating a rule. To create a simple rule, such as moving all messages received from your boss to a separate folder, use the **Using Folders** tab of the **Ways to Organize Inbox** pane. For more complex rules, click the **Rules Wizard** button in the top right corner of the **Ways to Organize Inbox** pane.

8 In the **Folder List**, click the **Home Show** folder.

The contents of the new folder are displayed.

9 In the **Folder List**, drag the **Home Show** folder to **Outlook Today**.

The new folder is now listed at the same level in the **Folder List** as the Inbox and in alphabetical order with the other items at this level.

10 In the **Folder List**, right-click the **Home Show** folder, and click **Rename "Home Show"** on the shortcut menu.

The name of the folder appears in the **Folder List** in an editable text box.

11 Type **Flower Show**, and press the Enter key.

The folder name is changed.

12 In the **Folder List**, click the **Flower Show** folder to display its contents.

Move to Folder

13 Click the **Upcoming show** message. Then click the **Move to Folder** button, and click **Move to Folder**.

The **Move Items** dialog box is displayed.

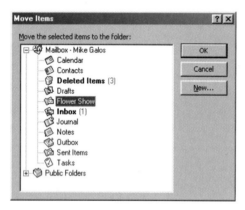

14 Click **Inbox**, and click **OK**.

The message is moved to the Inbox.

Delete

15 Now click the **New Supplier** message, and click the **Delete** button.

The message is deleted, and the folder is now empty.

16 In the **Folder List**, click the **Flower Show** folder, and click the **Delete** button.

17 When asked if you are sure you want to delete the folder, click **Yes**.

The folder is deleted. When you delete a folder, any messages contained within that folder are also deleted. (In this case, the folder is empty.)

Close

18 Close the **Folder List** by clicking its **Close** button.

The **Folder List** closes.

Important

When you delete any item in Outlook, it is moved to the Deleted Items folder. You can view your deleted items by clicking that folder in the **Folder List**. You can tell Outlook to empty the Deleted Items folder every time you close the program by setting that option in the **Options** dialog box. On the **Tools** menu, click **Options**, click the **Other** tab, and then select the **Empty the Deleted Items folder upon exiting** check box, clicking **OK** when you are finished. You can empty the **Deleted Items** folder at any time by right-clicking the folder in the **Folder List** and clicking **Empty "Deleted Items" Folder** on the shortcut menu.

Managing Messages with Color

OL2002e-7-3

Color-coding messages can help you easily distinguish messages sent to or received from certain people. You can also choose to have messages that were sent directly to you displayed in a different color to distinguish them from messages sent to a distribution list. For example, you might show all messages from your boss in red, and all messages from the finance department in green.

In this exercise, you will color-code messages.

Important

NextShow

If you haven't installed and copied the practice files for this book, please do so now. For details about installing and copying the practice files, see "Using the Book's CD-ROM" at the beginning of this book. If you want to complete only this exercise, follow the instructions in the "Using the Book's CD-ROM" section to copy just the practice file shown above the CD icon in the margin.

1 Display the **Folder List** by clicking **Folder List** on the **View** menu.

   The **Folder List** appears.

Inbox

2 In the **Folder List**, click **Inbox**, and on the **Tools** menu, click **Organize**.

   The **Ways to Organize Inbox** pane appears.

3 In the **Ways to Organize Inbox** pane, click **Using Colors**.

   The **Using Colors** tab is displayed, as shown on the next page.

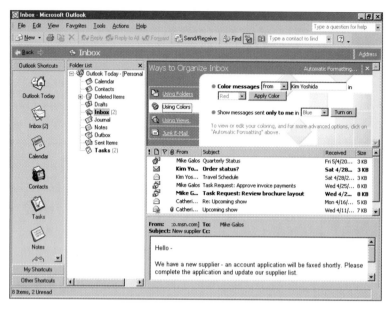

4 Click the **Upcoming show** message from Catherine Turner.

5 In the **Color Messages** section, make sure **From** is selected in the first box and Catherine Turner appears in the second box.

6 In the third box, select **Fuchsia** from the drop-down list, and click the **Apply Color** button.

The specified messages are displayed in the selected color.

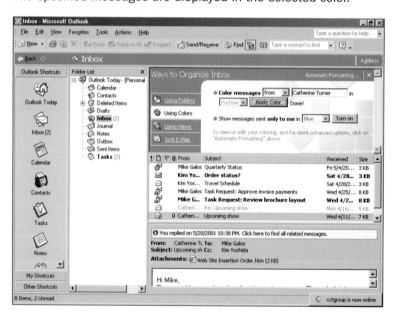

7　In the **Ways to Organize Inbox** pane, click **Automatic Formatting**.

The **Automatic Formatting** dialog box appears.

Delete

8　In the **Rules for this view** list, click **Mail received from Catherine Turner**, and then click the **Delete** button.

The Mail received from Catherine Turner rule is deleted.

9　In the **Automatic Formatting** dialog box, click OK.

The dialog box closes.

10　Click the **X** in the top right corner of the **Ways to Organize Inbox** pane to close it.

Close

11　Close the **Folder List** by clicking its **Close** button.

The **Folder List** closes.

Finding Messages

OL2002-3-2
OL2002-3-4

Find
new for
OfficeXP

If you are having trouble locating a message in your Inbox or other message folders, you can find it using Outlook's **Find** and **Advanced Find** features. You can look for messages in a single folder, a group of folders you select, or all of your folders. You also have the option of searching the text of the whole message or only the Subject field.

To make finding messages easier, you can create categories and assign messages to them. With categories, you group messages by a common characteristic. Outlook includes a set of predefined categories, and you can create your own. For example, you might assign all messages about invoices and payments to the Finance category, or you might create a Payroll category for all messages related to timesheets and pay-checks.

In this exercise, you will find a message using the Find feature, create a category, assign messages to it, and find messages using the Advanced Find feature.

Important

NextShow
ReNextShow

If you haven't installed and copied the practice files for this book, please do so now. For details about installing and copying the practice files, see "Using the Book's CD-ROM" at the beginning of this book. If you want to complete only this exercise, follow the instructions in the "Using the Book's CD-ROM" section to copy just the practice files shown above the CD icon in the margin.

1 On the toolbar, click the **Find** button.

The **Find** pane appears above the Inbox.

2 In the **Look for** box in the **Find** pane, type show, a word that you know is con-tained within a message in your Inbox. Then click the **Find Now** button.

Outlook searches your messages and displays only those that contain the word you typed.

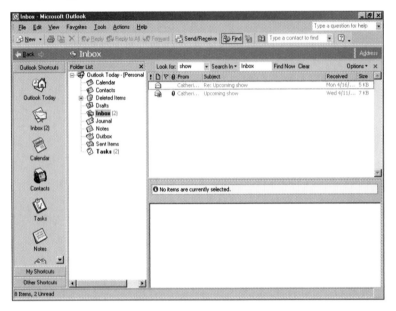

3 To show all messages again, click the **Clear** button.

All your messages are displayed.

4 In the Inbox, click the **Upcoming show** message from Catherine Turner, and on the **Edit** menu, click **Categories**.

The **Categories** dialog box appears.

5 In the **Item(s) belong to these categories** box, after **Practice Files**, type ; (a semicolon) and then Home Show as the name of a new category, and click the **Add to List** button.

The category is added to the list and automatically selected for the message.

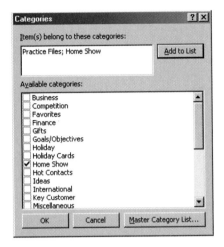

6 In the **Categories** dialog box, click **OK**.

The message is assigned to the new category.

7 In the **Find** pane, click the **Options** button, and then click **Advanced Find** in the **Options** drop-down list to display the **Advanced Find** window.

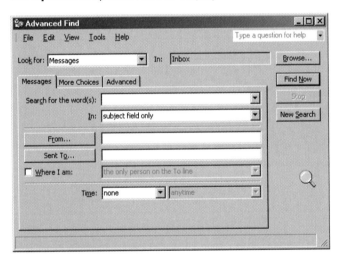

As you can see, you can search for messages in many ways.

8 In the **Advanced Find** window, click the **More Choices** tab.

The **More Choices** tab is displayed.

9 Click the **Categories** button.

The **Categories** dialog box appears.

10 In the **Available categories** list, select the **Home Show** check box, and click **OK**.

The **Categories** dialog box closes, and you return to the **Advanced Find** window. Your category appears in the **Categories** box, as shown on the next page.

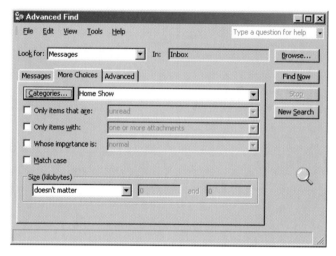

11 Click the **Find Now** button.

Outlook searches your messages and displays the matching items in a list at the bottom of the **Advanced Find** window.

Close

12 Close the **Advanced Find** window by clicking its **Close** button.

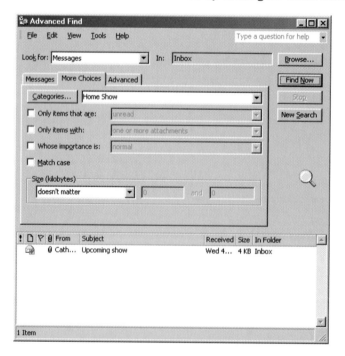

Storing and Archiving Messages

OL2002-3-3
OL2002-3-5

As messages accumulate in your Inbox and other message folders, you might need to consider other ways to store them. For example, you might want to **archive** all messages sent or received before a certain date, or save all messages related to a project as files on your hard disk. With Outlook, you can store your messages as text or HTML files on your hard disk, or archive your messages to an Outlook message file. Archiving messages in a separate Outlook message file helps you manage clutter and the size of your primary message file, while allowing easy access to archived messages from within Outlook.

Global
AutoArchive
settings
new for
OfficeXP

You can archive messages manually or automatically. When archived messages are moved to a separate message file, the messages are removed from their original folder. By default, Outlook automatically archives messages in all folders at regular intervals to a location determined by your operating system. You can change the default global settings for **AutoArchive** and choose settings for specific folders. Archive settings selected for a specific folder override the global settings for that folder. If you don't specify AutoArchive settings for a folder, Outlook uses the global settings.

In this exercise, you will save a message as a text file, save a message as an HTML file, archive messages manually, and set automatic archive options.

Important

OrderStatus
Schedule

If you haven't installed and copied the practice files for this book, please do so now. For details about installing and copying the practice files, see "Using the Book's CD-ROM" at the beginning of this book. If you want to complete only this exercise, follow the instructions in the "Using the Book's CD-ROM" section to copy just the practice files shown above the CD icon in the margin.

1   In the Inbox, click the **Order Status** message from Kim Yoshida, and on the **File** menu, click **Save As**.

The **Save As** dialog box appears, as shown on the next page.

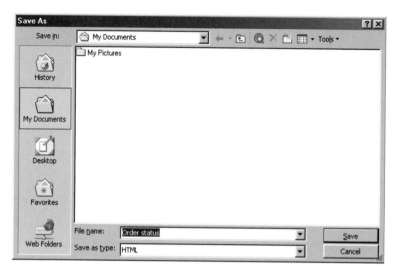

By default, messages are saved as HTML files in the My Documents folder.

Tip

Your **Save As** dialog box will reflect the contents of your My Documents folder. If you have file extensions turned on, the name in the **File Name** box will be *Order Status.htm*.

2   In the **Save As** dialog box, click **Save**.

The message is saved in the My Documents folder.

3   In the Inbox, click the **Travel Schedule** message from Kim Yoshida, and on the **File** menu, click **Save As**.

The **Save As** dialog box appears.

4   Click the down arrow to the right of the **Save as type** box, click **Text Only** in the drop-down list, and click **Save**.

The message is saved in the My Documents folder.

5   On the **Start** menu, point to **Documents**, and then click **My Documents**.

The My Documents folder opens, containing the messages you saved.

Web page

6   Double-click the HTML file you saved, which is indicated by a Web page icon.

The message opens in your Web browser.

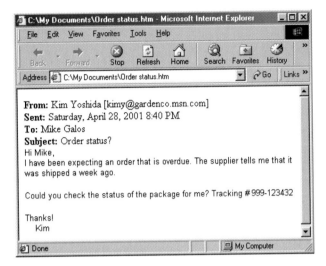

If the message contained any formatting, the HTML format would preserve it.

7 Close the browser window

8 In the My Documents folder, double-click the text file you saved, which is indicated by a Text page icon.

Text page

The message opens in Notepad.

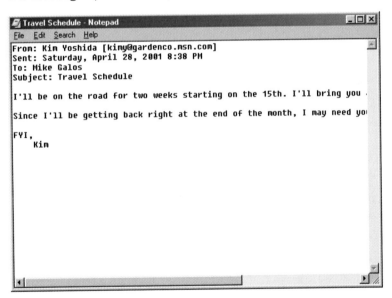

9 Close Notepad.

10 Close the My Documents folder.

11   Now you'll try archiving messages. In Outlook, on the **Tools** menu, click **Options**.

The **Options** dialog box appears.

12   Click the **Other** tab, and then click the **AutoArchive** button.

The **AutoArchive** dialog box appears.

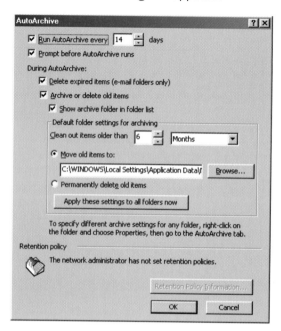

13   Review your AutoArchive default settings—particularly note the interval at which the archive will happen, the age at which items will be archived, and the location in the **Move old items to** box—and click **Cancel**.

The **AutoArchive** dialog box closes.

Tip

Mailbox Cleanup
new for
OfficeXP

With **Mailbox Cleanup**, you can see the size of your mailbox, find and delete old items or items that are larger than a certain size, start AutoArchive, or view and empty your Deleted Items folder. On the **Tools** menu, click **Mailbox Cleanup**.

14   In the **Options** dialog box, click **Cancel**.

The **Options** dialog box closes.

15 Open the **Folder List** by clicking **Folder List** on the **View** menu.

The **Folder List** appears.

16 In the **Folder List**, click **Sent Items**.

17 On the **File** menu, point to **Folder**, and click **Properties for "Sent Items"**.

The **Sent Items Properties** dialog box appears.

18 Click the **AutoArchive** tab.

The AutoArchive options are displayed.

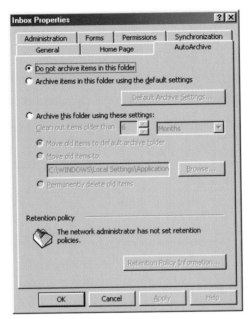

19 Select the **Archive this folder using these settings** option.

20 In the **Clean out items older than** box, select **4** and **Months**.

21 Be sure the option to **Move old items to default archive folder** is selected, and click **OK**.

The **Sent Items Properties** dialog box closes. Items in the Sent Items folder will be archived according to the new settings, whereas items in all other folders will be archived according to the default settings.

22 Now you'll set Outlook to archive your messages according to your settings. On the **File** menu, click **Archive**.

The **Archive** dialog box appears, as shown on the next page.

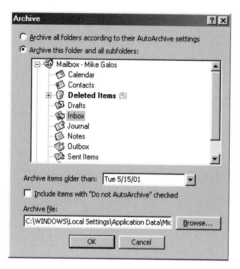

23 Be sure the **Archive this folder and all subfolders** option is selected and that the Sent Items folder is selected in the list.

24 In the **Archive items older than** list, select a date that you know is later than the date of some messages in your Sent Items folder, and click **OK**.

Outlook archives the messages in your Sent Items folder according to your settings.

25 In the **Folder List**, double-click **Archive Folders** to expand it, and click the **Sent Items** folder that appears within that folder.

The contents of the archived Sent Items folder are displayed. (Items that are copied to Outlook folders are archived based on the date they were copied rather than the date of the item itself.)

26 On the **Edit** menu, click **Select All**.

Outlook selects all the messages in the archived Sent Items folder.

Move to Folder

27 On the toolbar, click the **Move to Folder** button, and click **Sent Items** in the drop-down list.

The messages are returned to the Sent Items folder.

28 On the **Outlook Bar**, click the **Inbox** icon.

The contents of the Inbox are displayed.

29 In the **Folder List**, click **Sent Items**.

30 On the **File** menu, point to **Folder**, and click **Properties for "Sent Items"**.

The **Sent Items Properties** dialog box appears.

31 Click the **AutoArchive** tab.

The AutoArchive options are displayed.

32 Select the **Do not archive items in this folder** option, and then click **OK**.

The **Sent Items Properties** dialog box closes.

33 Close the **Folder List**, and then close the **Find** pane. Then on the **File** menu, click **Exit** to quit Outlook.

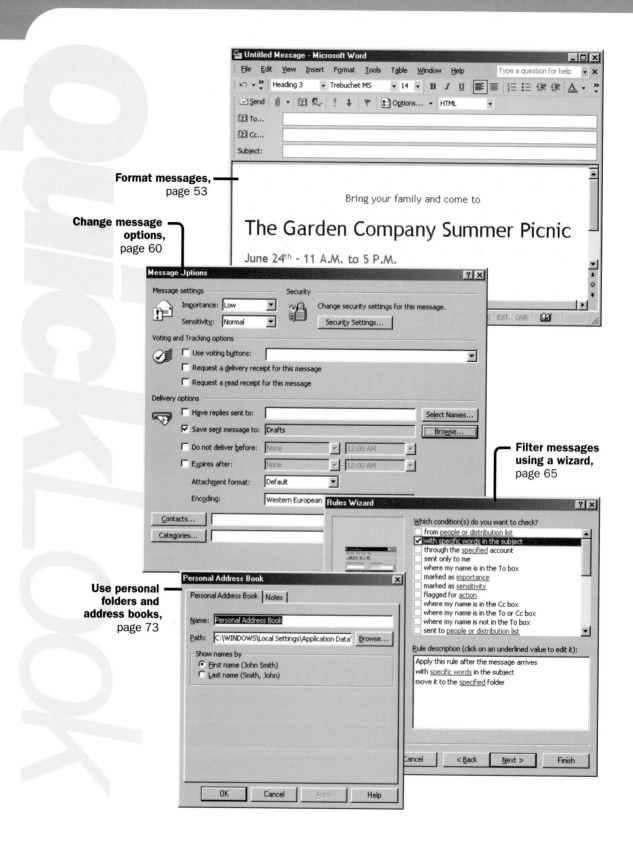

Format messages, page 53

Change message options, page 60

Filter messages using a wizard, page 65

Use personal folders and address books, page 73

Chapter 3
Customizing and Organizing E-mail Messages

After completing this chapter, you will be able to:

✔ **Format messages**
✔ **Change message options**
✔ **Filter messages**
✔ **Use personal folders and address books**

As you learn the fundamentals of sending, receiving, and managing your e-mail, you will see how using e-mail can help you work more efficiently. Because you can customize the format of your messages, select from a number of message and delivery options, filter messages, and set up personal folders and address books, you can configure Microsoft Outlook to be as convenient and useful as possible. For example, you might ask your project team to use a particular phrase in the subject line of messages related to the project. Then, when you need to focus on the project, you can filter messages to display only those items related to it.

 This chapter uses the practice files that you installed from this book's CD-ROM onto your hard disk and copied into Outlook. For details about installing and copying the practice files, see "Using the Book's CD-ROM" at the beginning of this book.

Formatting Messages

OL2002e-2-1

E-mail messages are sent in one of three formats: HTML, Plain Text, or Outlook Rich Text Format (RTF). Outlook supports all three formats. Other e-mail programs might be able to work with only some of them.

■ **HTML** is the default message format in Outlook. HTML supports text formatting, numbering, bullets, pictures and backgrounds in the message body, styles, and stationery. Most popular e-mail programs support HTML messages.

- **Outlook Rich Text Format** supports a host of formatting options including text formatting, bullets, numbering, background colors, borders, and shading. Rich Text Format is supported by some Microsoft e-mail clients, including Outlook 97 and Outlook 2000. Microsoft Outlook Express, which is distributed with several versions of Microsoft Windows, supports only HTML and Plain Text.

- **Plain Text** is supported by all e-mail programs, but as the name implies, messages in plain text do not include any formatting.

For the most part, HTML format will meet your needs. In fact, Microsoft recommends using the HTML format, whether you are sending messages over the Internet or using Microsoft Exchange Server. When you send an HTML message to someone whose e-mail program doesn't support HTML format, the message is displayed as plain text in the recipient's e-mail program. Outlook automatically converts RTF messages you send over the Internet into HTML format. When you reply to or forward a message, by default Outlook uses the format of the original message. However, you can choose the format for any message you send.

When sending messages in HTML format, you can enhance the appearance of your messages using **stationery** and **themes**. When you use stationery, you can specify the set of fonts, bullets, background color, horizontal lines, images, and other elements you want to use in outgoing e-mail messages. You can choose from a collection of predefined stationery, customize one of the patterns, create new stationery, or download new patterns from the Web. If you use Microsoft Word as your e-mail editor, you can choose from additional patterns available as Word themes.

Important

This book assumes that you use Microsoft Word as your default e-mail editor. If it's not, you can make it the default by clicking **Options** on the **Tools** menu, clicking the **Mail Format** tab, selecting the **Use Microsoft Word to edit e-mail messages** check box, and clicking **OK**.

Word as the default e-mail editor
new for
OfficeXP

In this exercise, you will use Word as the default e-mail editor to format messages in HTML, Rich Text, and Plain Text formats. You will also compose messages using stationery and themes. You don't need any practice files for this exercise.

1 If Outlook is not already open, start it now. Then if necessary, maximize the window.

Inbox

2 On the **Outlook Bar**, click the **Inbox** icon.

The contents of the Inbox are displayed.

New Mail
Message

3 On the toolbar, click the **New Mail Message** button.

A blank Message form appears.

Word's Formatting toolbar ⌐

⌐ **Message format** box

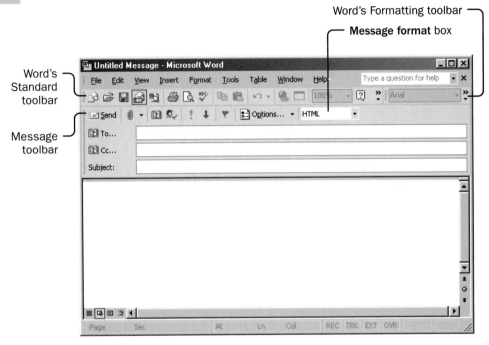

Word's
Standard
toolbar

Message
toolbar

4 Click in the body of the message, and type Wow! Have you seen the new roses?.

By default, the text is formatted in 10-point Arial (the Normal style).

5 Drag the gray bar at the left end of the Formatting toolbar to the left as far as it will go so that you can see more of its buttons.

Font Size

6 Select the word *Wow!*, and change its size by clicking the down arrow to the right of the **Font Size** box and clicking **16**.

Font Color

A

7 Click the down arrow to the right of the **Font Color** button, and click the red square.

8 On the Message form's toolbar, click the down arrow to the right of the **Message format** box, and click **Plain Text**.

A message box appears, indicating that **Plain Text** format does not support some of the formatting in the message, as shown on the next page.

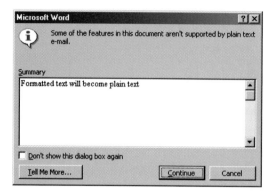

Tip

You can choose to bypass this message in the future. Before clicking **Continue**, select the **Don't show this dialog box again** check box.

9 Click the **Continue** button.

The text is formatted in 10-point Courier New (the Plain Text style), and the Formatting toolbar is unavailable.

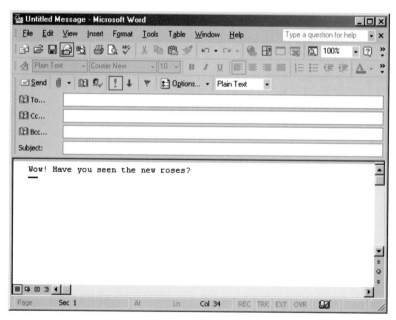

10 On the Message form's toolbar, click the down arrow to the right of the **Message format** box, and click **Rich Text**.

The message format is changed to Rich Text format, but the text remains in the Plain Text style. You can now use the Formatting toolbar to change the style or other text formatting.

Close

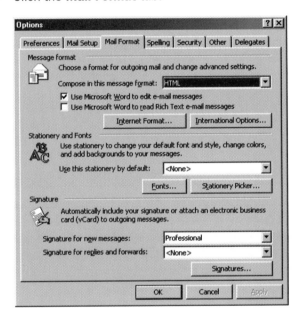

11 Click the Message form's **Close** button, and when asked if you want to keep a draft of the message, click **No**.

The Message form closes.

12 On the **Tools** menu, click **Options**.

The **Options** dialog box appears.

13 Click the **Mail Format** tab.

14 In the **Message format** area, click the down arrow to the right of the **Compose in this message format** box, click **Plain Text**, and then click **OK**.

The **Options** dialog box closes. The default message format for new messages is set to **Plain Text** format.

15 On the toolbar, click the **New Mail Message** button.

The Message form appears, with the **Plain Text** format selected.

16 Click the **Close** button.

The Message form closes.

17 On the **Tools** menu, click **Options**.

The **Options** dialog box appears.

18 Click the **Mail Format** tab.

19 In the **Message format** area, click the down arrow to the right of the **Compose in this message format** box, and then click **HTML**.

20 In the **Stationery and Fonts** area, click the down arrow to the right of the **Use this stationery by default** box, click **Clear Day**, and then click **OK**.

The **Options** dialog box closes. New messages will be formatted in HTML format using the Clear Day stationery.

21 On the toolbar, click the **New Mail Message** button.

The Message form appears, using the Clear Sky stationery.

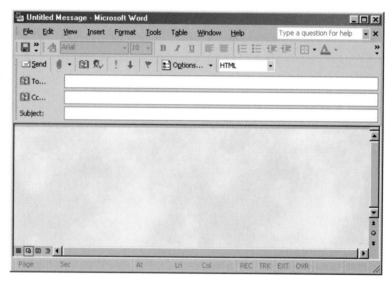

22 Click in the body of the message, and type **Bring your family and come to**.

By default, the text is formatted in 10-point Arial (the Normal style for this stationery).

Tip

You can customize message stationery. On the **Mail Format** tab of the **Options** dialog box, click the **Stationery Picker** button. To edit existing stationery, click the stationery design you want, click the **Edit** button, apply the font, background, and color formatting you want, and then click **OK**. To create new stationery, click the **New** button in the **Stationery Picker** dialog box, and follow the directions in the wizard that appears.

23 On the **Format** menu, click **Theme**.

The **Theme** dialog box appears.

24 In the **Choose a Theme** list, click **Artsy**.

A preview of the Artsy theme appears in the **Theme** dialog box.

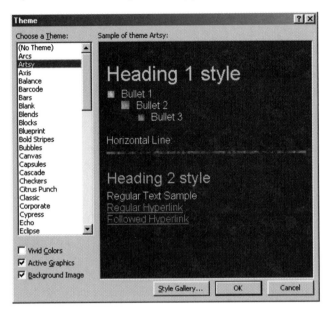

25 In the **Choose a Theme** list, click **Industrial**, and then click **OK**.

The **Theme** dialog box closes, and the Industrial theme is applied to the message, replacing the Clear Day stationery.

26 In the body of the message, press the [Enter] key, type **The Garden Company Summer Picnic**, press the [Enter] key, type **June 24th – 11 A.M. to 5 P.M.**, and then press the [Enter] key again.

Center

27 Click in the first line of text, and on the Formatting toolbar, click the **Center** button.

The line is now centered in the body of the message.

28 Click in the second line of text, and on the Formatting toolbar, click the down arrow to the right of the **Style** box, and then click **Heading 1**.

The line is now formatted with the Heading 1 style.

Tip

Toolbar Options

If you can't see the **Style** box, click the **Toolbar Options** button to display a drop-down menu of additional buttons, and set the style for the paragraph there. The **Style** box will then join the other buttons on the visible part of the Formatting toolbar.

29 Click the third line of text, and on the Formatting toolbar, click the down arrow to the right of the **Style** box, and then click **Heading 3**.

The line is now formatted with the Heading 3 style. The message looks like this:

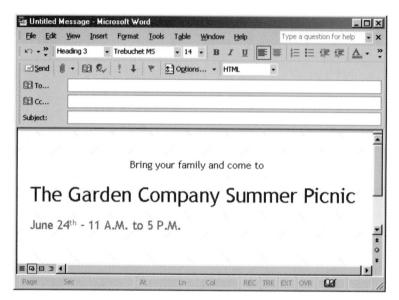

30 Click the **Close** button on the Message form, and when asked if you want to keep a draft of the message, click **No**.

The Message form closes, discarding the draft.

31 On the **Tools** menu, click **Options**, and then click the **Mail Format** tab.

32 In the **Stationery and Fonts** area, click the down arrow to the right of the **Use this stationery by default** box, click **<None>** at the top of the drop-down list, and then click **OK**.

The **Options** dialog box closes. New messages will now be formatted in HTML with no stationery applied.

Changing Message Settings and Delivery Options

OL2002-3-5

To help you manage your e-mail and convey the meaning of your messages more effectively, you can set the importance, sensitivity, and a number of delivery options for e-mail messages.

You can set a message to High, Normal, or Low **importance**. Messages sent with High importance are marked with a red exclamation point. Messages sent with Normal importance have no special marker. Messages sent with Low importance are marked with a blue arrow pointing downward. These markers show up in the **Importance** column in the Inbox.

You can also set message **sensitivity** to Normal, Personal, Private, or Confidential. Messages marked as Private cannot be modified after they are sent.

To help you manage messages you receive, you can choose to have people's replies to your messages sent to another e-mail address. For example, you might have replies sent to a new e-mail address as you transition from one to another. To help you manage messages you send, you can choose whether to save copies of your sent messages and in which folder they should be saved. You can also specify when a message will be delivered and make a message unavailable after a certain date.

In this exercise, you will set the importance of a message. You will also modify the delivery options for a message. You don't need any practice files for this exercise.

New Mail
Message

1 With your Inbox displayed in the Outlook window, on the toolbar, click the **New Mail Message** button.

A blank Message form appears.

Options...

2 On the Message form's toolbar, click the **Options** button.

The **Message Options** dialog box appears.

3 In the **Message settings** area, click the down arrow to the right of the **Importance** box, and click **High** in the drop-down list.

4 In the **Delivery options** area, select the **Have replies sent to** check box, delete the text in the adjacent box, and type kimy@gardenco.msn.com.

The dialog box looks like this:

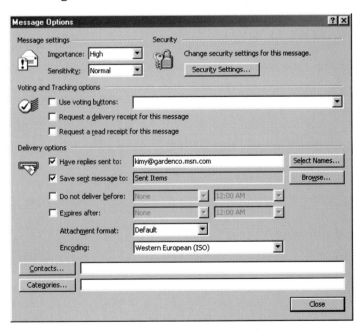

Close

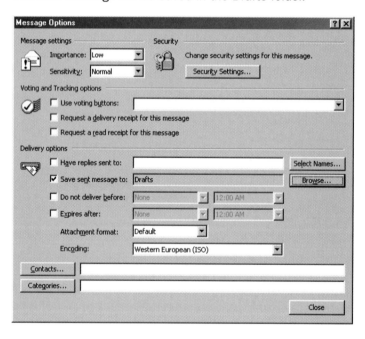

Send

5 Click the **Close** button.

The **Message Options** dialog box closes, and you return to the Message form.

6 In the **To** box, type your own e-mail address.

7 Click in the **Subject** box, type This is a message of high importance, and on the Message form's toolbar, click the **Send** button.

The Message form closes, and the message is sent.

8 On the toolbar, click the **New Mail Message** button.

A blank Message form appears.

9 On the Message form's toolbar, click the **Options** button.

The **Message Options** dialog box appears.

10 In the **Message settings** area, click the down arrow to the right of the **Importance** box, and click **Low** in the drop-down list.

11 In the **Delivery options** area, click the **Browse** button.

The **Select Folder** dialog box appears.

12 In the **Folders** list, click the **Drafts** folder, and click **OK**.

The sent message will be saved in the Drafts folder.

13 Click the **Close** button.

The **Message Options** dialog box closes, and you return to the Message form.

14 In the **To** box, type your own e-mail address.

15 Click in the **Subject** box, type **This is a message of low importance**, and on the Message form's toolbar, click the **Send** button.

The Message form closes, and the message is sent.

16 If the messages have not yet arrived in your Inbox, click the **Send/Receive** button.

Outlook downloads any new messages. The message sent with High importance is marked with a red exclamation point. The message sent with Low importance is marked with a blue arrow pointing downward.

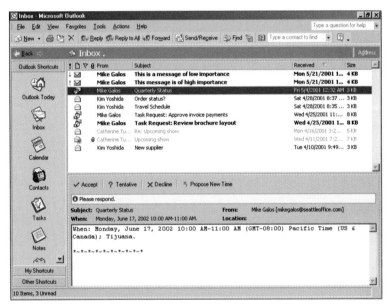

17 Double-click the message sent with High importance.

The Message window appears. The message header indicates that this message was sent with High importance.

18 On the toolbar, click the **Reply** button.

The Reply form appears. The **To** box contains the e-mail address you entered earlier, *kimy@gardenco.msn.com*, as shown on the next page.

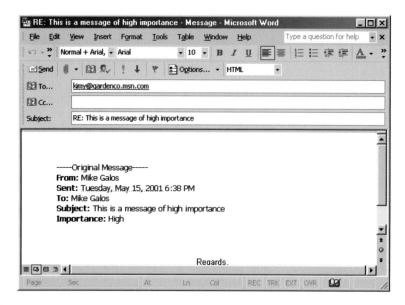

Close

19 Click the **Close** button.

The Reply form closes.

Recalling Messages

If you are connected to a network that uses Microsoft Exchange Server, you can recall messages you've sent. For example, if you discover errors in a message you've sent, you can recall the message so that you can correct the error and resend the message.

To recall a message:

1 If the **Folder List** is not open, click **Folder List** on the **View** menu.

2 In the **Folder List**, click **Sent Items**.

3 Double-click the message you want to recall to open it in a Message window.

4 On the **Actions** menu, click **Recall This Message**.

5 Select whether you want to delete unread copies of the message or delete unread copies and replace them with a new message, and then click **OK**.

You can recall or replace a message only if its recipient is logged on, is using Microsoft Outlook, and has not yet read the message or moved it from the Inbox.

20 Click the **Close** button on the Message window.

The Message window closes.

21 On the Folder banner, click the down arrow to the right of Inbox, and then click **Drafts** in the drop-down list.

The contents of the Drafts folder are displayed, including the copy of the message you sent with Low importance.

22 On the **Outlook Bar**, click the **Inbox** icon.

The contents of the Inbox are displayed.

Filtering Messages

OL2002e-2-2

As messages accumulate in your Inbox, it can be a challenge to find a message you need when you need it. To help meet this challenge, you can **filter** your messages by customizing views. When you filter messages, you display only those messages that meet common criteria, helping you identify a specific collection of messages. You can also create rules to move your messages to selected folders as you receive them, and you can filter out junk e-mail or e-mail with adult content.

In this exercise, you will create a view to filter messages and create a rule that will move messages out of the Inbox.

Important

NextShow
ReNextShow
Schedule

If you haven't installed and copied the practice files for this book, please do so now. For details about installing and copying the practice files, see "Using the Book's CD-ROM" at the beginning of this book. If you want to complete only this exercise, follow the instructions in the "Using the Book's CD-ROM" section to copy just the practice files shown above the CD icon in the margin.

1 With your Inbox displayed in Outlook, on the **View** menu, point to **Current View**, and click **Define Views**.

The **Define Views for "Inbox"** dialog box appears, as shown on the next page.

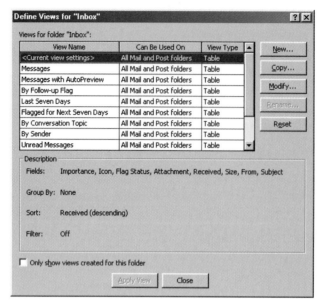

2 Click the **Copy** button.

The **Copy View** dialog box appears.

3 In the **Name of new view** box, type Filtered for Show, and click **OK**.

The **Copy View** dialog box closes, and the **View Summary** dialog box appears, showing the settings from the view you copied.

4 Click the **Filter** button.

The **Filter** dialog box appears.

5 In the **Search for the word(s)** box, type show, and click **OK**.

The **Filter** dialog box closes, and the **View Summary** dialog box appears, showing the new filter settings.

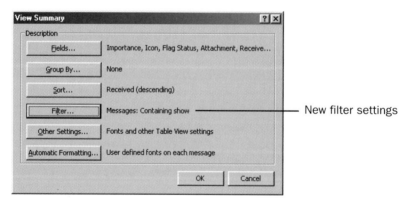

6 In the **View Summary** dialog box, click **OK**.

The **View Summary** dialog box closes, and you are returned to the **Define Views for "Inbox"** dialog box, which shows the new view in the **View Name** list.

7 Make sure **Filtered for Show** is highlighted in the **View Name** list, and click the **Apply View** button.

The **Define Views for "Inbox"** dialog box closes, and the Inbox is displayed, containing only the messages with the word *show* in the subject. The Folder banner indicates that a filter is applied.

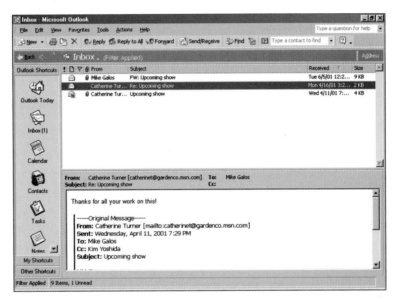

8 On the **View** menu, point to **Current View**.

The list of available views appears, including the new Filtered for Show view.

9 Click **Messages** on the **Current View** submenu.

The filter is removed, and all your messages appear in the Inbox.

10 Now you'll create a rule to manage messages that meet specific criteria. On the **Tools** menu, click **Rules Wizard**.

The first page of the **Rules Wizard** appears, as shown on next page.

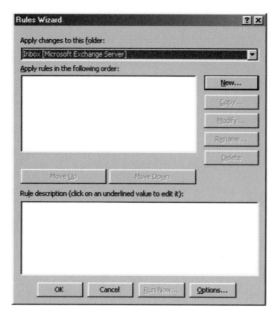

11 Click the **New** button.

The next page of the **Rules Wizard** appears. The **Start creating a rule from a template** option is selected. Take a moment to look over the types of rules you can create from a template. (If the Office Assistant offers to help you, click **No, don't provide help now**.)

12 Be sure that **Move new messages from someone** is selected, and click the **Next** button.

The next page of the **Rules Wizard** appears.

13 In the **Which condition(s) do you want to check?** list, clear the **from people or distribution list** check box, and select the **with specific words in the subject** check box.

The description in the **Rule description** box is updated to reflect the change. The underlined words in the description are values that you must specify to complete the rule.

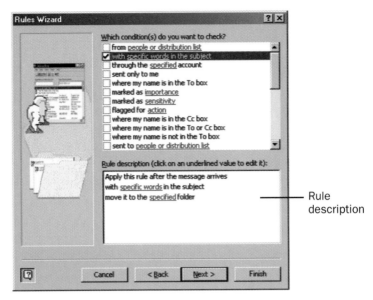

Rule description

14 In the **Rule description** box, click the underlined words **specific words**.

The **Search Text** dialog box appears.

15 In the **Specify words or phrases to search for in the subject** box, type Travel, click the **Add** button, and then click **OK**.

The **Rule description** box is updated to reflect the change.

16 Click the **Next** button.

The next page of the **Rules Wizard** is displayed.

17 In the **What do you want to do with the message?** box, be sure the **move it to the specified folder** check box is selected, and in the **Rule description** box, click the underlined word **specified**.

The **Rules Wizard** dialog box appears, showing a list of folders for you to choose from.

18 Click the **New** button.

The **Create New Folder** dialog box appears.

19 In the **Name** box, type Travel, and in the **Select where to place the folder** list, click **Inbox**.

The dialog box now looks like the graphic shown on the next page.

20 Click **OK**.

21 If prompted to add a shortcut to the **Outlook Bar**, click **No**, and then in the
Rules Wizard dialog box, click **OK**.

The dialog box closes, and the **Rule description** box is updated to reflect
your folder selection.

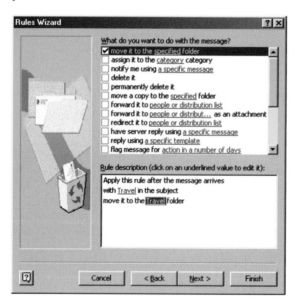

22 Click the **Next** button.

The next page of the **Rules Wizard** is displayed.

23 In the **Add any exceptions (if necessary)** list, select the **except if it is flagged for action** check box, and in the **Rule description** box, click the underlined word **action**.

The **Flagged Message** dialog box appears.

24 Click the down arrow to the right of the **Flag** box to see the available options, click **Any**, and click **OK**.

The **Rule description** box is updated to reflect your selection.

25 Click the **Next** button.

The final page of the **Rules Wizard** is displayed, summarizing the parameters you have set for the Travel rule.

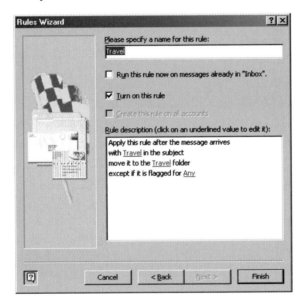

26 Select the **Run this rule now on messages already in "Inbox"** check box, and click the **Finish** button.

The rule is saved and is now listed in the **Rules Wizard** dialog box, as shown on the next page.

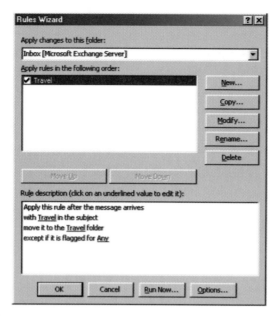

27 Click **OK**.

The rule is now active, and Outlook applies it to the messages in the Inbox.

28 In the **Folder List**, click the plus sign (+) to the left of the Inbox folder, and then click the **Travel** folder.

The contents of the Travel folder are displayed, including the Travel Schedule message from Kim Yoshida.

29 In the **Folder List**, click **Inbox**.

The contents of the Inbox are displayed.

Tip

If you are using Microsoft Exchange Server, you can filter messages even when you are away from the office by using the Out of Office Assistant. When you have more experience with Outlook, you might want to explore this feature by clicking **Out of Office Assistant** on the **Tools** menu.

Filtering Junk E-mail Messages

Outlook offers several options for managing junk e-mail messages—the unsolicited advertisements and solicitation letters that can swamp your Inbox if your e-mail address finds its way into the hands of unscrupulous mailing list vendors. You can color-code junk messages for easy identification, or you can move them to another folder to reduce clutter in your Inbox. You can manage messages with adult content in the same way.

To filter junk e-mail or adult-content messages:

1   On the toolbar, click the **Organize** button.

The **Ways to Organize Inbox** pane appears.

2   In the **Ways to Organize Inbox** pane, click **Junk E-Mail**.

3   To color-code junk messages, in the first line, set the first box to **color**, and in the second box, click a color in the drop-down list.

You can also set the first box to **move** and select a destination folder in the second box.

4   Click the **Turn On** button to turn on the rule for filtering junk messages.

5   To filter adult-content messages, in the second line, select either **color** or **move**, and then select a specific color or destination.

6   Click the **Turn On** button to turn on the rule for filtering messages with adult content.

7   Close the **Ways to Organize Inbox** pane.

The filtering rules remain in effect behind the scenes until you turn them off.

Using Personal Folders and Address Books

OL2002e-2-3

The items you create and receive in Outlook—messages, appointments, tasks, notes, and journal entries—are kept in a data file either on a server on your network or on the hard disk in your computer.

■   If your information is kept on a server, which is the case when you are working on a network that uses Microsoft Exchange Server, it is part of a file called a **private store**. You can access this store only when you are connected to your server.

■   If your information is kept on your computer, it is stored in a **Personal Folders file** that has a .pst file extension. The default Personal Folders file is Outlook.pst. You can access this file whether or not you are connected to your ISP.

Whether you are working on a networked or a stand-alone computer, you can create Personal Folders files to store Outlook items on the hard disk of your own computer. If you are working on a network, you might want to do this so that certain items are available whether or not you are connected to the server—if you work on a laptop that you use both in the office and at home, for example. If you are not working on a network, you might want to do this so that you can keep items related to a particular project in a separate Personal Folders file. Then you can back up that file separately from your other Outlook items, or you can copy that file to another computer.

For the same reason, you might want to create a **Personal Address Book** to store e-mail addresses and distribution lists separately from your Contacts folder. Personal Address Book files have a .pab file extension and can be stored on your local computer.

In this exercise, you will create a Personal Folders file, move messages and folders to the new file, add a Personal Address Book, and create a personal distribution list.

Important

NextShow
ReNextShow
Travel
GardenCo

If you haven't installed and copied the practice files for this book, please do so now. For details about installing and copying the practice files, see "Using the Book's CD-ROM" at the beginning of this book. If you did not work through the previous exercise in this chapter, you also need to complete steps 1 through 7 of this exercise to import the Travel folder into Outlook. If you did work through the previous exercise, you can skip these steps. You will also use the GardenCo Personal Address Book located in the SBS\Outlook\Personal folder, which is probably on drive C.

1   On the **File** menu, click **Import and Export**.

The **Import and Export Wizard** appears.

2   In the **Choose an action to perform** list, click **Import from another program or file**, and then click **Next**.

The next page of the **Import and Export Wizard** appears.

3   In the **Select file type to import from** list, click **Personal Folder File (.pst)**, and then click **Next**.

4   On the next page of the **Import and Export Wizard**, click the **Browse** button.

The **Open Personal Folders** dialog box appears.

5   Click the down arrow to the right of the **Look in** box, browse to the SBS\Outlook\Address folder, click **Travel**, and then click the **Open** button.

The **Open Personal Folders** dialog box closes, and the path to the folder you selected appears in the **File to import** box.

6   In the **Import and Export Wizard**, make sure the **Replace duplicates with items imported** option is selected, and click **Next**.

7 In the **Select the folder to import from** list, click the **Travel** folder, and then click **Finish**.

The Travel folder is added to your **Folder List**. (If the **Folder List** is not visible, display it by clicking **Folder List** on the **View** menu.)

8 On the **Tools** menu, click **Options**, and then click the **Mail Setup** tab.

The **Options** dialog box appears, with the **Mail Setup** options displayed.

9 Click the **Data Files** button to display the **Outlook Data Files** dialog box.

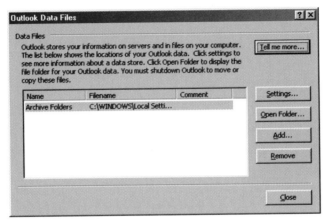

10 Click the **Add** button, and in the **New Outlook Data File** dialog box, click **OK** to create a new Personal Folders file.

The **Create or Open Outlook Data File** dialog box appears.

11 In the **File name** box, type **personal.pst**, and click **OK**.

The **Create Microsoft Personal Folders** dialog box appears.

12 In the **Name** box, type MikeG as a distinct name for this file, and click **OK**.

The **Outlook Data Files** dialog box is displayed, showing the new Personal Folders file.

13 Click the **Close** button, and in the **Options** dialog box, click **OK**.

The **Options** dialog box closes.

14 In the **Folder List**, double-click **MikeG**.

The contents of the Personal Folders file are displayed in the Inbox (currently the file is empty), and the folder is expanded in the **Folder List**. By default, the Personal Folders file contains its own Deleted Items folder.

New Personal ———
Folders file

15 In the **Folder List**, click **Inbox**.

The contents of the Inbox are displayed.

16 Click the **Upcoming show** message from Catherine Turner, and then hold down the Ctrl key and click the **RE: Upcoming show** message.

The messages are selected.

Move to Folder

17 On the toolbar, click the **Move to Folder** button, and then click **Move to Folder** on the drop-down menu.

The **Move Items** dialog box appears.

18 In the **Move the selected items to the folder** list, click **MikeG**, and then click **OK**.

The **Move Items** dialog box closes, and the messages are moved to the new Personal Folders file.

19 In the **Folder List**, click **MikeG**.

The contents of the new Personal Folders file, including the two messages you just moved, are displayed.

20 In the **Folder List**, drag the **Travel** folder to the **MikeG** folder.

The folder and its contents are moved to the new Personal Folders file.

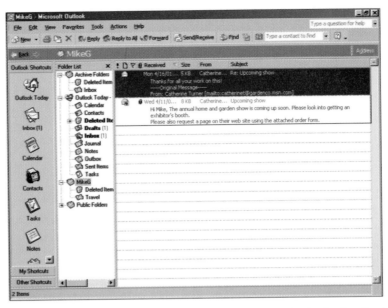

21 Now you will add a Personal Address Book to Outlook. On the **Tools** menu, click **E-mail Accounts** to display the **E-mail Accounts** dialog box.

22 Select the **Add a new directory or address book** option, and click **Next**.

The **Directory or Address Book Type** page appears.

23 Select the **Additional Address Books** option, and click **Next**.

The **Other Address Book Types** page appears.

24 In the **Additional Address Book Types** list, click **Personal Address Book**, and then click **Next**.

The **Personal Address Book** dialog box appears.

25 Click the **Browse** button to open the **Use Personal Address Book** dialog box.

26 Click the down arrow to the right of the **Look in** box, browse to the SBS \Outlook\Personal folder, which is probably on drive C, click **GardenCo**, and then click the **Open** button.

In the **Personal Address Book** dialog box, the path to the GardenCo file appears in the **Path** box.

27 Click **OK**, and in the **Add E-mail Account** message box, click **OK** again.

The address book is added, but you must restart Outlook to use it.

28 On the **File** menu, click **Exit** to quit Outlook.

Microsoft
Outlook

29 On your desktop, double-click the **Microsoft Outlook** icon to start Outlook.

30 On the **Tools** menu, click **Address Book**. Then click the down arrow to the right of the **Show Names from the** box, and click **Personal Address Book**.

The contents of the Personal Address Book are displayed, including entries for Catherine Turner and Kim Yoshida.

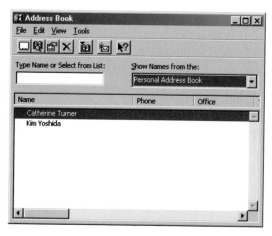

New Entry

31 On the toolbar, click the **New Entry** button.

The **New Entry dialog** box appears.

32 In the **Put this entry** area, click the down arrow to the right of the **In the** box, and then click **Personal Address Book** in the drop-down list.

33 In the **Select the entry type** list, click **Personal Distribution List**, and then click **OK**.

The **New Personal Distribution List Properties** dialog box appears.

34 In the **Name** box, type Team, and click the **Add/Remove Members** button.

The **Edit Members of Team** dialog box appears.

35 In the **Show Names from the** list, click **Personal Address Book**.

The names in the Personal Address Book appear in the **Name** list.

Tip

You can also add contacts to your personal distribution lists. In the **Edit Members** dialog box, click **Contacts** in the **Show Names from the** list to show names from the Contacts folder, and then click the names you want.

36 In the **Name** list, click **Catherine Turner**, hold down the ⌈shift⌋ key and click **Kim Yoshida**, and then click the **Members** button.

The names are added to the **Personal Distribution List** box.

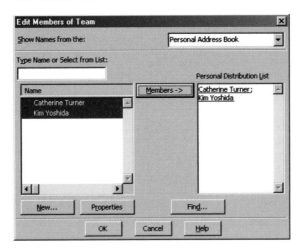

37 Click **OK**, and in the **New Personal Distribution List Properties** dialog box, click **OK**.

The Address Book shows the new distribution list. Distribution lists appear in bold and are marked with an icon, as shown on the next page.

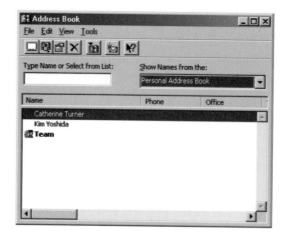

New Mail
Message

39 On the toolbar, click the **New Mail Message** button.

A new, blank Message form appears.

40 Click the **To** button, click the down arrow to the right of the **Show Names from the** box, and then click **Personal Address Book** in the drop-down list.

The contents of the Personal Address Book are displayed in the **Name** list.

41 In the **Name** list, click the **Team** distribution list, click the **To** button, and then click **OK**.

The **Team** distribution list appears in the **To** box.

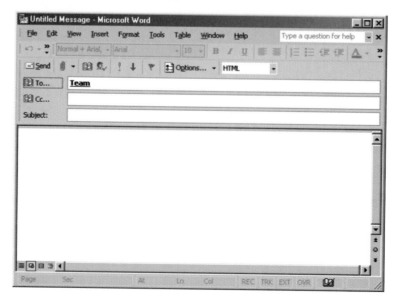

42 Click the **Close** button, and click **No** when prompted to save the message draft.

The Message form closes, discarding the draft.

43 Close the **Folder List** by clicking its **Close** button. If you are not continuing on to the next chapter, close any open messages, and on the **File** menu, click **Exit** to quit Outlook.

Checking Addresses

By default, Outlook will check any e-mail address you type against the entries in the Outlook Address Book. If the address book does not contain an entry for a name that you type in the **To**, **Cc**, or **Bcc** boxes of a new message, when you send the message, Outlook will prompt you to select an address book entry or provide a full address.

To have Outlook check entries from your Personal Address Book:

1 On the **Tools** menu, click **Address Book**.

2 On the **Address Book** window's **Tools** menu, click **Options**.

3 In the **Addressing** dialog box, click the **Add** button.

4 In the **Add Address List** dialog box, click **Personal Address Book**, and then click the **Add** button.

5 Click the **Close** button.

6 In the **Addressing** dialog box, click **OK**.

7 In the **Address Book** window, click the **Close** button.

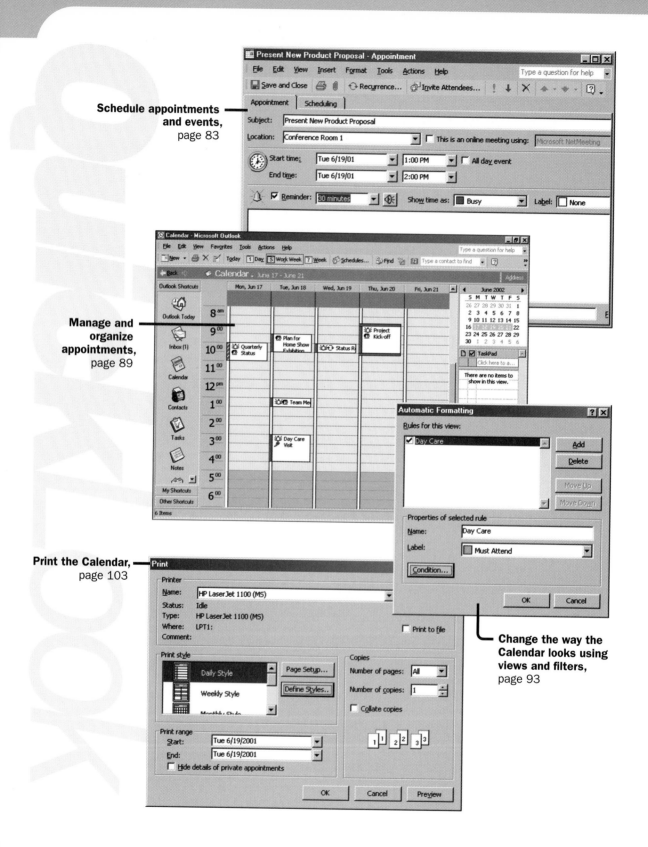

Schedule appointments and events, page 83

Manage and organize appointments, page 89

Print the Calendar, page 103

Change the way the Calendar looks using views and filters, page 93

Chapter 4
Managing Your Calendar

After completing this chapter, you will be able to:
✔ **Schedule appointments and events**
✔ **Manage and organize appointments**
✔ **Change the way the Calendar looks**
✔ **Print your Calendar**

Managing time effectively is a constant challenge for most people today. Microsoft Outlook's **Calendar** makes it easy for you to manage your schedule, including both appointments and events, as well as to view and print your schedule for a day, a week, or a month.

This chapter uses the practice files that you installed from this book's CD-ROM onto your hard disk and copied into Outlook. For details about installing and copying the practice files, see "Using the Book's CD-ROM" at the beginning of this book.

Scheduling Appointments and Events

OL2002-2-1
OL2002e-3-2

Adding your time commitments to a calendar can help you manage your daily schedule. You can use Outlook's Calendar to schedule **appointments** (which typically last just part of a day) or **events** (which typically last all day long). For example, you might create an appointment in your Outlook Calendar for the time you will spend seeing your doctor, and you might schedule an event for an all-day seminar you plan to attend. Both appointments and events can be **recurring**, meaning they occur repeatedly at regular intervals—for example, daily, weekly, or monthly. You can specify a subject and location for each Calendar item as well as the date and time. You can indicate your availability as available, tentative, busy, or out of the office during the scheduled time, and you can choose to receive a reminder of an appointment or event. Reminders appear in a small dialog box that appears as the time of the appointment or event approaches. Outlook must be open for you to receive reminders.

You can also mark an appointment as **private**. Private appointments appear on your Calendar, but the details are hidden from others.

By default, your Calendar looks like this:

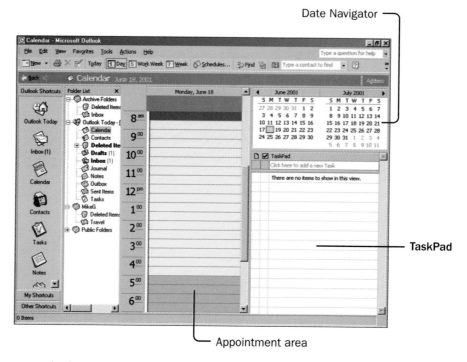

Date Navigator

TaskPad

Appointment area

In Outlook's Calendar, the day is broken into half-hour increments, with the hours between 8 A.M. and 5 P.M. on weekdays highlighted as the default **work week**. You can change the Calendar's work week to reflect your own working hours, and you can schedule appointments for any time of any day.

The **Date Navigator** serves as a handy month calendar and an easy way to view your schedule for specific dates. To view your schedule for a particular date, simply click that date in the Date Navigator. You can use the **Task Pad** to view your current tasks and add new ones without opening the Tasks folder.

In this exercise, you will view and move around your Calendar, schedule an appointment, make a recurring appointment, and schedule an event. You don't need any practice files for this exercise.

1 If it is not already open, start Outlook, and then maximize its window.

Calendar

2 On the **Outlook Bar**, click the **Calendar** icon.

Your Calendar is displayed, showing today's schedule.

3 If necessary, close the **Folder List** by clicking **Folder List** on the **View** menu. Then in the Date Navigator, click tomorrow's date.

Tomorrow's schedule is displayed.

4   Double-click the 1 P.M. time slot.

The Appointment form appears.

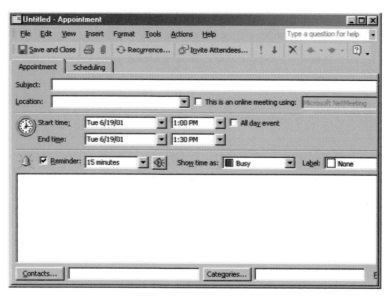

5   In the **Subject** box, type **Present New Product Proposal**.

6   Press the ⇥ key, and in the **Location** box, type **Conference Room 1**.

7   Click the down arrow to the right of the second **End time** box, and click **2:00 PM** in the drop-down list to extend the meeting duration to an hour.

8   Click the down arrow to the right of the **Reminder** box, and click **30 minutes** in the drop-down list to allow time to set up for your presentation.

The Appointment form now looks like this:

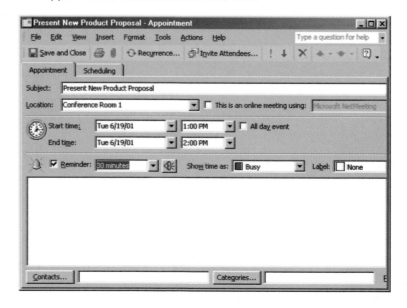

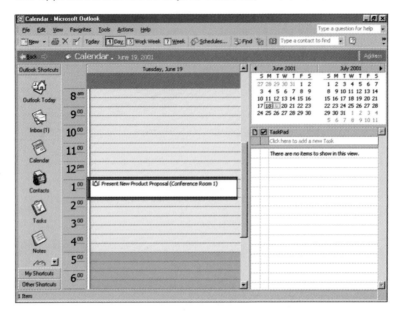

🔲 Save and Close   **9**   Click the **Save and Close** button.

The appointment is saved in your Calendar, where it looks like this:

Tip

You can quickly create an appointment by clicking the appropriate place on the Calendar. Appointments created this way will use the default reminder setting and won't list a meeting location.

10   In the Date Navigator, click the Wednesday of the third week of next month.

The schedule for the selected day of the month is displayed.

11   Double-click the 10 A.M. time slot.

The Appointment form appears.

12   In the **Subject** box, type **Status Report**.

13   Press the ⊞ key, and in the **Location** box, type **Boss's Office**.

↻ Recurrence...   **14**   Click the **Recurrence** button.

The **Appointment Recurrence** dialog box appears.

15   In the **Recurrence pattern** area, select the **Monthly** option, and then select **The third Wednesday of every 1 month(s)** option.

The dialog box now looks like this:

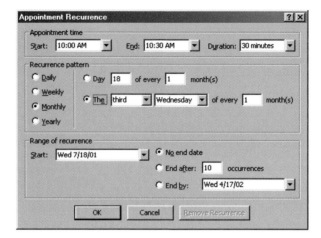

16 Click **OK**.

The recurrence settings are added to the Appointment form.

Recurrence settings ⌐

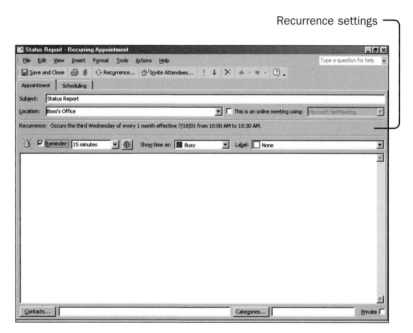

17 Click the **Save and Close** button.

The recurring appointment is added to your Calendar.

18 In the Date Navigator, click the right arrow.

The Date Navigator shows the next month, with the third Wednesday appearing bold, indicating that an appointment is scheduled for that day.

19 On the **View** menu, point to **Go To**, and click **Go to Date**.

The **Go To Date** dialog box appears, as shown on the next page.

20 In the **Date** box, type 12/23/02, and click **OK**.

The schedule for December 23rd, 2002, is displayed.

21 Right-click the 9 A.M. time slot, and click **New All Day Event** on the shortcut menu.

The Event form appears.

22 In the **Subject** box, type Out for the Holidays.

23 Clear the **Reminder** check box.

24 Click the down arrow to the right of the **Show time as** box, and click **Out of Office** in the drop-down list.

25 In the bottom right corner of the Event form, select the **Private** check box.

The form now looks like this:

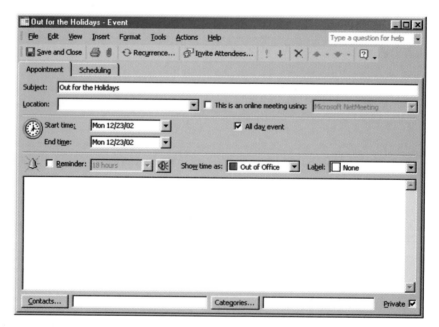

Tip

You can easily mark an existing appointment as private. Simply right-click the appointment in the Calendar, and click **Private** on the shortcut menu.

26 Click the **Save and Close** button.

The new event is added to your Calendar, with a key icon indicating that the appointment is marked as private.

Tip

By default, Outlook adds the typical holidays for your country as events on your Calendar, but you can add the holidays of other countries. On the **Tools** menu, click **Options**. On the **Preferences** tab, click **Calendar Options**, and click the **Add Holidays** button. Select the countries whose holidays you want to add, and then click **OK**. Click **OK** again to close the confirmation message that appears, and then click **OK** twice to close the remaining dialog boxes.

27 Navigate to the location of the Status Report appointment and right-click the appointment.

28 On the shortcut menu, click **Delete**. In the **Confirm Delete** dialog box that appears, select the **Delete the series** option.

The appointment is deleted.

29 Navigate to the location of the Present New Product Proposal appointment, and right-click the appointment.

30 On the shortcut menu, click **Delete**.

The appointment is deleted.

31 On the toolbar, click the **Today** button.

Today's schedule is displayed.

Managing and Organizing Appointments

OL2002-2-4

You can use the Outlook Calendar to manage and organize your appointments in a variety of ways. You can enter details about an appointment to help you remember important information, such as the agenda for a meeting or directions to a client's office. And as with e-mail messages, you can assign categories to help you sort your appointments. For example, you might assign a dentist appointment to the Personal category. Outlook includes a selection of useful categories, including Business, Personal, and Miscellaneous, but you can create additional categories to meet your needs. When your schedule changes, you can also move, copy, and delete appointments.

In this exercise, you will add details to an appointment, assign a category to an appointment, and move, copy, and delete an appointment. You don't need any practice files for this exercise.

1   With your Calendar displayed in Outlook, click tomorrow's date in the Date Navigator.

Tomorrow's schedule is displayed.

2   Click the 9 A.M. time slot, type **Budget Meeting**, and press the [Enter] key.

The appointment is added to the Calendar.

3   Double-click the appointment to edit it.

The Appointment form appears.

4   Click in the **Location** box, and type **Conference Room 1**.

Tip

Outlook remembers the locations you type in the **Location** box. Instead of typing the location again, you can click the down arrow to the right of the **Location** box and then click the location you want.

5   Click the down arrow to the right of the second **Start time** box, and click **9:30 AM** in the drop-down list.

6   Click the down arrow to the right of the second **End time** box, and click **10:30 AM** in the drop-down list.

7   Be sure the **Reminder** check box is selected, and in the **Reminder** list, click **1 hour**.

8   Click the comments area below the reminder, and type a rough agenda for the meeting like the one shown here:

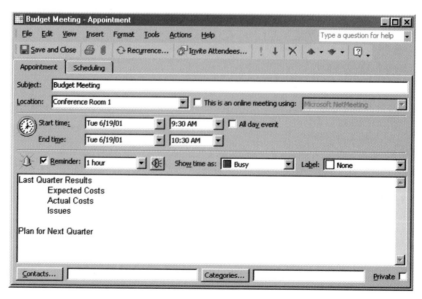

9 At the bottom of the Appointment form, click the **Categories** button.

The **Categories** dialog box appears.

10 Click in the **Item(s) belong to these categories** box, type Finance, and click the **Add to List** button.

The **Finance** category is added to the list and is selected.

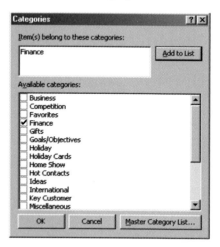

11 In the **Available categories** list, select the **Business** check box, and click **OK**.

The selected categories are added to the **Categories** box in the Appointment form.

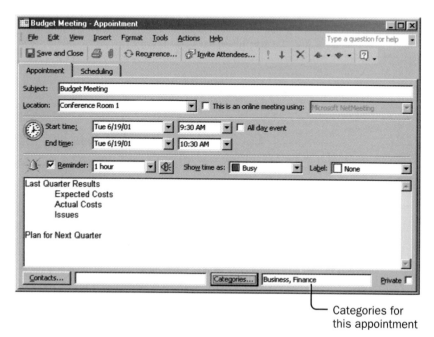

Categories for
this appointment

Save and Close

12 Click the **Save and Close** button.

The updated appointment is added to the Calendar.

13 Click the 12 P.M. time slot, and type **Lunch with Susan**.

14 Point to the bottom border of the appointment, and when the pointer changes to a vertical double-headed arrow, drag the bottom of the appointment to 1 P.M., and then press the ⌈Enter⌋ key.

The appointment is added to the Calendar.

Today

15 On the toolbar, click the **Today** button.

The schedule for today is displayed. In the Date Navigator, tomorrow's date appears in bold, indicating that appointments are scheduled for that day.

16 In the Date Navigator, click tomorrow's date.

Tomorrow's schedule is displayed.

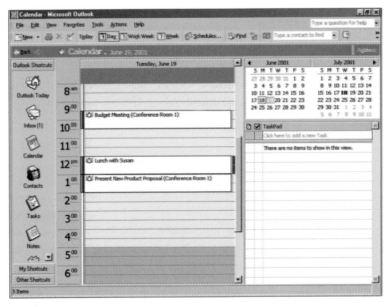

17 Point to the left border of the **Lunch with Susan** appointment.

The pointer becomes a four-headed arrow.

18 Drag the appointment to the 11:30 A.M. time slot.

The lunch appointment is rescheduled for 11:30 A.M.

19 Point to the left border of the **Budget Meeting** appointment.

The pointer becomes a four-headed arrow.

20 Using the right mouse button, drag the appointment to the same day of the following week in the Date Navigator.

A shortcut menu appears.

21 On the shortcut menu, click **Copy**.

The schedule for the same day next week is displayed, showing the Budget Meeting appointment.

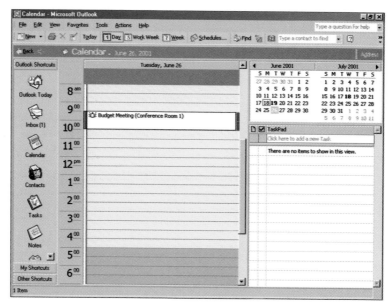

22 In the Date Navigator, click tomorrow's date.

Tomorrow's schedule is displayed, showing the original Budget Meeting appointment.

Delete

23 Click the **Lunch with Susan** appointment, and on the toolbar, click the **Delete** button.

The appointment is removed from your Calendar.

Changing the Way the Calendar Looks

OL2002-2-2

To help you stay on top of your schedule, Outlook provides a variety of ways to view your Calendar. For daily use, you can look at one day at a time. For short-term planning, you can see a five-day work week or a seven-day week. You can view an entire month for long-term planning. You can set your default work schedule as well as choose how appointments are displayed using a set of customizable views and filters, similar to those available for e-mail messages.

Calendar coloring
new for
OfficeXP

To make important appointments stand out in your Calendar, you can color-code them using labels. Labels allow you to color-code appointments so that you know the type of an appointment at a glance. The available labels include Important, Business, and Personal. Labels can help you get ready for your appointments. You can apply the Travel Required label to remind you that an appointment takes place away from your office or apply the Needs Preparation label to an appointment for which you must prepare a presentation.

About Calendar Views

Outlook offers a number of ways to view your Calendar. To select the view, on the **View** menu, point to **Current View**, and then click the view you want.

Click this view	To see
Day/Week/Month	A calendar-like view of appointments, events, and meetings for the period of time you specify. This is the default view, and it includes the **TaskPad**.
Day/Week/Month With AutoPreview	The Day/Week/Month view with the addition of the first line of comment text for each Calendar item.
Active Appointments	A list of appointments and meetings scheduled for today and in the future, showing details in columns.
Events	A list of events, showing details in columns.
Annual Events	A list of annual events, showing details in columns.
Recurring Appointments	A list of recurring appointments, showing details in columns.
By Category	A list of all items, grouped by category, showing details in columns.

In this exercise, you will view items during a specified period of time, change your Calendar view, add colors to appointments manually and by using a rule, and change your default work week schedule.

Important

DayCareVisit
TeamMeeting

If you haven't installed and copied the practice files for this book, please do so now. For details about installing and copying the practice files, see "Using the Book's CD-ROM" at the beginning of this book. If you want to complete only this exercise, follow the instructions in the "Using the Book's CD-ROM" section to copy just the practice file shown above the CD icon in the margin.

1   With your Calendar displayed in Outlook, point to the right frame of the Calendar. When you pointer changes to a double-sided arrow, drag the frame to the right until only one month is visible in the Date Navigator.

5 Work Week   **2**   Navigate to June 2002 in the Date Navigator, click **18**, and then click the **Work Week** button on the toolbar.

The Calendar shows the schedule for Monday through Friday of the week containing the date you selected.

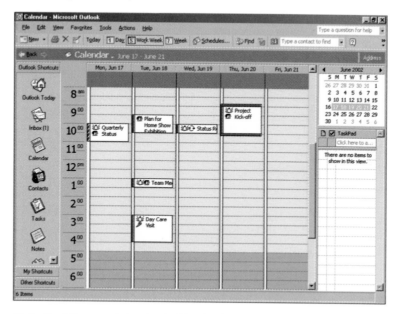

Note that the week is shaded in the Date Navigator.

7 Week   **3**   On the toolbar, click the **Week** button.

The Calendar now shows the schedule for the seven-day week containing the date that was selected when you clicked the **Week** button. The week is shaded in the Date Navigator.

4   In the Date Navigator, click in the margin to the left of Sunday of the next week.

The Calendar now shows the schedule for next week.

31 Month   **5**   On the toolbar, click the **Month** button. (If necessary, click the **Toolbar Options** button at the right end of the toolbar, and click the **Month** button on the drop-down menu.)

The Calendar shows the schedule for the current month, as shown on the next page.

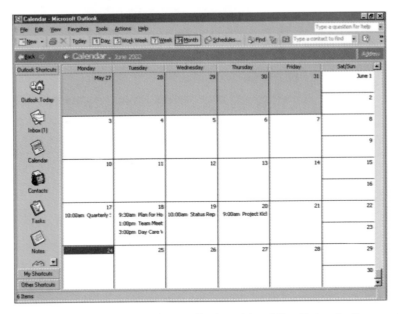

Dates in the current month are displayed in white. Dates in the months immediately preceding or following are displayed in gray. Gray and white alternate for each month thereafter.

6 On the toolbar, click the **Day** button.

You see the familiar display for a single day—in this case, showing any appointments scheduled for the date you selected in step 2.

7 Click the **Today** button.

The Calendar displays today's schedule.

8 On the **View** menu, point to **Current View**, and click **Day/Week/Month View With AutoPreview**.

9 Click tomorrow's date in the Date Navigator.

Calendar items are displayed with the first line of comment text. If you have no appointments on the date shown, click any Tuesday after July 2001 in the Date Navigator to see the Team Meeting appointment, which contains comment text.

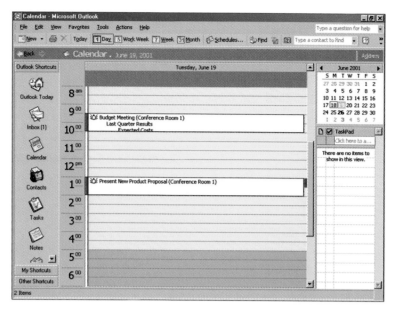

10 On the **View** menu, point to **Current View**, and click **By Category**.

Calendar items are displayed in a columnar list, grouped by category.

11 Click the plus (+) sign to the left of the **Personal** category.

The item in the Personal category is displayed.

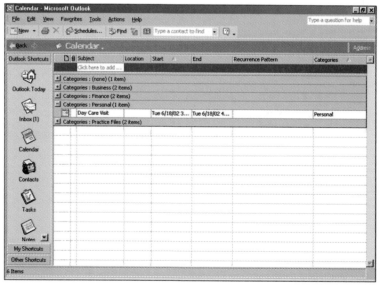

12 On the **View** menu, point to **Current View**, and click **Day/Week/Month**.

The Calendar displays today's schedule.

Save and Close

13 Navigate to June 18, 2002, add an appointment at 11:00 A.M. called **Budget Meeting**, and then double-click the **Budget Meeting** appointment.

The Appointment form appears.

14 Click the down arrow to the right of the **Label** box, click **Business**, and then click the **Save and Close** button.

The updated appointment is saved in your Calendar, appearing in blue to indicate it is business related.

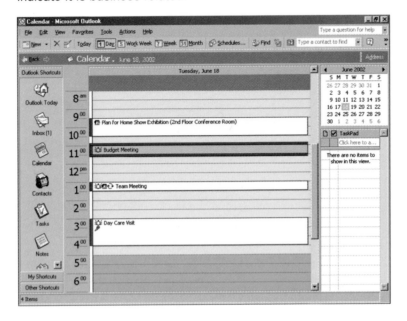

Calendar Coloring

15 On the toolbar, click the **Calendar Coloring** button, and then click **Automatic Formatting**.

The **Automatic Formatting** dialog box appears so that you can create a new formatting rule.

16 Click the **Add** button, and in the **Name** box, type **Day Care**.

The rule is added to the **Rules for this view** area.

17 In the **Label** list, click **Must Attend**, and click the **Condition** button.

The **Filter** dialog box is displayed.

18 In the **Search for the word(s)** box, type **Day Care**, and click **OK**.

The condition specifying that the formatting should be applied to items that include the words *Day Care* is saved, and you return to the **Automatic Formatting** dialog box, which looks like this:

19 Click **OK**.

Outlook applies the automatic formatting rule to your Calendar and displays the Day Care Visit appointment in orange, indicating that you must attend.

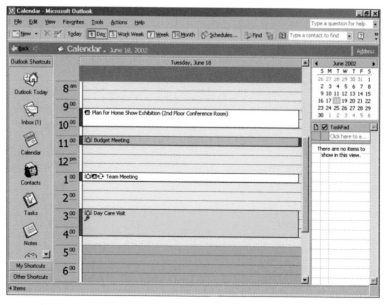

20 Now you'll change your work week. On the **Tools** menu, click **Options**.

The **Options** dialog box appears.

21 On the **Preferences** tab, click the **Calendar Options** button.

The **Calendar Options** dialog box appears.

22 In the **Calendar work week** area, select the **Sun** check box and clear the **Fri** check box.

23 Make sure that the **Start time** setting is **8:00 AM**. Then click the down arrow to the right of the **End time** box, and click **4:30 PM**.

The dialog box now looks like this:

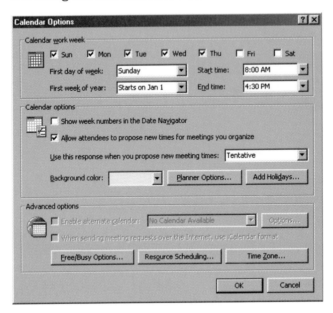

24 Click **OK**, and in the **Options** dialog box, click **OK** again.

The Calendar is displayed with your new default work hours—only the hours between 8 A.M. and 4:30 P.M. are highlighted.

25 On the toolbar, click the **Work Week** button.

The Work Week view displays Sunday through Thursday, according to your default work week settings.

26 On the toolbar, click the **Calendar Coloring** button, and then click **Automatic Formatting**.

The **Automatic Formatting** dialog box appears.

27 Click the **Day Care** rule, and click the **Delete** button.

The rule is deleted.

28 Click **OK**.

The **Automatic Formatting** dialog box closes.

29 On the **Tools** menu, click **Options**.

The **Options** dialog box appears.

30 On the **Preferences** tab, click the **Calendar Options** button.

The **Calendar Options** dialog box appears.

31 In the **Calendar work week** area, clear the **Sun** check box and select the **Fri** check box.

32 Click **OK**, and in the **Options** dialog box, click **OK** again.

Both dialog boxes close.

33 Drag the right frame of the Calendar to the left until two months are visible in the Date Navigator again.

34 On the toolbar, click the **Day** button.

The schedule for the date selected in the Date Navigator is displayed.

Tip

Each time zone is measured in reference to Greenwich Mean Time (GMT) or Universal Time (UTC). GMT is defined as the time at the Greenwich Observatory in England.

Note that changing your time zone in Outlook is equivalent to changing your time zone in Control Panel. It affects the time displayed on the Windows taskbar and in any other Windows programs.

Time Zones in Your Calendar

If you frequently work with people from other countries or regularly travel internationally, you might want to change the time zone or view a second time zone in your Calendar.

To change your current time zone:

1 On the **Tools** menu, click **Options**.

2 On the **Preferences** tab, click the **Calendar Options** button.

3 In the **Calendar Options** dialog box, click the **Time Zone** button.

4 Click the down arrow to the right of the **Time zone** box, click a time zone other than your own, and then click **OK** three times to close all the dialog boxes.

To show a second time zone in your Calendar:

1 On the **Tools** menu, click **Options**.

2 On the **Preferences** tab, click the **Calendar Options** button.

3 In the **Calendar Options** dialog box, click the **Time Zone** button.

4 Select the **Show an additional time zone** check box.

(continued)

(continued)

5 Click in the **Label** box, and type the label you want for this time zone. (For example, if you are adding the Eastern Time Zone, you would type *EST*.)

6 Click the down arrow to the right of the **Time zone** box, click the time zone you want, and click **OK** three times to close all the dialog boxes. Your Calendar will look something like this:

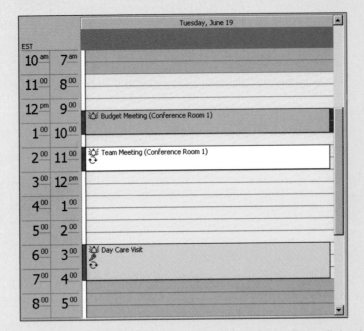

You can use the **Swap Time Zones** button in the **Time Zone** dialog box to replace the current time zone with the second one. Swapping time zones changes all time-related fields, such as when messages are received or the time of appointments, to the new time zone.

To reset the time zone display to its original settings:

1 On the **Tools** menu, click **Options**.

2 On the **Preferences** tab, click the **Calendar Options** button.

3 In the **Calendar Options** dialog box, click the **Time Zone** button.

4 Select the **Show an additional time zone** check box.

5 Clear the **Show an additional time zone** check box.

6 Click the down arrow to the right of the **Time zone** box, click your own time zone, and then click **OK** three times to close all the dialog boxes.

Printing Your Calendar

OL2002-2-5

When your schedule is full and you find yourself running from one appointment to the next, you might not always be able to check your Outlook Calendar. By printing your Calendar, you can take your schedule with you. You can print your Calendar in a variety of formats, called **print styles**. You can select from a list of pre-defined print styles, including Daily, Weekly, and Monthly, or create your own. You can also select the range of dates to be printed.

In this exercise, you will print your Calendar in the Daily, Weekly, and Monthly styles, and then create a new print style for your Calendar. You don't need any practice files for this exercise.

Important

To complete this exercise, you must have a printer installed. If you are working on a network, your administrator can provide the information you need to install a printer. If you are working on a stand-alone computer, click the **Start** button, point to **Settings**, and click **Printers**. Then click the **Add Printer** icon, and follow the wizard's instructions.

1   With your Calendar displayed in Outlook, click tomorrow's date in the Date Navigator.

The Calendar displays your schedule for tomorrow.

Print

2   On the toolbar, click the **Print** button. (If the **Print** button is not visible, click the **Toolbar Options** button to display it.)

The **Print** dialog box appears, with the **Daily Style** format and tomorrow's date as the default options.

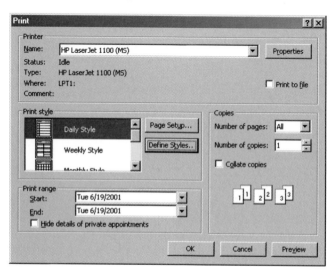

3 Click **OK**.

Outlook prints today's schedule in the **Daily Style** format, which approximates the Day view.

4 On the toolbar, click the **Print** button again.

The **Print** dialog box appears, with **Daily Style** and tomorrow's date as the default options.

5 In the **Print style** list, click **Weekly Style**.

6 In the **Print range** area, click the down arrow to the right of the **End** box, and click the date seven days from today.

The **Print** dialog box now looks like this:

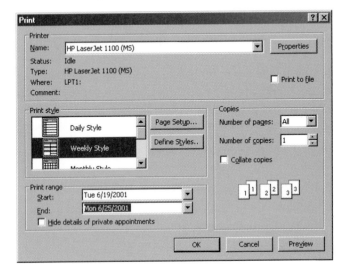

7 Select the **Hide details of private appointments** check box, and click **OK**.

Outlook prints the schedule for the selected dates in the **Weekly Style** format, which approximates the Week view.

8 On the toolbar, click the **Print** button again.

Note that Outlook doesn't retain your settings from one print session to the next.

9 In the **Print style** list, click **Monthly Style**, and then click the **Page Setup** button.

The **Page Setup** dialog box appears, showing the options for the **Monthly Style** format.

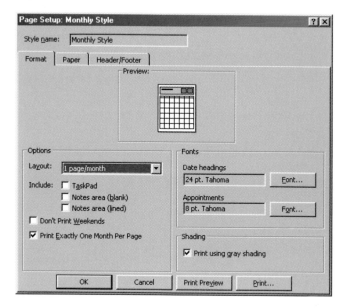

Tip

Each print style has a unique set of page setup options. When selecting a print style, be sure to click the **Page Setup** button to investigate these options.

10 On the **Format** tab, select the **Don't Print Weekends** check box, and click **OK**.

The **Page Setup** dialog box closes.

11 In the **Print** dialog box, click **OK**.

Outlook prints the Calendar for the current month.

12 Now you'll copy a built-in style and customize it to create your own print style. On the toolbar, click the **Print** button.

13 In the **Print** dialog box, click the **Define Styles** button.

The **Define Print Styles** dialog box appears.

14 In the **Print styles** list, make sure **Daily Style** is selected, and click the **Copy** button.

The **Page Setup** dialog box appears, showing the options for your copy of the **Daily Style** format.

15 Click in the **Style name** box at the top of the dialog box, delete the text in the box, and type **2 Per Day**.

16 Click the down arrow to the right of the **Layout** box, and click **2 pages/day**.

17 Clear the **Notes area (blank)** check box, and select the **Notes area (lined)** check box.

The dialog box now looks like this:

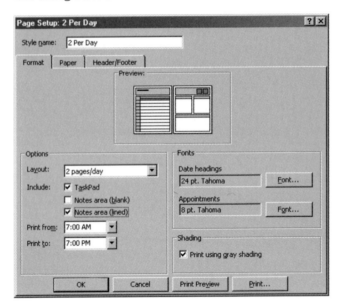

18 Click the **Paper** tab.

The options on the **Paper** tab are displayed.

19 In the **Orientation** area in the bottom right corner, click the **Landscape** option, and then click the **Print Preview** button.

The **Print Preview** window opens, showing your print style applied to today's schedule.

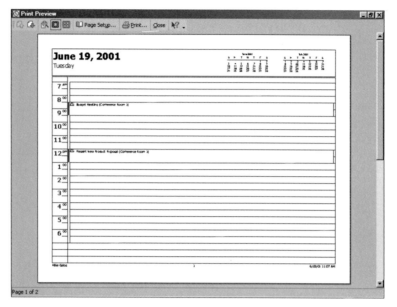

20 On the Print Preview toolbar, click the **Close Preview** button.

The **Print Preview** window closes.

21 On the toolbar, click the **Print** button.

The **Print** dialog box appears.

22 In the **Print style** list, make sure the **2 Per Day** style is selected, and then click **OK**.

Outlook prints the selected day's schedule in the **2 Per Day** format.

23 If you are not continuing on to the next chapter, on the **File** menu, click **Exit** to quit Outlook.

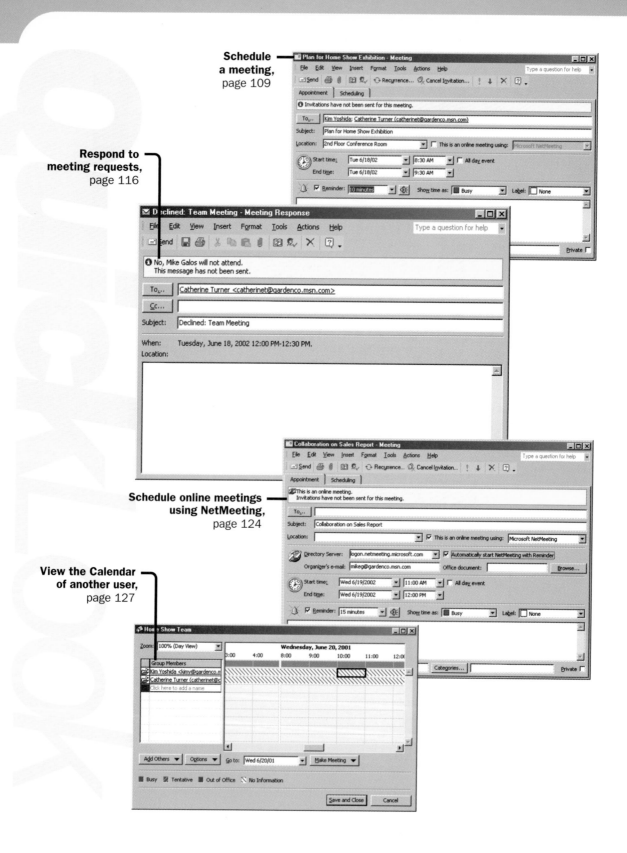

Schedule a meeting, page 109

Respond to meeting requests, page 116

Schedule online meetings using NetMeeting, page 124

View the Calendar of another user, page 127

Chapter 5
Scheduling and Managing Meetings

After completing this chapter, you will be able to:

✔ **Schedule a meeting**

✔ **Respond to meeting requests**

✔ **Update and cancel meetings**

✔ **Schedule online meetings with NetMeeting**

✔ **View the Calendar of another user**

Microsoft Outlook can help you with the often onerous task of organizing meetings. You can check the availability of attendees, find a location, distribute the meeting invitations, and track attendee responses. And as schedules change, you can update or cancel scheduled meetings. You can also respond to meeting invitations manually or automatically and view other users' calendars to check their availability.

This chapter uses the practice files that you installed from this book's CD-ROM and copied into Outlook. For details about installing and copying the practice files, see "Using the Book's CD-ROM" at the beginning of this book.

Scheduling Meetings

OL2002e-3-2
OL2002-2-1

With Outlook, you can schedule meetings, invite attendees—both those who work for your organization and those who don't—and reserve resources such as conference rooms or equipment. To choose a date and time for your meeting, you can check the availability of attendees and resources by viewing their free/busy information. Attendees who don't work for your organization must make this information available over the Internet.

You also can have Outlook select the meeting time for you. You can indicate whether the attendance of each invitee is required or optional. Outlook uses this information to find the best meeting times for required attendees and to optimize the availability of optional attendees.

After you have selected a time, you send a **meeting request**—a type of e-mail message—to each invited attendee and requested resource. Responses from attendees and those responsible for scheduling the resources you requested are automatically tracked as you receive them.

In this exercise, you will plan a meeting, invite attendees, and set and then remove a meeting reminder.

Important

CatherineT
KimY

If you haven't installed and copied the practice files for this book, please do so now. For details about installing and copying the practice files, see "Using the Book's CD-ROM" at the beginning of this book. For this exercise, you will need contact information for Catherine Turner and Kim Yoshida in your **Contacts** list. If you didn't add this information to your **Contacts** list in an earlier chapter, follow the instructions in "Using the Book's CD-ROM" to copy the CatherineT and KimY practice files from the SBS\Outlook\Meeting folder to the **Contacts** icon on the **Outlook Bar.**

1 If it is not already open, start Outlook, and then maximize its window.

Calendar

2 On the **Outlook Bar**, click the **Calendar** icon.

The Calendar is displayed.

3 If Outlook displays reminders about appointments entered in your Calendar in previous exercises, click **Dismiss All**, and then click **Yes** to close them.

4 In the Date Navigator, scroll to June 2002, and click **17** to display the Calendar for that day.

5 On the **Actions** menu, click **Plan a Meeting**.

The Plan a Meeting form appears, listing you as the only attendee in the **All Attendees** list.

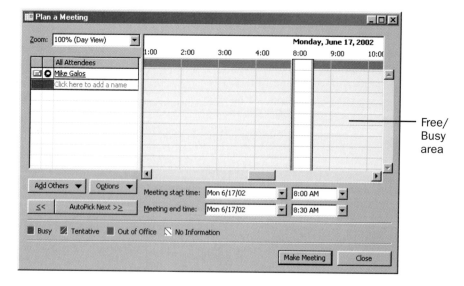

6 Click the **Add Others** button, and in the drop-down list, click **Add from Address Book**.

The **Select Attendees and Resources** dialog box appears.

7 If necessary, click the down arrow to the right of the **Show Names from the** box, and then click **Contacts**.

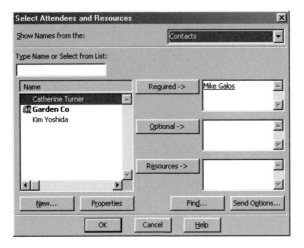

In this exercise, you have been provided with contact information for fictitious employees of The Garden Company. If you want, you can use the names of your co-workers or other contacts to plan an actual meeting.

8 In the **Name** list, click **Kim Yoshida**, and click the **Required** button.

The name is added to the **Required Attendees** box.

9 In the **Name** list, click **Catherine Turner**, and click the **Optional** button.

The name is added to the **Optional Attendees** box.

10 Click **OK**. If prompted to join the **Microsoft Office Internet Free/Busy Service**, click **Cancel**.

The attendees are added to the **All Attendees** list, with icons that indicate whether their attendance is required or optional.

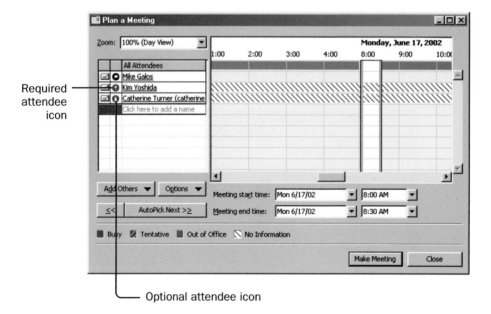

Required attendee icon

Optional attendee icon

11 Use the horizontal scroll bar in the Free/Busy area to view attendee availability for June 18, 2002.

This area shows whether attendees are free, tentatively scheduled, busy, or out of the office. Busy time appears in blue, tentative time in stripes, and time out of the office in purple, as shown on the next page. (If you are using fictitious names, free/busy information will not be available.)

12 Click the 9:30 time slot in the Free/Busy area to select that time.

The half-hour time slot you clicked appears as a vertical white bar. The **Meeting start time** and **Meeting end time** lists reflect the date and time you selected.

Tip

You can quickly find the next available free time for all attendees and resources. Click the **AutoPick Next** button in the **Plan a Meeting** dialog box or on the **Scheduling** tab of the Meeting form.

13 In the Free/Busy area, click the red bar on the right edge of the selected meeting time and drag it one half hour to the right.

The second **Meeting end time** setting reflects the change—the meeting is now scheduled to last for one hour.

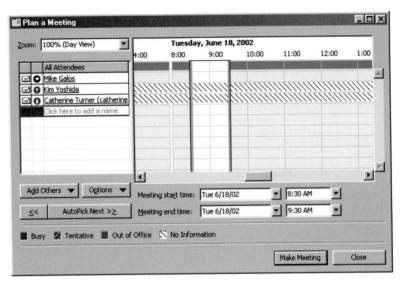

14 Click the **Make Meeting** button.

The Meeting form appears.

15 In the **Subject** box, type **Plan for Home Show Exhibition**, press the `Tab` key, and in the **Location** box, type **2nd Floor Conference Room**.

16 Be sure the **Reminder** check box is selected, click the down arrow to the right of the **Reminder** box, and then click **10 minutes**.

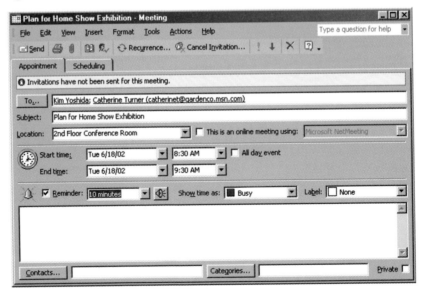

17 On the toolbar, click the **Send** button.

The meeting request is sent.

Important

If the attendees you provided are fictitious, e-mail messages you send to them will be returned as undeliverable. You can delete the returned messages at any time.

Close

18 Click the **Close** button.

The Plan a Meeting form closes.

19 In the Calendar, click June 18, 2002, in the Date Navigator.

The schedule for tomorrow is displayed, with the meeting request in the 9:30-10:30 time slot.

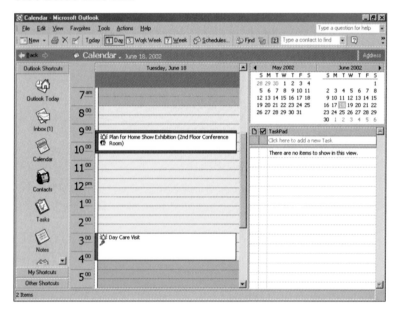

20 Double-click the **Plan for Home Show Exhibition** meeting.

The Meeting form opens.

21 Clear the **Reminder** check box, and on the toolbar, click the **Save and Close** button.

The updated meeting is saved. You will not receive a reminder for the meeting, but your meeting attendees will.

Scheduling Resources for a Meeting

If you are working on a network that uses Microsoft Exchange Server and your system administrator has added resources, such as conference rooms or projection equipment, to the organization's **Global Address List**, you can reserve those resources for your meeting. You reserve resources by inviting them to your meeting. Your invitation is sent to the person designated by your administrator to manage the schedule for the resource. That person responds to your meeting request based on the availability of the resource at the time you requested.

To schedule a resource for a new meeting:

1   On the **Outlook Bar**, click the **Calendar** icon.

2   On the **Actions** menu, click **Plan a Meeting**.

The Plan a Meeting form appears.

3   Click the **Add Others button**, and then click **Add from Address Book**.

The **Select Attendees and Resources** dialog box appears.

4   In the **Show Names from the** box, be sure that **Global Address List** is selected.

5   In the **Name** list, select the required and optional attendees as usual. Then click the resource you want, and click the **Resources** button.

6   Repeat step 5 for as many resources as you need, and then click **OK**.

7   In the Plan a Meeting form, click the **Make Meeting** button, and then click the **Close** button.

To schedule a resource for an existing meeting:

1   In the Calendar, double-click the meeting to open it, and then click the **Scheduling** tab.

2   Click the **Add Others** button, and then click **Add from Address Book**.

3   In the **Show Names from the** box, be sure that **Global Address List** is selected.

4   In the **Name** list, click the resource you want, and then click the **Resources** button.

5   Repeat step 4 for as many resources as you need, and then click **OK**.

6   Click the **Send Update** button.

Responding to Meeting Requests

OL2002-2-3

Just as you can send meeting requests, you can receive meeting requests from others. When you do, you can respond in one of three ways. You can accept the request and inform the requester that you will attend. Meetings that you accept are automatically entered in your Calendar. You can tentatively accept a request, indicating that you might or might not be able to attend the meeting. Meetings that you accept tentatively are also entered in your Calendar, but your free/busy information will show you as only tentatively scheduled for that time. Finally, you can decline a meeting, in which case the request is deleted and no entry is made in your Calendar. When you decline a meeting, you can choose whether Outlook notifies the person who sent the request.

In this exercise, you will accept a meeting request, decline a meeting request, and propose a new meeting time in response to a meeting request.

Important

Kickoff
Status
TeamMeet

If you haven't installed and copied the practice files for this book, please do so now. For details about installing and copying the practice files, see "Using the Book's CD-ROM" at the beginning of this book. If you want to complete just this exercise, copy only the files above the CD icon in the margin.

Inbox

1 On the **Outlook Bar**, click the **Inbox** icon.

The contents of the Inbox are displayed.

2 Double-click the **Quarterly Status** message.

The Meeting form appears.

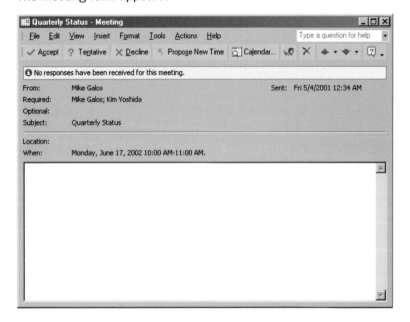

3 To view the meeting in your Calendar before you respond, click the **Calendar** button on the toolbar.

Your Calendar appears in a new window, with the requested meeting shown on the desired date.

Close

4 In the Calendar's window, click the **Close** button.

The Calendar closes.

✓ Accept

5 On the Meeting form, click the **Accept** button.

A message box appears, prompting you to choose how you want to respond.

6 With the **Send the response now** option selected, click **OK**.

Your response is sent to the person who requested the meeting, the Meeting form closes, the meeting is entered in your Calendar, and the next message in the Inbox opens.

Tip

When accepting or declining a meeting, you can choose to send a standard response, send a response that you compose yourself, or send no response.

7 Close the open message by clicking its **Close** button.

8 In the Inbox, double-click the **Team Meeting** message.

The Meeting form appears.

✕ Decline

9 On the toolbar, click the **Decline** button.

A message box appears, prompting you to choose how you want to respond.

10 With the **Edit the response before sending** option selected, click **OK**.

The Meeting Response form appears. The **Subject** box indicates that you are declining the Team Meeting request, as shown on the next page.

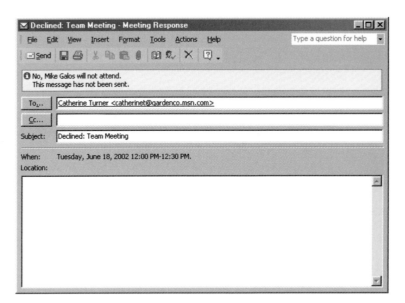

11 In the message body, type **I will be out of the office on this day**.

12 On the toolbar, click the **Send** button.

Your response is sent, and the Meeting form closes. The meeting is not added to your Calendar.

13 In the Inbox, double-click the **Project Kick-off** message.

The Meeting form appears.

Propose
new time
new for
OfficeXP

14 On the toolbar, click the **Propose New Time** button. If prompted to join the Microsoft Office Internet Free/Busy Service, click **Cancel**.

The **Propose New Time** dialog box appears.

15 In the Free/Busy area, click the **11:00** column, and drag the right edge of the meeting time to 12:00.

The time in the **Meeting end time** box is updated to 12:00 P.M. to reflect your changes.

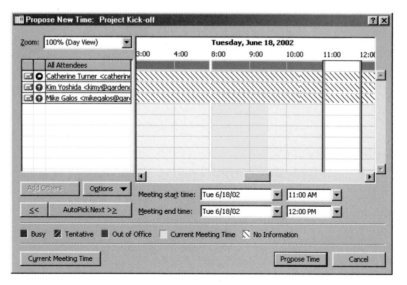

16 Click the **Propose Time** button.

The **Propose New Time** dialog box closes, and the Meeting Response form appears. The subject of the response indicates that you are proposing a new time for the meeting.

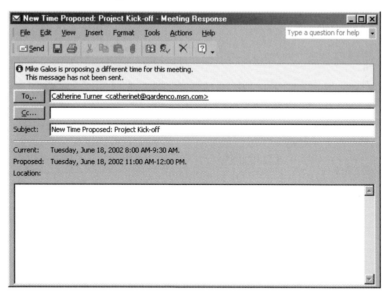

17 In the body of the message, type **I cannot attend meetings scheduled before 9 A.M.**, and on the toolbar, click the **Send** button.

Your response is sent, and the Meeting form closes. The meeting is added to your Calendar as tentatively scheduled for the original meeting time.

Responding to Meeting Requests Automatically

You can choose to respond to meeting requests automatically. Outlook will process meeting requests and cancellations as you receive them, responding to requests, adding new meetings to your calendar, and removing cancelled meetings from your calendar. If you choose, Outlook will automatically decline meeting requests that conflict with existing items on your calendar. You can also choose to automatically decline any request for a recurring meeting.

1   On the **Tools** menu, click **Options**.

   The **Options** dialog box appears.

2   On the **Preferences** tab, click the **Calendar Options** button, and then click the **Resource Scheduling** button.

   The **Resource Scheduling** dialog box appears.

3   Select the **Automatically accept meeting requests and process cancellations** check box.

4   Select the **Automatically decline conflicting meeting requests** and the **Automatically decline recurring meeting requests** check boxes if desired, and click **OK**.

5   In the **Calendar Options** dialog box, click **OK**, and in the **Options** dialog box, click **OK**.

Updating and Cancelling Meeting Requests

OL2002e-3-3
OL2002e-3-4

Project schedules can shift on a daily basis. Consequently, your meetings must be flexible. Outlook makes it easy to update or cancel meetings as your needs change. For example, you might learn that a required attendee is unavailable at the time you requested. In this case, you can change the date or time of the meeting or cancel the meeting altogether. You can also add people to or remove people from the list of attendees.

In this exercise, you will reschedule a meeting, revise a list of meeting attendees, and cancel a meeting.

Important

HomeShow

If you haven't installed and copied the practice files for this book, please do so now. For details about installing and copying the practice files, see "Using the Book's CD-ROM" at the beginning of this book. For this exercise, you will work with the Plan for Home Show Exhibition meeting. If you didn't create this meeting in an earlier exercise, follow the instructions in "Using the Book's CD-ROM" to copy the HomeShow practice file from the SBS\Outlook\Meeting folder to the **Calendar** icon on the **Outlook Bar**.

Calendar

1 On the **Outlook Bar**, click the **Calendar** icon.

The Calendar is displayed.

2 Using the Date Navigator, click June 18, 2002—the date of the Plan for Home Show Exhibition meeting.

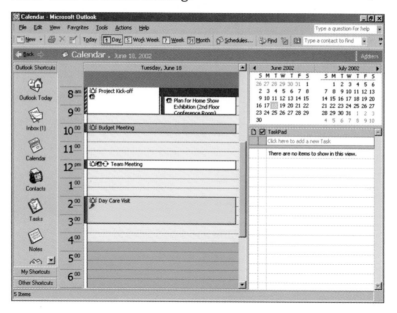

3 Double-click the **Plan for Home Show Exhibition** meeting.

The Plan for Home Show Exhibition - Meeting form appears.

4 Click the **Scheduling** tab, and in the Free/Busy area, scroll to the next business day.

5 Click the **11:00 A.M.** time slot, and drag the right edge of the shaded area to 12:00 P.M. to schedule the meeting to last for one hour.

The start and end times reflect the changes you made to the date and time.

6 Click the **Add Others** button, and then click **Add from Address Book** in the drop-down list.

The **Select Attendees and Resources** dialog box appears.

7   In the **Optional** box, click **Catherine Turner**, and press the ⌨Del⌨ key.

Catherine Turner is removed from the **Optional** box.

Tip

If you are working with an actual meeting and using the names of your co-workers, pick any one of the optional attendees to delete. You can add that person back to the meeting request at any time.

8   Click **OK**.

The **Select Attendees and Resources** dialog box closes. The Plan for Home Show Exhibition – Meeting form reflects your change in attendees.

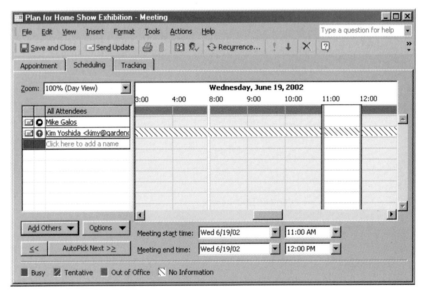

9   On the toolbar, click the **Send Update** button.

The updated Meeting form is sent.

10   In the Date Navigator, click the next business day.

The schedule for the next business day is displayed, including the rescheduled Plan for Home Show Exhibition meeting.

11   Double-click the **Plan for Home Show Exhibition** meeting.

The Plan for Home Show Exhibition - Meeting form appears.

12   Click the **Tracking** tab.

The **Tracking** tab is displayed, indicating the response received from each attendee. If you are using the practice files for this exercise, this tab will not reflect any responses to the meeting request because the attendees are fictitious people.

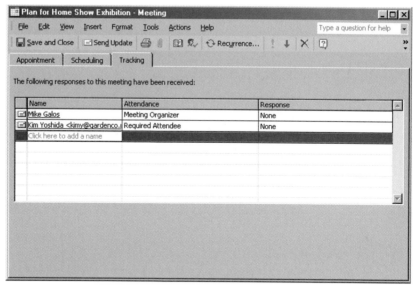

13 On the **Actions** menu, click **Cancel Meeting**.

A message box appears, asking you if you want to send a cancellation notice to the attendees.

14 With the **Send cancellation and delete meeting** option selected, click **OK**.

15 Click the **Appointment** tab.

The Plan for Home Show Exhibition - Meeting form is updated to indicate that the meeting has been cancelled.

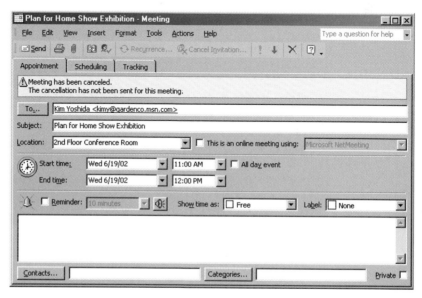

16 On the toolbar, click the **Send** button.

The cancellation notice is sent to all remaining attendees (Kim Yoshida), the Meeting form closes, and the meeting is removed from your Calendar.

Tip

You can easily send a new e-mail message to all attendees of a particular meeting. Simply open the meeting, and on the **Actions** menu, click **New Message to Attendees**. (This method works only on meetings for which attendees have already been invited.)

Scheduling Online Meetings Using NetMeeting

OL2002e-3-5

With **NetMeeting**, a program that comes with Microsoft Internet Explorer, you can conduct online meetings via the Internet. NetMeeting allows you to conduct both audio and video conferences with one or more people. NetMeeting conference participants can share applications, collaborate on documents, draw on a shared electronic whiteboard, or transfer files.

Important

To take full advantage of NetMeeting's audio and video capabilities, you need an audio card, video card, speakers, microphone, and camera connected to your computer. Without a camera, you can view other people's video, but they cannot view yours.

In this exercise, you will schedule an online meeting using NetMeeting.

Important

CatherineT
KimY

If you haven't installed and copied the practice files for this book, please do so now. For details about installing and copying the practice files, see "Using the Book's CD-ROM" at the beginning of this book. For this exercise, you will need contact information for Catherine Turner and Kim Yoshida in your **Contacts** list. If you didn't add this information to your **Contacts** list in an earlier chapter, follow the instructions in "Using the Book's CD-ROM" to copy the CatherineT and KimY practice files from the SBS\Outlook\Meeting folder to the **Contacts** icon on the **Outlook Bar.**

1 In the Calendar, display the schedule for June 19, 2002, and select the 11:00-12:00 time slot.

New Appointment

2 On the toolbar, click the down arrow to the right of the **New Appointment** button, and then click **Meeting Request**.

A blank Meeting form appears.

3   Click in the **Subject** box, and type Collaboration on Sales Report.

4   Select the **This is an online meeting using** check box, and be sure **Microsoft NetMeeting** is selected in the adjacent box. You might have to enlarge the window to see its entire contents.

5   Click in the **Directory Server** box, type logon.netmeeting.microsoft.com (the name of the Microsoft Internet Directory server), and then select the **Automatically start NetMeeting with Reminder** check box.

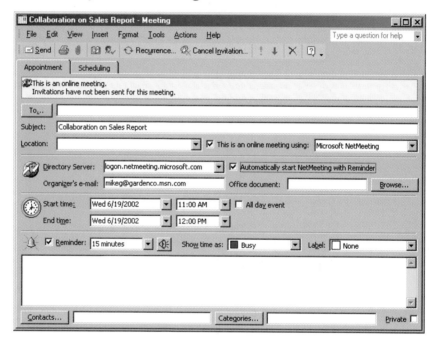

Your organization might use another **directory server**. Contact your system administrator or ISP for more information.

6   Click the **Scheduling** tab.

7   Click the **Add Others** button, and then click **Add from Address Book** in the drop-down list.

The **Select Attendees and Resources** dialog box appears.

8   If necessary, click the down arrow to the right of the **Show names from the** list, and then click **Contacts**.

9   In the **Name** list, click **Kim Yoshida**, hold down the ⌗ key, and click **Catherine Turner**.

Both names are selected.

10 Click the **Required** button, and then click **OK**. If prompted to join the Microsoft Office Internet Free/Busy Service, click **Cancel**.

The names are added to the **All Attendees** list.

11 In the Free/Busy area, scroll to the next business day, click the **2:00 P.M.** time slot and drag the right edge of the selected time slot to 3:30 P.M. (halfway between 3:00 P.M. and 4:00 P.M.).

The meeting start and end times reflect the date and time you chose.

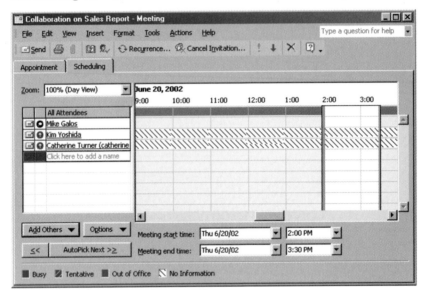

12 On the toolbar, click the **Send** button.

The meeting request is sent. When the meeting time arrives, NetMeeting will start automatically so that you and the other attendees can connect to the conference.

Hosting a NetMeeting

To host a meeting in NetMeeting, start NetMeeting, and on the **Call** menu, click **Host Meeting**. In the **Host Meeting** dialog box that appears, you can give the meeting a name and password, and set the options for the meeting, including who can place outgoing calls, accept incoming calls, and use NetMeeting features. You can also choose whether or not to require security for the meeting.

Find Someone in a Directory

Once the meeting has started, you can place calls to other meeting attendees by clicking **New Call** on the **Call** menu. If you don't know an attendee's address, you can find it by clicking the **Find Someone in a Directory** button and searching for the person's address in the directory.

Tip

For more information on using NetMeeting, start NetMeeting, and on the **Help** menu, click **Help Topics**. To start NetMeeting, click the **Start** button, point to **Programs**, point to **Accessories**, point to **Communications**, and click **NetMeeting**.

Viewing the Calendar of Another User

OL2002e-3-1

When organizing a meeting, it's helpful to be able to see when attendees are available without having to contact each person individually. With Outlook, you can see when people are free or busy by inviting them to a meeting, adding them to a group schedule, or viewing an Internet or intranet location where schedules are published.

A group schedule shows you the combined schedules of a number of people or resources at a glance. For example, you might create a group schedule containing all the people on your project team so you can quickly see when the entire team is available for an impromptu discussion.

If you are working on a network that uses Exchange Server, the free/busy information of others is available to you by default. In addition, if a person connected to your network has shared his or her Calendar, you can open that person's calendar directly. You share a calendar just as you would any other folder—using permissions or by granting **delegate access** to it.

Important

To complete this exercise, you will need access to a co-worker's calendar. See Chapter 11, "Sharing Information and Working Offline" later in this book, and consult your system administrator for more information.

In this exercise, you will create a group schedule, create a meeting from that schedule, and open another person's calendar directly.

Important

CatherineT
KimY

If you haven't installed and copied the practice files for this book, please do so now. For details about installing and copying the practice files, see "Using the Book's CD-ROM" at the beginning of this book. For this exercise, you will need contact information for Catherine Turner and Kim Yoshida in your **Contacts** list. If you didn't add this information to your **Contacts** list in an earlier chapter, follow the instructions in "Using the Book's CD-ROM" to copy the CatherineT and KimY practice files from the SBS\Outlook\Meeting folder to the **Contacts** icon on the **Outlook Bar**.

View Group
Schedules

Schedules...

1 With the Calendar displayed, on the toolbar, click the **View Group Schedules** button.

The **Group Schedules** dialog box appears.

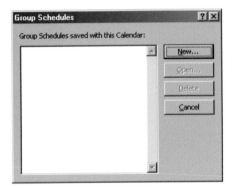

Group
schedules
new for
OfficeXP

2 Click the **New** button.

The **Create New Group Schedule** dialog box appears.

3 In the **Type a name for the new Group Schedule** box, type Home Show Team, and click **OK**.

The Home Show Team group schedule appears.

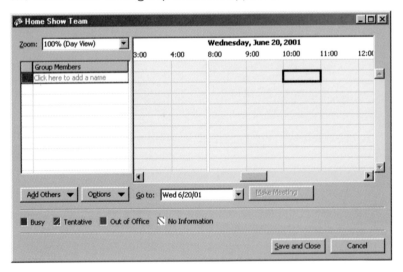

4 Click the **Add Others** button, and click **Add from Address Book** in the drop-down list.

The **Select Members** dialog box appears.

5 If necessary, click the down arrow to the right of the **Show Names from the** list, and then click **Contacts**.

6 In the **Name** box, click **Kim Yoshida**, hold down the ⌃ key, click **Catherine Turner**, and then click the **To** button.

The names are added to the **To** list.

7 Click **OK**. If prompted to join the **Microsoft Office Internet Free/Busy Service**, click **Cancel**.

8 In the Home Show Team group schedule, click the **Save and Close** button.

The Home Show Team group schedule is saved.

9 On the toolbar, click the **View Group Schedules** button.

The **Group Schedules** dialog box appears.

10 In the **Group Schedules saved with this Calendar** list box, click **Home Show Team**, and then click the **Open** button.

The Home Show Team group schedule appears.

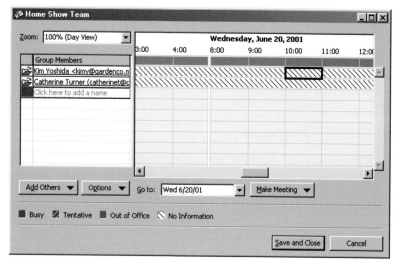

11 To see the most recent schedule information, click the **Options** button, and then click **Refresh Free/Busy**.

The Free/Busy area is updated. Outlook gathers information from wherever the free/busy information for your group members is stored—your Microsoft Exchange Server, the Microsoft Office Internet Free/Busy Service, or the Internet or Intranet locations selected by group members.

12 Click the down arrow to the right of the **Go to** box, and click the next Monday.

The Free/Busy area shows the data for the date you selected.

13 Click the **Make Meeting** button, and click **New Meeting with All** in the dropdown list.

A new Meeting form appears, with the attendees' names in the **To** box.

Close

14 Click the **Close** button, and when prompted to save your changes, click **No**.

The Meeting form closes, discarding the meeting request.

15 In the **Home Show Team** group schedule, click the **Cancel** button.

The group schedule closes.

Important

The remaining steps in this exercise require that you be connected to a network that is running Microsoft Exchange Server.

16 On the **File** menu, point to **Open**, and click **Other User's Folder**.

The **Open Other User's Folder** dialog box appears.

17 Click the **Name** button, click the name of a person who has granted you sharing or delegate access permission to his or her Calendar, and then click **OK**.

18 Be sure **Calendar** appears in the **Folder** box, and then click **OK**.

The other user's calendar is displayed.

19 If you are not continuing on with the next chapter, on the **File** menu, click **Exit** to quit Outlook.

Viewing Other People's Schedules on the Internet or an Intranet

Outlook free/busy sharing

new for **Office**XP

Microsoft offers a Web-based service that enables you to publish information about your free and busy times to a designated, secure Internet location. This service is called the Microsoft Office Internet Free/Busy Service. If you and your colleagues don't have access to each other's calendars but do have access to the Internet, each of you can join this service and publish your free/busy information for others to view. Easy access to this information can save you a lot of time when you need to coordinate the schedules of a group of busy people.

To start using the Microsoft Office Internet Free/Busy Service:

1 On the **Tools** menu, click **Options**.

2 In the **Calendar** area, click the **Calendar Options** button, and then in the **Advanced options** area, click the **Free/Busy Options** button.

3 In the **Free/Busy Options** dialog box, select the **Publish and search using Microsoft Office Internet Free/Busy Service** check box.

4 To see free/busy information for others who have shared their schedules with you, select the **Request free/busy information in meeting invitations** check box, and click **OK**.

5   If prompted to install the feature, click **Yes**.

6   When installation is complete, in the **Calendar Options** dialog box, click **OK**.

7   In the **Options** dialog box, click **OK**.

You can also choose to publish your free/busy information to an intranet location you specify. Your administrator can provide you with the path to the appropriate location on your organization's intranet.

To publish your schedule to an intranet location:

1   On the **Tools** menu, click **Options**.

2   In the **Options** dialog box, click the **Calendar Options** button, and then in the **Calendar Options** dialog box, click the **Free/Busy Options** button.

3   In the **Free/Busy Options** dialog box, select the **Publish at my location** check box, and type the name of the server where your free/busy information should be stored. (E.g. *file://servername/schedules/yourname.vfb*. This name might include **FTP**, **HTTP**, or file **URL**s.)

4   Click in the **Search Location** box, type the name of the server, and click **OK**.

5   In the **Calendar Options** dialog box, click **OK**, and in the **Options** dialog box, click **OK**.

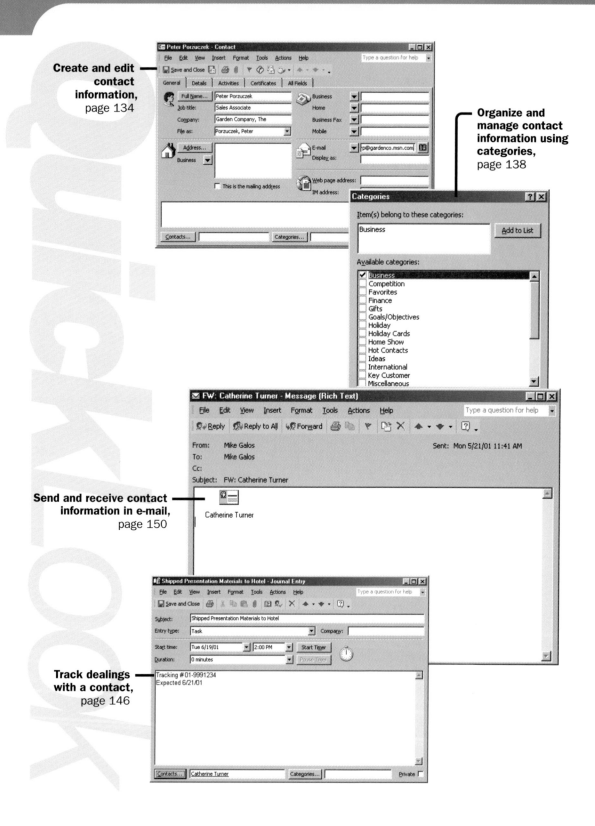

Create and edit contact information, page 134

Organize and manage contact information using categories, page 138

Send and receive contact information in e-mail, page 150

Track dealings with a contact, page 146

Chapter 6
Creating and Organizing a List of Contacts

After completing this chapter, you will be able to:

✔ **Create, edit, and print a list of contacts**

✔ **Organize and manage contact information**

✔ **Track dealings with a contact**

✔ **Send and receive contact information in e-mail**

✔ **Import and export contact information**

Managing the information you have about your **contacts** is crucial for staying organized and connected. To communicate effectively, you must have instant access to current, accurate contact information, including phone numbers, addresses, and e-mail addresses. Microsoft Outlook 2002 makes it easy to build and maintain your contacts list. You have many options for viewing, sorting, and printing your contact information, as well as the ability to keep track of your dealings with a particular contact and share contact information with other people through e-mail or with other programs.

Outlook gives you several options for storing addresses and other contact information in the **Outlook Address Book**.

■ The **Global Address List** is available if you are working on a network that includes Microsoft Exchange Server. It contains all the e-mail addresses and distribution lists in your organization. Your administrator maintains the Global Address List. You can view it, but you cannot change it.

■ The **Contacts** list is created automatically when you configure your Outlook profile. It contains information about the people you have added to your Contacts folder.

■ The **Personal Address Book** might also be part of your profile. You can create a Personal Address Book for personal contacts and distribution lists, rather than work-related contacts. The e-mail addresses and distributions lists in this address book are stored in a file with a *.pab* extension.

Tip

If a Personal Address Book is part of your Outlook profile, you can access it in the **Address Book** dialog box by displaying the **Show items in this list** drop-down list and clicking **Personal Address Book**.

In this chapter, you will learn how to work with contacts in your Outlook Address Book. This chapter uses the practice files you should already have installed from this book's CD-ROM onto your hard disk and copied them into Outlook. For details about installing and copying the practice files, see "Using the Book's CD-ROM" at the beginning of this book.

Creating and Editing Contact Information

OL2002e-4-6
OL2002-4-1

Think of your Outlook contacts as a powerful electronic Rolodex, where you can store all the information you need to stay in touch with and manage contacts. For each contact, you can store the following:

- Name, job title, and company name
- Business, home, and other addresses
- Business, home, fax, mobile, and other phone numbers
- E-mail, Web page, and instant messaging addresses

You can also store the following details for each contact:

- Professional information, including department, manager's names, and assistant's names
- Personal information, including nickname, spouse's name, birth and anniversary dates
- Online meeting settings
- Location of free/busy information

You can create a contact with as little as a name or as much information as you choose. You can add to or change the information for a contact at any time. To save time, you can create contact entries for people who work for the same company based on an existing contact from that company.

In this exercise, you will view your Contacts folder, create a contact, create multiple contacts from the same company, and edit a contact.

Important

CatherineT
KimY

If you haven't installed and copied the practice files for this book, please do so now. For details about installing the practice files on your hard disk and copying them into Outlook, see "Using the Book's CD-ROM" at the beginning of this book. For this exercise, you will need contact information for Catherine Turner and Kim Yoshida in your **Contacts** list. If you didn't add this information to your **Contacts** list in an earlier chapter, follow the instructions in "Using the Book's CD-ROM" to copy the CatherineT and KimY practice files from the SBS\Outlook\Contacts folder to the **Contacts** icon on the **Outlook Bar**.

1 If it is not already open, start Outlook, and then maximize its window.

Contacts

2 On the **Outlook Bar**, click the **Contacts** icon.

The contents of the Contacts folder are displayed, showing **address cards** for each of your contacts.

New Contact

3 On the toolbar, click the **New Contact** button.

The Contact form appears.

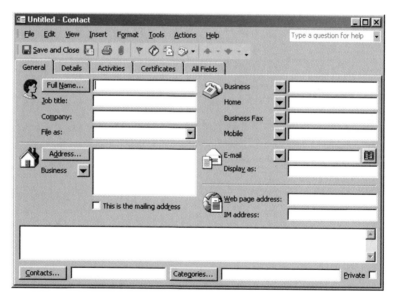

4 In the **Full Name** box, type Peter Porzuczek.

5 Press the ⇥ key, and in the **Job title** box, type Sales Associate. Press the ⇥ key again, and in the **Company** box, type The Garden Company.

After you type the person's name, Outlook completes the **File As** box, indicating that the contact entry will be filed by the person's last name. After you type the company name, Outlook formats the name to appear as *Garden Company, The*.

6 Click in the **Business** box, and type **(206) 555-0100**. Then click in the **Address** box, type **1234 Oak Street**, press the Enter key, and type **Seattle WA 10101**.

Tip

Outlook automatically checks addresses for standard elements such as street address, city, state, and zip code. If Outlook cannot identify these elements, the **Check Address** dialog box will appear, allowing you to enter each item in its own box. You can open the **Check Address** dialog box by clicking the **Address** button.

7 Click in the **E-mail** box, and type **peterp@gardenco.msn.com**.

Tip

In a networked organization (e.g. if you are connected to a Microsoft Exchange Server), you don't need to type the full e-mail address—you can use the internal e-mail alias for your contact instead. For this contact, that address might be simply *peterp*.

The Contact form looks like this:

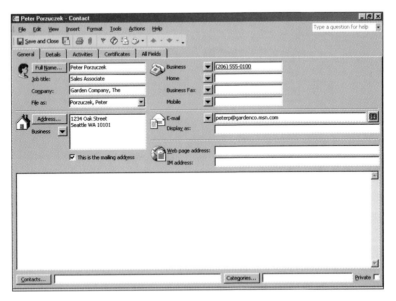

Save and Close **8** Click the **Save and Close** button.

The Contact form closes, and your Contacts folder is displayed, containing the contact entry for Peter Porzuczek.

9   In the Contacts folder, double-click the entry for **Kim Yoshida**.

The Kim Yoshida – Contact form appears.

10   Click in the **Job title** box, and type Head Buyer. Then press ⒯, and in the **Company** box, type The Garden Company.

11   Click in the **Business** box, and type (206) 555-0100. Then click in the **Address** box, and type 1234 Oak Street, press ⒠ⁿᵗᵉʳ, and type Seattle, WA 10101.

12   On the **Actions** menu, click **New Contact from Same Company**.

A new Contact form opens, containing the company name, address, and phone number.

13   In the **Full Name** box, type Britta Simon, press the ⒯ key, and in the **Job title** box, type Associate Buyer.

14   Click in the **E-mail** box, type brittas@gardenco.msn.com, and click the **Save and Close** button twice to close both open forms.

The Contact forms close, and the Contacts folder is displayed. Your screen now looks similar to this one:

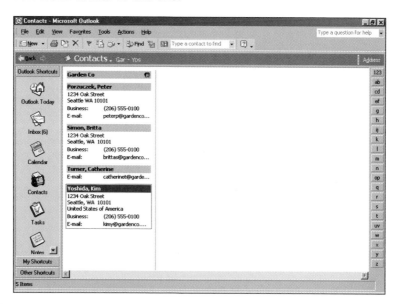

15   In the Contacts folder, double-click the entry for **Catherine Turner**.

The Catherine Turner – Contact form appears.

16   Click the **Details** tab.

17 Click in the **Spouse's name** box, and type James. Then click the down arrow to the right of the **Birthday** box, scroll forward two months, and click **18**.

The contact form looks like this:

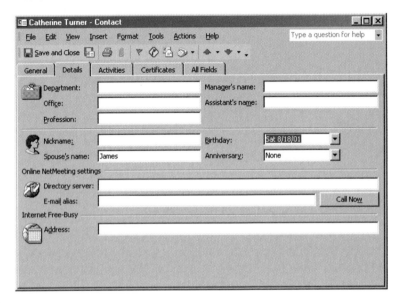

18 Click the **General** tab.

19 Click in the **Job title** box, and type Owner. Then press [Tab], and in the **Company** box, type The Garden Company.

20 Click in the **Web page address** box, and type www.gardenco.msn.com.

The address is automatically formatted as blue and underlined to show that it is a Web address, or URL.

21 Press the [Tab] key twice to move to the comments area, type Member of Washington Society of Women in Business, and click the **Save and Close** button.

The Contact form closes, saving the updated information, and the Contacts folder is displayed.

Managing and Organizing Contact Information

OL2002-4-2

As your collection of contacts grows, managing and organizing contact information can become a challenge. With Outlook, you can delete contact information you no longer need and restore information that has been inadvertently deleted. You can view and sort your contact information in a number of ways to help you find what you need more quickly. Address Card view displays contact information as it might appear on a business card. Detailed Address Card view displays contact information in a similar format, but includes details about the contact including the job title and company name. In both of these views, contact entries are displayed in alphabetical order by first or last name, depending on how each entry is filed. Phone List view is a columnar list showing key contact information, primarily the phone number. Additional columnar views list contacts by category, company, location, and follow-up flag. You can sort these views by any column and customize each view to display the specific information (columns) that you find most useful.

Another way to organize and find contacts is to assign them to categories. For example, you might assign entries for potential new customers to the Hot Contacts category. Then, when you are ready to follow up on your initial sales call, you could use this category to find only those entries that require follow up.

In this exercise, you will delete and restore contacts, view and sort contacts, and organize contacts using categories.

Important

CatherineT
KimY

If you haven't installed and copied the practice files for this book, please do so now. For details about installing and copying the practice files, see "Using the Book's CD-ROM" at the beginning of this book. For this exercise, you will need contact information for Catherine Turner and Kim Yoshida in your **Contacts** list. If you didn't add this information to your **Contacts** list in an earlier chapter, follow the instructions in "Using the Book's CD-ROM" to copy the CatherineT and KimY practice files from the SBS\Outlook\Organize folder to the **Contacts** icon on the **Outlook Bar**.

1   With your Contacts folder displayed in Outlook, click the entry for **Kim Yoshida**.

Delete

2   On the toolbar, click the **Delete** button.

The entry is removed from the Contacts folder and placed in the Deleted Items folder.

Tip

You can also delete a contact entry using the keyboard. Simply click the entry, and press the [Del] key.

3   Click the down arrow to the right of **Contacts** in the Folder banner to display the drop-down **Folder List**, as shown on the next page.

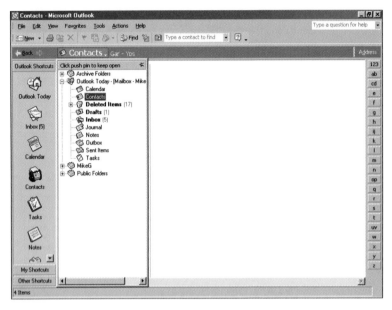

4   Click the **Deleted Items** folder.

The contents of the Deleted Items folder are displayed. The contact entry you deleted appears in the folder, with a subject line of *Kim Yoshida*.

Contacts

5   In the Deleted Items folder, click the contact item for **Kim Yoshida** and drag it to the **Contacts** icon on the **Outlook Bar**.

The deleted contact is restored to the Contacts folder.

Tip

You can also restore deleted items using the Undo feature. Immediately after deleting the item, on the **Edit** menu, click **Undo Delete**, or press Ctrl+Z on the keyboard.

6   On the **Outlook Bar**, click the **Contacts** icon.

The contents of the Contacts folder are displayed, including the restored entry for Kim Yoshida.

Tip

You can create a new message to a contact at any time by right-clicking the contact entry and clicking **New Message to Contact**.

7   On the **View** menu, point to **Current View**, and click **Detailed Address Cards**.

Additional information for each contact is displayed, like this:

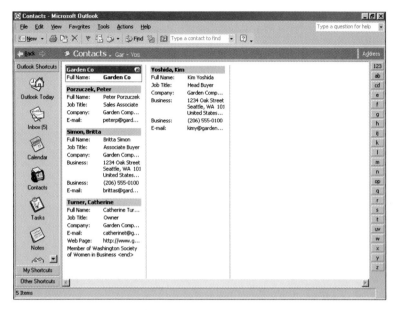

8 On the **View** menu, point to **Current View**, and click **Phone List**.

The contacts are displayed in a grid of columns and rows and are in ascending order based on the **File As** column.

Editable row for adding new contacts

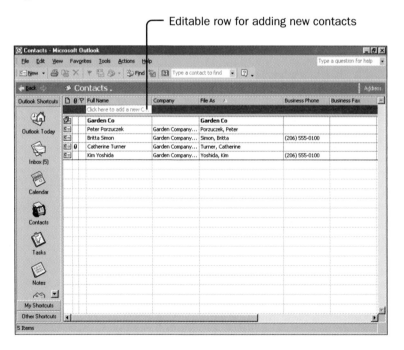

Tip

In the **Phone** list and other list views, you can quickly add a new contact using the row at the top of the list. Simply type the information in each cell, press the `Tab` key to move from one column to the next, and press the `Enter` key when you have finished.

9 Click the **Full Name** column heading.

The contacts are sorted in ascending order based on the **Full Name** column, as indicated by the up arrow to the right of the column heading.

Sort arrow

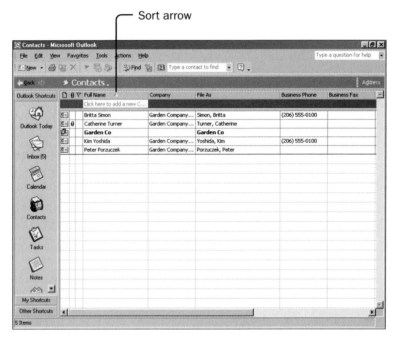

10 Click the **Full Name** column heading again.

The contacts are sorted in descending order based on the **Full Name** column. The sort arrow now points downward.

11 On the **View** menu, point to **Current View**, and click **By Company**.

The contacts are now displayed in a grid that is grouped by company and sorted by the **File As** column.

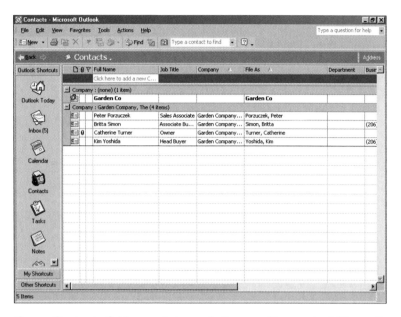

If your Contacts folder contains only the practice contact files, all your individual contacts are from the same company and the company groups are expanded by default. If you have contacts from other companies, the company groups are collapsed by default. To see the individual contacts for a company, click the plus (+) sign to the left of the company name.

12 Double-click the contact entry for **Catherine Turner**.

The Catherine Turner – Contact form appears.

Tip

Display Map
of Address

From the Contact form, you can access a contact's Web site. Simply click the link in the **Web page address** box. You can also get a map to the contact's address. On the toolbar, click the **Display Map of Address** button.

13 Click the **Categories** button.

The **Categories** dialog box appears.

14 In the **Available categories** list, select the **Business** check box. Your results should look like the graphic on the next page.

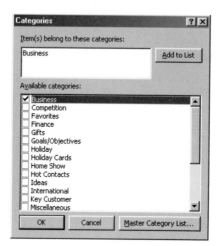

15 Click **OK**.

The Categories dialog box closes.

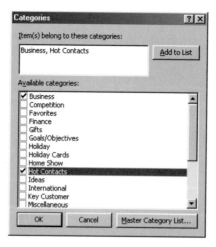
Save and Close

16 On the toolbar of the Catherine Turner – Contact form, click **Save and Close**.

The Contact form closes, and the contents of the Contacts folder are displayed, including the updated entry for Catherine Turner.

17 Double-click the contact entry for **Kim Yoshida**.

The Kim Yoshida – Contact form appears.

18 Click the **Categories** button.

The **Categories** dialog box appears.

19 In the **Available categories** list, select the **Business** check box, and then select the **Hot Contacts** check box.

20 Click **OK** to close the **Categories** dialog box.

21 On the toolbar for the Kim Yoshida – Contact form, click the **Save and Close** button.

The Contact form closes, and the contents of the Contacts folder are displayed, including the updated entry for Kim Yoshida.

22 On the **View** menu, point to **Current View**, and click **By Category**.

The contacts are displayed in a grid grouped by category and sorted by the **File As** column.

23 Click the plus (+) sign to the left of the **Business** category.

The contacts in the Business category are displayed.

24 Click the plus (+) sign to the left of the **Hot Contacts** category.

The contacts in the Hot Contacts category are displayed. Note that the entry for Kim Yoshida appears in both categories.

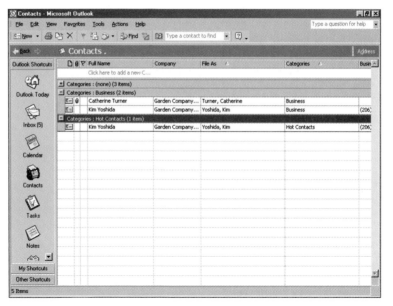

25 On the **View** menu, point to **Current View**, and click **Address Cards**.

The contacts are displayed as address cards.

Tip

You can customize the existing contact views or define your own new view from scratch. To get started, on the **View** menu, point to **Current View**, and click **Customize Current View** or **Define Views**.

Tracking Dealings with Contacts

OL2002-4-3

Keeping track of what's been done or needs to be done in connection with a particular contact can be challenging. For example, you might have agreed to provide additional information for a sales contact and want to follow up after the material has been received. With Outlook, you can link contacts to other Outlook items including appointments or events, journal entries, notes, and e-mail messages. You can also track all items related to a contact and flag contacts for follow up at a specified time.

In this exercise, you will link items to a contact, track the items linked to a contact, flag a contact for follow up, and resolve the follow-up flag.

Important

Package
CatherineT

If you haven't yet installed and copied the practice files for this book, please do so now. For details about installing and copying the practice files, see "Using the Book's CD-ROM" at the beginning of this book. For this exercise, you will need contact information for Catherine Turner in your **Contacts** list. If you didn't add this information to your **Contacts** list in an earlier chapter, follow the instructions in "Using the Book's CD-ROM" to copy the CatherineT practice file from the SBS\Outlook\Tracking folder to the **Contacts** icon on the **Outlook Bar**.

Journal

1 On the **Outlook Bar**, click the **My Shortcuts** button, click the **Journal** icon, and if presented with a message box asking if you want to turn on Journal tracking, click **No**.

The contents of the Journal folder are displayed.

Tip

You can use the Journal to record the dates and times of your interactions with contacts—manually or automatically. In addition to Outlook items such as e-mail and meetings, you can track Microsoft Office documents and other interactions like phone conversations, letters, and faxes. Journal entries are presented in a timeline.

2 On the **View** menu, point to **Go To**, and then click **Go to Date**.

3 In the **Date** box, type 6/19/02 and click **OK**.

The Journal entries for June 19th, 2002, are displayed.

4 Click the plus (+) sign next to **Entry Type: Task** to expand its entries.

The entries appear expanded.

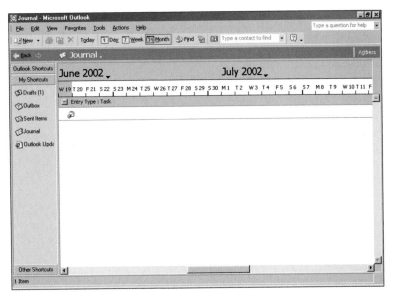

5   Double-click the entry entitled **Shipped Presentation Materials to Hotel**.

The Journal Entry form appears.

6   In the bottom left corner, click the **Contacts** button.

The **Select Contacts** dialog box appears.

7   In the **Items** list, click **Turner, Catherine**, and click **OK**.

The contact is added to the Journal Entry form, indicating that this Journal entry is linked to the contact entry for Catherine Turner.

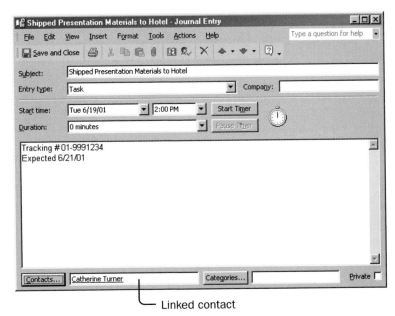

└─ Linked contact

Save and Close

8 On the Journal Entry form's toolbar, click the **Save and Close** button.

Tip

You can link appointments, notes, and even other contacts to a contact in much the same way. Open the entry, and click the **Contacts** button in the bottom left corner. E-mail messages sent to a contact are automatically linked to the contact.

Contacts

9 On the **Outlook Bar**, click the **Outlook Shortcuts** button, and then click the **Contacts** icon.

The contents of the Contacts folder are displayed.

10 Double-click the contact entry for **Catherine Turner**.

The Catherine Turner – Contact form appears.

11 Click the **Activities** tab.

The **Activities** tab is displayed, showing that the Shipped Presentation Materials to Hotel journal entry is linked to this contact.

Important

The **Activities** tab also shows a Calendar item for Catherine's birthday. This item was created by Outlook when Catherine's birth date was added to the **Details** tab of the contact entry.

Follow Up

12 On the toolbar, click the **Follow Up** button.

The **Flag for Follow Up** dialog box appears.

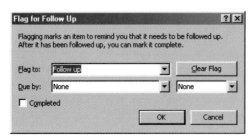

13 Click the down arrow to the right of the **Due by** box, scroll to and click **June 21, 2002**, and click **OK**. (If you are completing this step on a date later than June 21, 2002, click a date that is a few days in the future rather than clicking June 21.)

14 Click the **General** tab.

The Contact form is updated to indicate that a **follow-up flag** has been set.

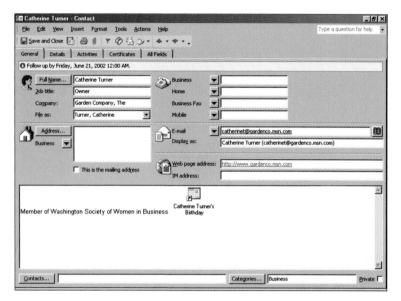

15 On the Contact form's toolbar, click the **Save and Close** button.

The Contact form closes. In the Contacts folder, the entry for Catherine Turner indicates that a follow-up flag has been set.

16 On the **View** menu, point to **Current View**, and click **Phone List**.

The contacts are displayed in the Phone List view. A red flag icon to the left of the entry for Catherine Turner indicates that a follow-up flag has been set.

17 Double-click the contact entry for **Catherine Turner**.

The Catherine Turner – Contact form appears.

18 On the toolbar, click the **Follow Up** button.

The **Flag for Follow Up** dialog box appears.

19 Select the **Completed** check box, and click **OK**.

The Contact form is updated to show that the follow up is complete.

20 On the Contact form's toolbar, click the **Save and Close** button.

The Contact form closes. In the Contacts folder, the flag icon to the left of the entry for Catherine Turner is gray, indicating that follow up is complete, as shown on the next page.

Flag indicating that follow up is complete

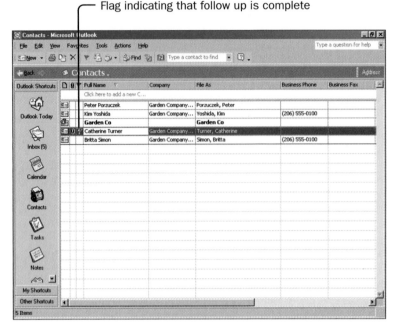

21 On the **View** menu, point to **Current View** and then click **Address Cards**.

The contact information is displayed in Address Cards view.

Tip

When viewing contact information in a list, you can quickly mark a follow-up flag as complete by clicking the flag icon and clicking **Completed** in the drop-down list. If you've inadvertently set or need to remove a follow up flag, you can clear the flag by displaying the **Follow-Up Flag** dialog box and clicking the **Clear Flag** button.

Sending and Receiving Contact Information via E-mail

Sharing contact information with your co-workers can save you and your co-workers a considerable amount of time and reduce the possibility of errors because the information needs to be entered only once. With Outlook, you can send and receive contact information via e-mail. If the recipient uses Outlook, you can send contact information as an Outlook contact. Otherwise, you can send the contact information as a **vCard**, the Internet standard for creating and sharing virtual business cards.

In this exercise, you will send a contact via e-mail, send a vCard via e-mail, and receive both types of contact via e-mail.

Important

CatherineT
KimY

If you haven't yet installed and copied the practice files for this book, please do so now. For details about installing and copying the practice files, see "Using the Book's CD-ROM" at the beginning of this book. For this exercise, you will need contact information for Catherine Turner and Kim Yoshida in your **Contacts** list. If you didn't add this information to your **Contacts** list in an earlier chapter, follow the instructions in "Using the Book's CD-ROM" to copy the CatherineT and KimY practice files from the SBS\Outlook\Sending folder to the **Contacts** icon on the **Outlook Bar**.

1 With your Contacts folder displayed in Outlook, right-click the entry for **Catherine Turner**, and click **Forward**.

The Forward Message form appears, with the contact entry for Catherine Turner in the message body.

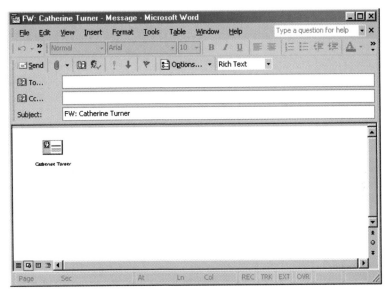

2 In the **To** box, type your e-mail address, and click the **Send** button.

The message is sent.

3 On the **Outlook Bar**, click the **Inbox** icon.

The contents of the Inbox are displayed.

Important

If your computer is not connected to a network with a mail server, the next step requires that you be connected to the Internet.

4 If the forwarded message has not arrived, on the toolbar, click the **Send/Receive** button.

The forwarded message appears in your Inbox, with the paper clip icon indicating that the message contains an attachment.

5 Double-click the forwarded message.

The Message form appears, showing that the contact entry is attached to the message.

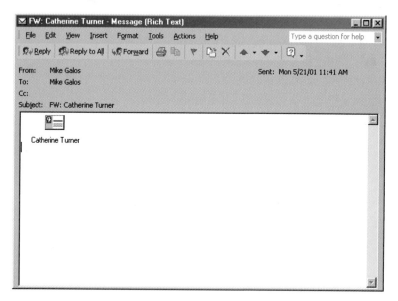

6 Double-click the contact entry.

The Catherine Turner – Contact form appears.

7 Click the **Save and Close** button.

The contact information is saved in your Contacts folder. Since an entry for Catherine Turner already existed, the folder now contains two entries with that name.

8 Close the e-mail message.

Contacts

9 On the **Outlook Bar**, click the **Contacts** icon.

The contents of the Contacts folder are displayed, including the new contact entry for Catherine Turner.

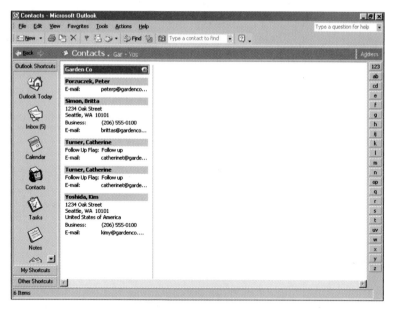

10 Double-click the entry for **Kim Yoshida**.

The Kim Yoshida – Contact form appears.

11 On the **Actions** menu, click **Forward as vCard**.

The Forward Message form appears, with the vCard for Kim Yoshida attached to the message.

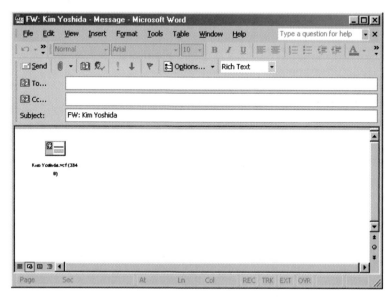

12 In the **To** box, type your own e-mail address, and click the **Send** button to send the message.

13 Click the **Save and Close** button to close the Kim Yoshida – Contact form.

Inbox

14 On the **Outlook Bar**, click the **Inbox** icon.

The contents of the Inbox are displayed.

Important

If your computer is not connected to a network with a mail server, the next step requires that you be connected to the Internet.

15 If the forwarded message has not arrived, on the toolbar, click the **Send/ Receive** button.

The forwarded message appears in your Inbox, with the paper clip icon indicating that the message contains an attachment.

16 Double-click the forwarded message.

The Message form appears, showing the vCard as an attachment.

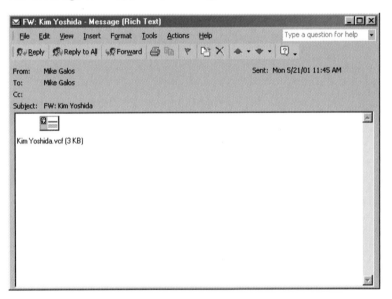

17 Double-click the vCard, and if prompted to open the attachment or save it on your hard disk, click the **Open it** option, and click **OK**.

The Kim Yoshida – Contact form appears.

18 Click the **Save and Close** button. If the **Duplicate Contact Detected** dialog box appears, make sure the **Add this as a new contact anyway** option is selected, and click **OK**.

The contact information is saved in your Contacts folder.

19 Close the e-mail message.

20 On the **Outlook Bar**, click the **Contacts** icon.

The contents of the Contacts folder are displayed, including the new contact entry for Kim Yoshida.

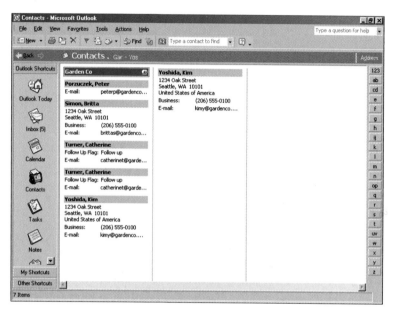

Delete

21 Click the second **Catherine Turner** contact, hold down the [Ctrl] key, and click the second **Kim Yoshida** contact. On the toolbar, click the **Delete** button.

Both contacts are deleted.

Sending Multiple Contact Entries

You can send the information for more than one contact in the same e-mail message. Here are the steps:

1 In the Inbox, create a new message, and address it.

2 On the **Insert** menu, click **Item**.

3 In the **Insert Item** dialog box, click the **Contacts** folder.

4 Select the contact entries you want to send. (To select multiple contact entries, hold down the [Ctrl] key, and click each entry in turn.)

5 Click **OK** to close the **Insert Item** dialog box, and on the Message form, click **Send**.

The contact entries are sent as attachments to the message.

Printing Contacts

To make it easy to take contact information with you while you are away from your computer, you can print your **Contacts** list. You can print contact information from any of the available views, and for the Address Card views, you can select from a number of print styles. For all views, you can define your own print styles, specifying the layout, the margins, orientation, and more. The print options available to you vary based on the view selected when you chose to print.

In this exercise, you will print a phone list and print a number of key contact entries as address cards.

Important

CatherineT
BrittaS

If you haven't yet installed and copied the practice files for this book, please do so now. For details about installing and copying the practice files, see "Using the Book's CD-ROM" at the beginning of this book. For this exercise, you will need contact information for Catherine Turner and Britta Simon in your **Contacts** list. If you didn't add this information to your **Contacts** list in an earlier chapter, follow the instructions in "Using the Book's CD-ROM" to copy the CatherineT and BrittaS practice files from the SBS\Outlook\Printing folder to the **Contacts** icon on the **Outlook Bar**.

Tip

To complete this exercise, you must have a printer installed. If you don't have a printer installed, see your administrator or the printer manufacturer's documentation for assistance.

1 With your Contacts folder displayed in Outlook, on the **View** menu, point to **Current View**, and click **Phone List**.

The contact entries are displayed in a columnar list.

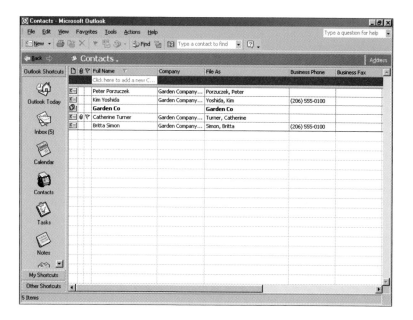

Print

2 On the toolbar, click the **Print** button.

The **Print** dialog box appears.

3 In the **Print range** box, be sure that the **All rows** option is selected, and click **OK**.

The contact entries are printed in the table style.

4 On the **View** menu, point to **Current View**, and click **Address Cards**.

The contact entries are displayed as address cards.

5 On the toolbar, click the **Print** button.

The **Print** dialog box appears.

6 Scroll the **Print style** box, click **Phone Directory Style**, and then click the **Preview** button.

The Print Preview window appears, showing how the contact entries will appear printed in **Phone Directory Style** format. This style is an alternative to printing the Phone List view, as shown on the next page.

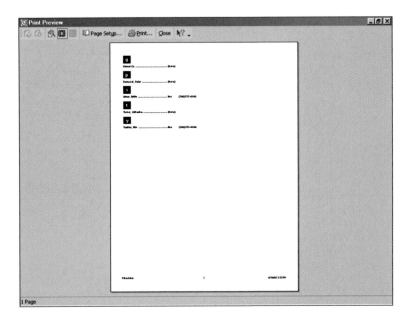

Close

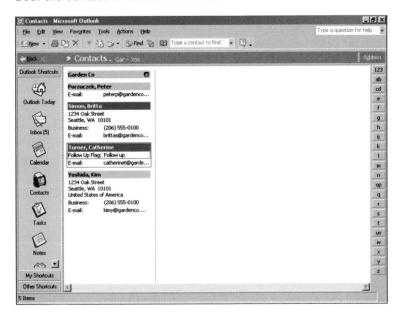

7 On the **Print Preview** window's toolbar, click the **Close** button.

The **Print Preview** window closes.

8 In the Contacts folder, click the **Britta Simon** contact entry to select it, hold down the Ctrl key, and click the **Catherine Turner** contact entry to add it to the selection.

Both the contact entries are selected.

9 On the toolbar, click the **Print** button.

The **Print** dialog box appears.

10 In the **Print style** box, be sure that **Card Style** is selected.

11 In the **Print range** box, click the **Only selected items** option, and click **OK**.

The contacts you selected are printed in **Card Style** format.

Inbox

12 If you are not continuing on with the next chapter, close any open contacts or messages, click the **Inbox** icon on the **Outlook Bar**, and on the **File** menu, click **Exit** to quit Outlook.

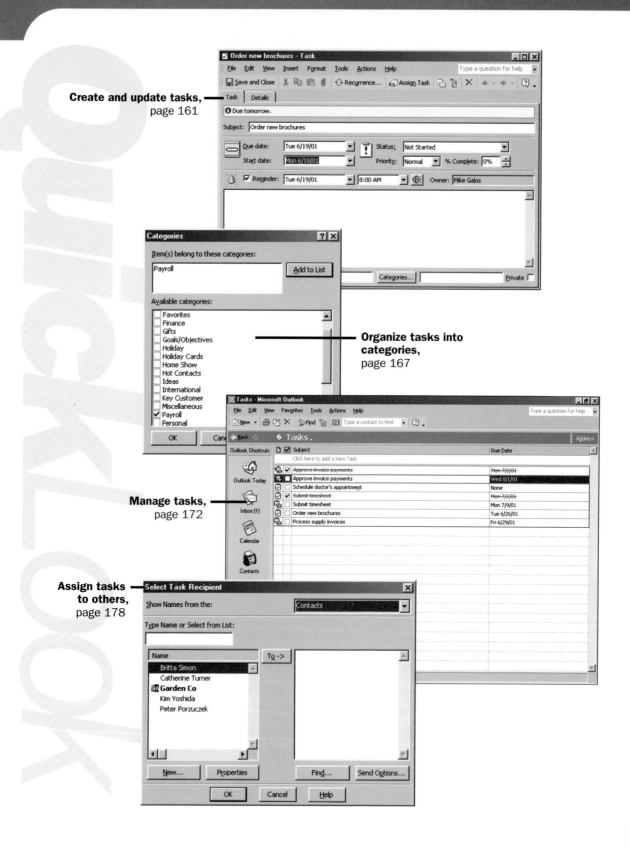

Create and update tasks, page 161

Organize tasks into categories, page 167

Manage tasks, page 172

Assign tasks to others, page 178

Chapter 7
Creating and Organizing Tasks

After completing this chapter, you will be able to:

✔ **Create and update tasks**

✔ **Organize and manage tasks**

✔ **Assign tasks to others**

To-do lists written on scraps of paper or stored in bulky paper planners are often difficult to maintain and easy to lose. With Microsoft Outlook, you can replace these lists with a **Tasks** list that is easy to maintain, and much more powerful. You can use Outlook to create a list of **tasks**, track the progress of tasks, and assign tasks to others. Plus, Outlook offers ways to organize your tasks to help you manage them more efficiently.

In addition to creating a few files from scratch, in this chapter you will use the practice files that you installed from this book's CD-ROM onto your hard disk and copied into Outlook. For details about installing and copying the practice files, see "Using the Book's CD-ROM" at the beginning of this book.

Creating and Updating Tasks

OL2002-5-1
OL2002e-5-3
OL2002e-5-4

You can create and store a list of tasks for any activity that you want to remember and track to completion. For each task, you can specify a due date and a start date. A task is displayed in your **Tasks** list beginning on the start date. A task that is incomplete past its due date is displayed in red to indicate that it is overdue. You can also set the priority of a task—High for urgent tasks, and Normal and Low for less important tasks. And you can choose to set a reminder for a task, much like reminders on appointments.

Tasks can recur either at regular intervals or at intervals based on the date on which you mark the task complete. For example, you might create a task to remind yourself to review the status of a project every seven days. If you perform your review on a Friday and mark the task as complete, Outlook creates the next instance of the task as due on the following Friday. If you perform your next review on a Thursday, Outlook creates the next instance of the task as due on the following Thursday. A task that you create to recur at a regular interval will be regenerated at that interval regardless of the status of earlier instances of the task. For example, you might create a task for submitting your employees' expense reports to the finance department on the fifth of each month. When you mark the task as complete, regardless of the day, Outlook creates the next instance of the task and marks it as due on the fifth of the following month.

You can create and modify tasks in the Tasks folder or in the **TaskPad** that appears in the default Calendar view.

In this exercise, you'll create a task, create a recurring task, set a reminder, update a task, and modify task settings. You don't need any practice files for this exercise.

1   If it is not already open, start Outlook, and then maximize its window.

Tasks
2   On the **Outlook Bar**, click the **Tasks** icon.

The contents of the Tasks folder are displayed in the default Simple List view.

New Task
3   On the toolbar, click the **New Task** button.

The Task form appears.

4   In the **Subject** box, type Order new brochures.

5   Click the down arrow to the right of the **Due date** box, and then click tomorrow's date.

6   Click the down arrow to the right of the **Start date** box, and click today's date.

The Task form looks like this:

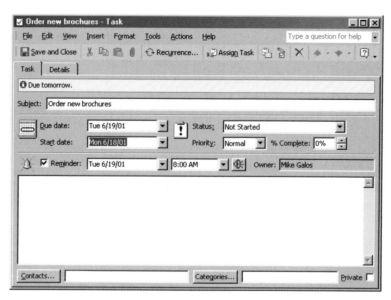

Save and Close
7   Click the **Save and Close** button.

The Task form closes. The new task appears in the Tasks folder.

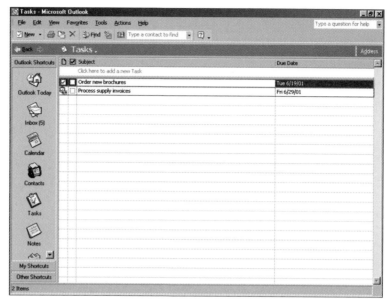

8 On the toolbar, click the **New Task** button to open a Task form.

9 In the **Subject** box, type **Submit timesheet**.

10 Click the down arrow to the right of the **Due date** box, and then click the Monday after next.

11 Click the down arrow to the right of the **Start date** box, and then click the next Monday.

12 Click the down arrow to the right of the **Priority** box, and then click **High**.

13 On the toolbar, click the **Recurrence** button.

The **Task Recurrence** dialog box appears.

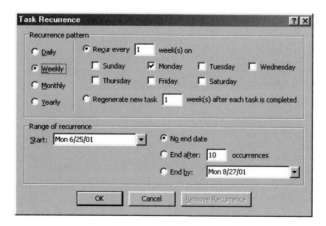

14 In the **Recurrence pattern** area, be sure that the **Weekly** option is selected, and that the **Monday** check box is selected.

As you complete the task each week, the task is regenerated for the next Monday.

15 In the **Range of recurrence** area, select the **End after** option, type **8** in the **occurrences** box, and click **OK**.

Outlook will generate eight instances of the task over the next eight weeks. The Task form looks like this:

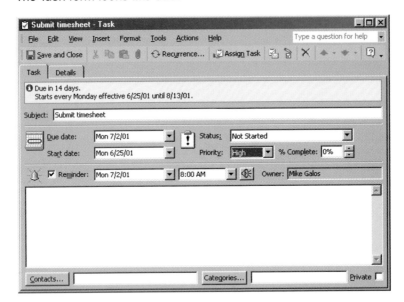

16 Click the **Save and Close** button.

The Task form closes. The new task appears in the Tasks folder.

Tip

You can quickly create a new task directly in the Tasks folder. Simply click in the **Click here to add a new Task** box. Then type the task subject, press the Tab key, type the due date, and press the Enter key.

17 Double-click the **Order new brochures** task.

The Order new brochures – Task form appears.

18 Click the down arrow to the right of the **Due date** box, and then click the date one week later than the current due date. The current due date is indicated by a gray box.

19 Click the down arrow to the right of the **Status** box, and then click **In Progress**.

20 Be sure the **Reminder** check box is selected. Then click the down arrow to the right of the first **Reminder** box, and click the date two business days before the new due date.

21 Click the down arrow to the right of the second **Reminder** box, and then click **10:00 AM**.

22 Click in the comments area, type **Contact marketing for layout materials**, and click the **Save and Close** button.

The Task form closes. The updated task appears in the Tasks folder.

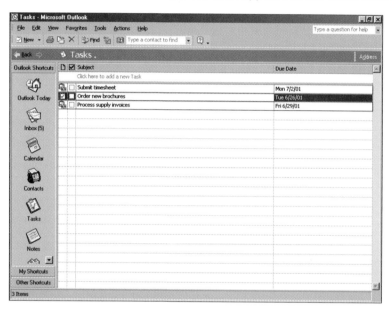

23 On the **Tools** menu, click **Options**.

The **Options** dialog box appears.

24 In the **Tasks** area, click the down arrow to the right of the **Reminder time** box, and then click **9:00 AM**.

Reminders for all tasks you create will be set for 9 A.M. on the date you choose to be reminded.

25 Click the **Task Options** button.

The **Task Options** dialog box appears.

26 Click the down arrow to the right of the **Completed task color** box, scroll up, and then click navy blue (the fifth color from the top of the list).

27 Clear the **Send status reports when assigned tasks are completed** check box.

The dialog box looks similar to the one shown on the next page.

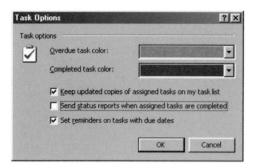

28 Click **OK**, and in the **Options** dialog box, click **OK**.

The **Options** dialog box closes. The Tasks folder is displayed.

29 To mark the Submit timesheet task as complete, select the check box to its left.

The **Tasks** list is updated to show the completed task in navy blue and crossed out. The **Tasks** list also displays the next instance of the recurring Submit timesheet task.

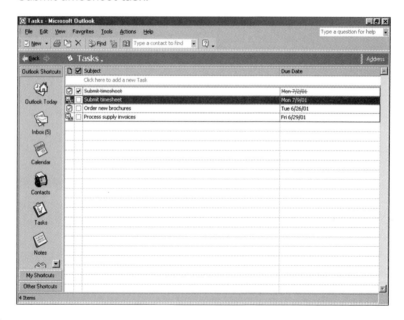

Tip

You can quickly create a task from an e-mail message. Simply drag the message to the **Tasks** icon on the **Outlook Bar**, and complete the Task form that appears.

Organizing Tasks

OL2002-5-2
OL2002-5-5

Staying on top of your tasks can be a challenge as the list grows. To help you organize your tasks, Outlook offers several ways to view and sort them. You can also organize your tasks using folders and categories. For example, if you fall behind, you can view only your overdue tasks to get caught up quickly. Or, you might assign all tasks related to milestones for a key project to the Goals/Objectives category and then view only the tasks in that category to check the progress of the project.

In this exercise, you will change your task view, sort your tasks, assign categories to a task, view your tasks by category, and view your tasks in the **TaskPad**.

Important

Timesheet
Brochures
Invoices

If you haven't installed and copied the practice files for this book, please do so now. For details about installing and copying the practice files, see "Using the Book's CD-ROM" at the beginning of this book. If you have not completed the previous exercise in this chapter, also copy the Timesheet and Brochures files from the SBS\Outlook \Tasks folder, which is probably on drive C, to the **Tasks** icon on the **Outlook Bar**.

1 With the Tasks folder displayed, on the **View** menu, point to **Current View**, and click **Detailed List**.

The details of the tasks, including the status, percent complete, and categories, are displayed.

2 On the **View** menu, point to **Current View**, and click **Active Tasks**.

Only tasks that are not complete are shown. The Folder banner indicates that the tasks are filtered.

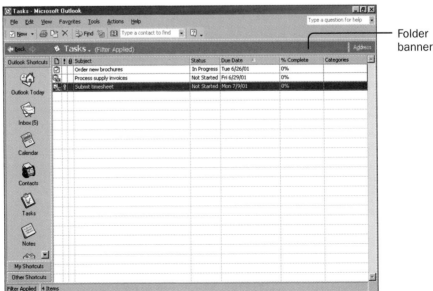

Folder banner

3   Click the **Subject** column heading.

The tasks are sorted in ascending order based on the **Subject** column.

Tip

To manage a list of many tasks, you can organize your tasks in folders. To move a task to a folder, simply drag it from the **Tasks** list to a folder in the **Folder List**. (If you drag the task to the Inbox folder, a Message form opens with the task's subject entered in the **Subject** box.)

4   On the **View** menu, point to **Current View**, and click **Simple List**.

The contents of the Tasks folder are displayed in the default view.

5   Double-click the **Process supply invoices** task.

The Process supply invoices – Task form appears. If the date in the **Due date** box is in the past, change it to a date two weeks in the future.

6   Click the **Categories** button.

The **Categories** dialog box appears.

7   In the **Available categories** list, select the **Miscellaneous** check box.

The dialog box now looks like this:

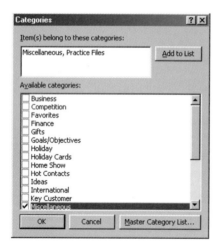

8   Click **OK**.

The **Available Categories** dialog box closes. The **Miscellaneous** category is added to the Process supply invoices – Task form.

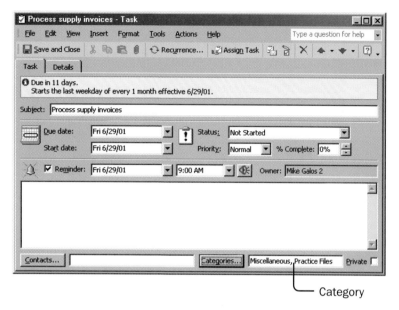

Category

9 Click the **Save and Close** button.

The updated task is saved in the Tasks folder.

10 Double-click the new **Submit timesheet** task.

The Submit timesheet – Task form appears.

11 Click the **Categories** button.

The **Categories** dialog box appears.

12 Click in the **Item(s) belong to these categories** box, type Payroll, and click the **Add to List** button.

The Payroll category is added to the **Available categories** list.

13 In the **Available categories** list, scroll down to see the **Payroll** category.

The check box next to the Payroll category is selected, as shown on the next page.

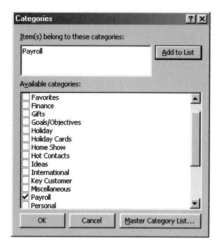

14 In the **Categories** dialog box, click **OK**.

The **Categories** dialog box closes. The **Payroll** category is added to the Submit timesheet – Task form.

15 On the Task form's toolbar, click the **Save and Close** button.

The updated task is saved in the Tasks folder.

16 On the **View** menu, point to **Current View**, and click **By Category**.

The tasks are displayed, grouped by category.

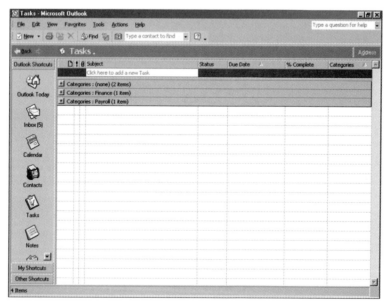

17 Click the plus (+) sign to the left of the **Payroll** category.

The task in the **Payroll** category (Submit timesheet) is displayed.

18 On the **View** menu, point to **Current View**, and click **Simple List**.

The contents of the Tasks folder are displayed in the default view.

Tip

You can easily organize tasks with folders, categories, and views by using the **Ways to Organize Tasks** pane. While viewing the Tasks folder, click the **Organize** button on the toolbar to display this pane.

To organize tasks in folders, click **Using Folders**, select the task(s), select the folder, and click the **Move** button.

To assign categories to tasks, click **Using Categories**, select the task(s), select the category, and click the **Add** button.

To change the way you view tasks, click **Using Views**, and select the view you want.

Calendar

19 On the **Outlook Bar**, click the **Calendar** icon.

The Calendar is displayed, and the **TaskPad** is shown in the bottom right corner of the Outlook window.

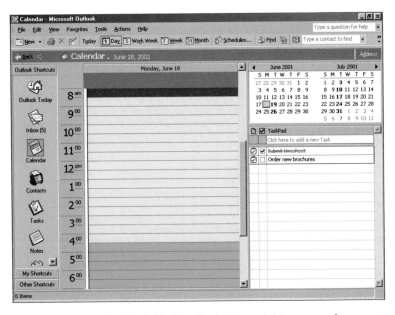

If you don't see the **Task Pad** in the bottom right corner of your screen, point to **Current View** on the **View** menu, and then click **Day/Week/Month View with AutoPreview**.

20 In the **TaskPad**, click the **Click here to add a new Task** box, type Schedule doctor's appointment, and press the ⌜Enter⌝ key.

The new task is added to the **Tasks** list in the **TaskPad**.

21 Double-click the **Schedule doctor's appointment** task.

The Schedule doctor's appointment – Task form appears.

22 Select the **Reminder** check box. Then click the down arrow to the right of the **Reminder** box, and click tomorrow's date.

23 Click the **Save and Close** button.

The Task form closes, and the updated task is saved. You return to the Calendar and the **TaskPad**.

Managing Your Tasks

OL2002-5-3
OL2002e-5-6

As you complete your tasks, you will want to remove them from your to-do list. You might find that some tasks were not necessary and can be deleted. You might also acquire new tasks that other Outlook users assign to you, asking that you report back on your progress. Outlook makes it easy to manage changes to your tasks and send status reports for tasks requested by others.

When you receive a task request, you must accept or decline the task. For example, you might decline a request for a task that is due when you are scheduled to be out of the office.

Tip

If you set reminders for tasks, you will start receiving **reminder messages** as task due dates approach. When a reminder pops up on your screen, you can respond in one of three ways. Clicking the **Dismiss** button closes the task—you will receive no further reminders for this task. Clicking the **Snooze** button sets the reminder to appear again in a specified amount of time. You can also open the item, which closes the reminder.

To track the progress of a task, you can indicate the status and percentage complete. New tasks have the status of *Not Started*. When you begin work on a task, you can mark the task as *In Progress*. You can also enter the percentage of the work that is complete. For example, if you are halfway through a document that you must review, you would mark the task as 50 percent complete. If a task is zero percent complete, the status of the task is set to *Not Started*. When you enter 100 as the percentage complete, the status of the task is set to *Completed*. If the percent complete contains any number between 0 and 100, the task status is *In Progress*. When you have finished the task, you mark the task as *Completed* or enter the percent complete as 100. If work on a task has stalled, you can mark the task as *Deferred* or *Waiting on someone else*.

In this exercise, you will accept a task assigned to you, decline a task assigned to you, send a status report on a task assigned to you, mark a task as complete, stop a task from recurring, and delete a task.

Important

Timesheet
Brochures
Invoices
Task Payments
Task Layouts

If you haven't installed and copied the practice files for this book, please do so now. For details about installing and copying the practice files, see "Using the Book's CD-ROM" at the beginning of this book. If you have not completed the previous exercises in this chapter, also copy the Timesheet and Brochures files from the SBS\Outlook \Tasks folder, which is probably on drive C, to the **Tasks** icon on the **Outlook Bar**.

Inbox

1 On the **Outlook Bar**, click the **Inbox** icon.

The contents of the Inbox are displayed.

2 If your Inbox is not sorted on the **Received** column, click the **Received** column header to sort the messages in ascending order by date and time.

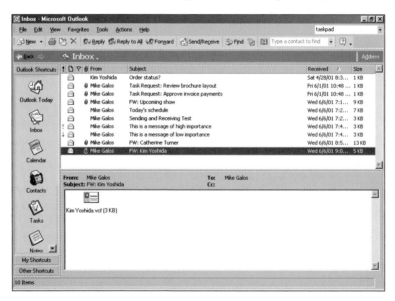

3 Double-click the **Approve invoice payments** task request.

The Approve invoice payments – Task form appears, as shown on the next page.

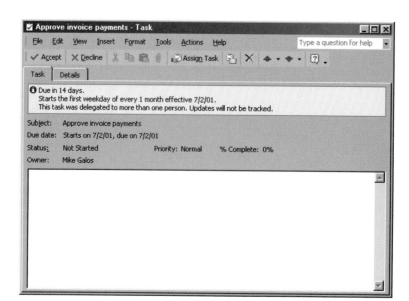

4   On the toolbar, click the **Accept** button.

The Task form closes, the task request disappears from your Inbox, and the next message in the Inbox appears in the open form. The new task is added to your **Tasks** list, and a notice of your acceptance is sent to the requester.

5   Close the message.

6   Double-click the **Review brochure layout** task request.

The Review brochure layout – Task form appears.

7   On the toolbar, click the **Decline** button.

The Task form closes, the task request disappears from your Inbox, and the next message in the Inbox appears in the open form. A notice that you have declined the request is sent to the requester.

8   Close the message.

9   On the **Outlook Bar**, click the **Tasks** icon.

The contents of the Tasks folder are displayed.

10   Double-click the **Approve invoice payments** task.

The Approve invoice payments – Task form appears.

11   Click the down arrow to the right of the **Status** box, and click **In Progress**. Then click in the % **Complete** box, and type **50**.

12   Select the **Reminder** check box. Then click the down arrow to the right of the **Reminder** box, and select the last business day before the due date. The due date is indicated by a gray box.

The Task form now looks like this:

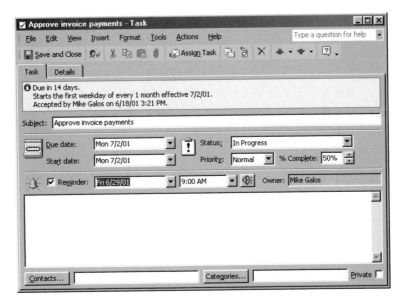

Send Status
Report

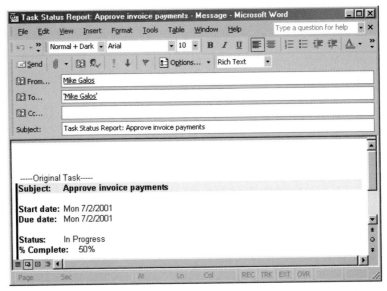

13 On the toolbar, click the **Send Status Report** button.

The Task Status Report: Approve invoice payments - Message form appears, addressed to the task requester and containing the current status of the task.

14 In the body of the message, above the existing text, type **Approved payments marked in accounting program**, and click the **Send** button.

The Message form closes, sending the status report to the task requester.

175

Save and Close   **15**   In the Approve invoice payments – Task form, click the **Save and Close** button.

The Task form closes. The updated task is saved to your **Tasks** list.

Tip

You can quickly create an appointment from a task. Simply drag the task to the **Calendar** icon on the **Outlook Bar**, and then complete the Appointment form.

16   Double-click the **Approve invoice payments** task.

The Approve invoice payments – Task form appears.

Mark Complete   **17**   On the toolbar, click the **Mark Complete** button.

The Task form closes. A status report is automatically sent to the task requester. The task appears as completed in your **Tasks** list, and because this task is recurring, the next month's task is added to your list.

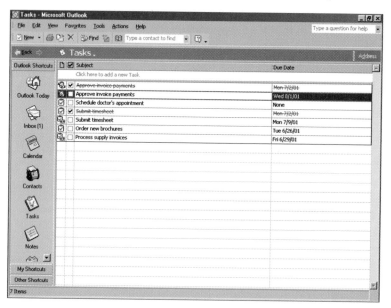

18   In the **Tasks** list, double-click the new **Approve invoice payments** task.

The Approve invoice payments – Task form appears.

19   Click the **Details** tab.

20   Click the down arrow to the right of the **Date completed** box, and then click the task's due date, **8/1/02**.

21   Click in the **Actual work** box, delete the existing text, type **8**, and then press the ⎇Tab⎈ key.

Outlook converts the 8 (hours) you entered to **1 day**, because one workday is eight hours long. The Task form now looks like this:

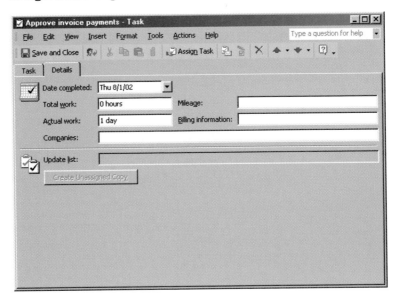

22 Click the **Save and Close** button.

The Task form closes. A status report is automatically sent to the task requester. The task appears as completed in your **Tasks** list, and the next month's task is added to your list.

23 In the **Tasks** list, double-click the new **Submit timesheet** task.

The Submit timesheet – Task form appears.

⟳ Recurrence... **24** On the toolbar, click the **Recurrence** button.

The **Task Recurrence** dialog box for this task appears.

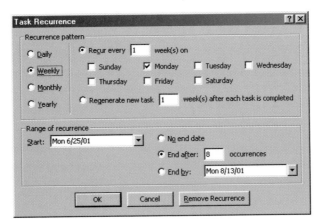

25 Click the **Remove Recurrence** button.

The **Task Recurrence** dialog box closes, and you return to the updated Task form.

26 On the Task form's toolbar, click the **Save and Close** button.

The Task form closes. The updated task is saved in your **Tasks** list.

27 In the **Tasks** list, click the new **Submit timesheet** task to select it.

Delete

28 On the toolbar, click the **Delete** button.

The task is removed from your **Tasks** list.

29 In the **Tasks** list, click the **Approve invoice payments** task to select it.

30 On the toolbar, click the **Delete** button.

This time, the **Delete Incomplete Task** dialog box appears.

31 Click the **Mark complete and delete** option, and click **OK**.

A message box asks if you want to delete all occurrences of this task.

32 In the message box, click the **Delete all** option, and click **OK**.

The task is marked as completed in the **Tasks** list, and no further tasks are created.

Tip

You can quickly mark a task as completed in the **Tasks** list in Simple List view or in the **TaskPad** in the default Calendar view. Simply select the check box that appears to the left of the task.

Assigning Tasks to Others

OL2002e-5-1
OL2002e-5-2
OL2002e-5-4
OL2002e-5-5

You can create a task in Outlook but assign it to someone else for completion. You might delegate a task to your assistant, or when your project depends on receiving something from another department, you might assign a task to your contact in that department.

Although you can update the tasks you create for yourself, when you assign a task to someone else, only that person can update it. However, you can keep a copy of the task in your **Tasks** list, and your copy will be updated as the other person updates the tasks. For example, if the other person changes the status or the percent complete, your copy of the task will be updated. You can also specify that you want to receive status reports for the task. Status reports are special e-mail messages that reflect the current status of a task.

In this exercise, you will assign a task to a contact and view and track the task you have assigned. You don't need any practice files for this exercise.

New Task

1 With the Tasks folder displayed in Outlook, on the toolbar, click the **New Task** button.

The Task form appears.

2 In the **Subject** box, type **Submit report**.

3 Click the down arrow to the right of the **Due date** box, and click the date two weeks from today.

4 Click the down arrow to the right of the **Start date** box, and click the date one week from today.

The Task form looks similar to this one:

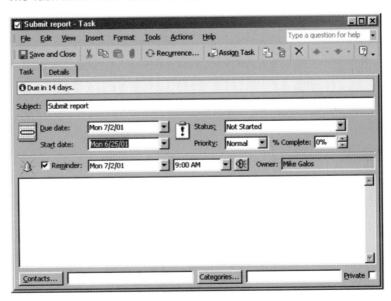

Assign Task

5 On the toolbar, click the **Assign Task** button.

The Task form is updated to include a **To** box.

6 In the **To** box, type **kimy@gardenco.msn.com**.

The Task form now looks as shown on the next page.

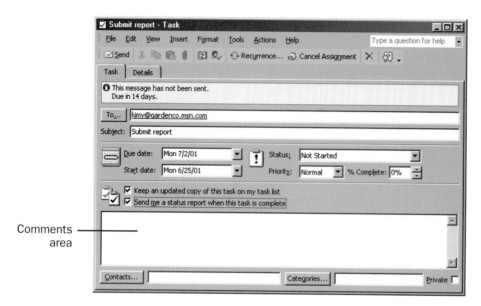

Comments area

Note that the **Keep an updated copy of this task on my task list** and **Send me a status report when this task is complete** options are selected.

7 Click in the comments area, and type **Inventory report** to describe the type of report you are requesting.

8 On the toolbar, click the **Send** button. If a message appears to notify you that the task reminder has been turned off, click **OK**.

The task request is sent. You will be notified when the assignee accepts or declines the task.

Important

The e-mail addresses used in these exercises are not valid. Any items you send to these addresses will be returned as undeliverable. You can delete the returned messages at any time.

9 On the **View** menu, point to **Current View**, and click **Assignment**.

The Tasks folder shows only those tasks that you have assigned to others. For each task, the **Subject**, **Owner**, **Due Date**, and **Status** columns are shown.

Important

If you assign a task to more than one person, you cannot keep a copy of the task in your **Tasks** list. To be able to track the progress on tasks assigned to more than one person, create duplicate tasks, and assign each of them to one person.

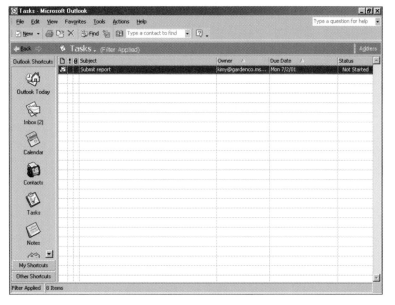

10 In the **Tasks** list, double-click the **Submit report** task.

The Submit report – Task form appears. As work on the task progresses, its status will be reflected in the header on the **Task** tab.

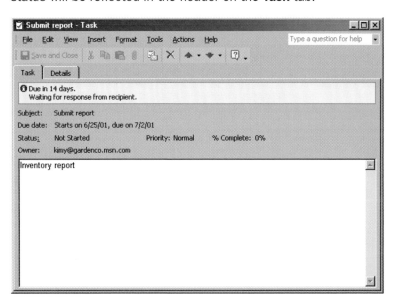

11 Click the **Details** tab.

The **Details** tab is displayed. As work on the task progresses or the task is completed, any work-related information or the date the task was completed will appear in the header on this tab, as shown on the next page.

181

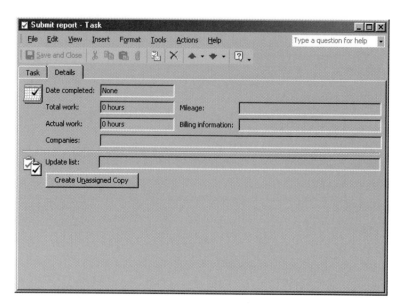

Close

12 Click the **Close** button.

The Task form closes, and you return to the **Tasks** list.

Tip

If you want another person to perform a task but don't need to track the progress of that task, you can send the task as an attachment to an e-mail message rather than assigning a task to another person. In the **Tasks** list, right-click the task, and click **Forward** on the shortcut menu. Address the message, and then click the **Send** button. The recipient can then save the attached task to his or her **Tasks** list. Tasks received in this manner are just like tasks you created for yourself.

13 On the toolbar, click the **New Task** button.

The Task form appears.

14 On the toolbar, click the **Assign Task** button.

The Task form is updated to include a **To** box.

15 Click the **To** button.

The **Select Task Recipient** dialog box appears.

16 If **Contacts** is not the active address book, click the down arrow to the right of the **Show Names from the** box, and click **Contacts** in the drop-down list.

The result looks like this:

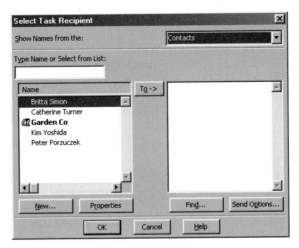

17 In the **Name** list, click any contact, click the **To** button, and click **OK**.

The name and e-mail address of the contact is added to the **To** box.

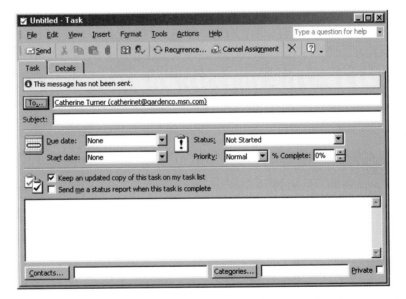

18 Click the **Close** button, and when prompted to save the changes, click **No**.

The task is discarded without being saved.

Inbox

19 If you are not continuing on with the next chapter, close any open tasks, appointments, or messages. Then on the **Outlook Bar**, click the **Inbox** icon, and on the **File** menu, click **Exit**.

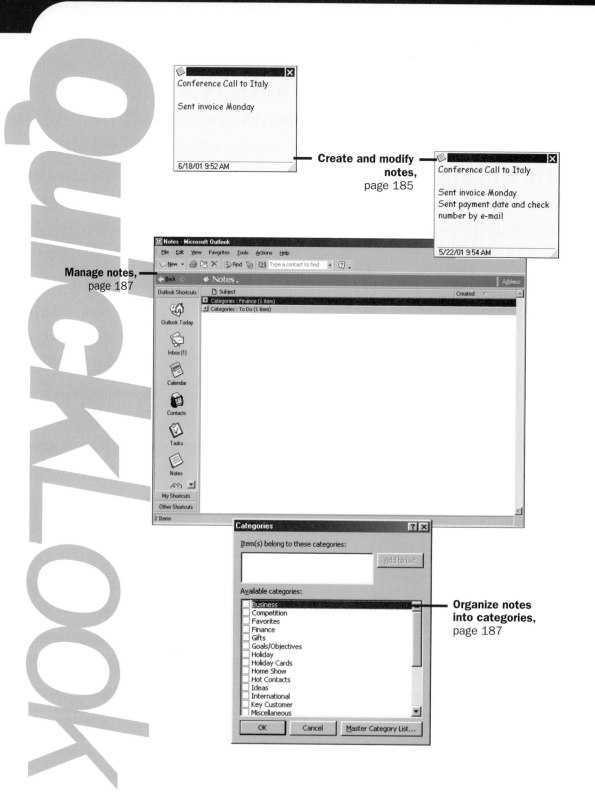

Create and modify notes, page 185

Manage notes, page 187

Organize notes into categories, page 187

Chapter 8
Creating and Organizing Notes

After completing this chapter, you will be able to:

✔ **Create and modify notes**

✔ **Organize and manage notes**

As you work, you might think of ideas, remember small tasks, or jot down messages on notepads or sticky notes. Microsoft Outlook allows you to record these items in the form of electronic notes that you can save, edit, and organize.

This chapter uses the practice files that you installed from this book's CD-ROM onto your hard disk and copied into Outlook. For details about installing and copying the practice files, see "Using the Book's CD-ROM" at the beginning of this book.

Creating and Modifying Notes

OL2002-5-4

You can use Outlook's **Notes** feature to record questions, ideas, reminders, messages, or anything else that you might otherwise write down. Because you can leave notes open on your screen even while Outlook is minimized, they are especially useful for storing small bits of information that you might need as you work. For example, you might open a Note form to record your notes during a phone conference, or you might use a note to jot down useful references you find while doing research on the Web.

In this exercise, you will create and edit notes. You don't need any practice files for this exercise.

1   If it is not already open, start Outlook, and then maximize its window.

Notes

2   On the **Outlook Bar**, click the **Notes** icon.

If you have copied this book's practice files, you will see one sample note displayed.

New Note

New

3   On the toolbar, click the **New Note** button.

The Note form appears, showing the current date and time at the bottom.

4   In the body of the Note form, type **Conference Call to Italy**, press the [Enter] key twice, and type **Sent invoice Monday**.

Your Note form looks like the one shown on the next page.

Close

5 To save your note, click the **Close** button.

Your note is saved in the Notes folder, and the first line appears as the note's title.

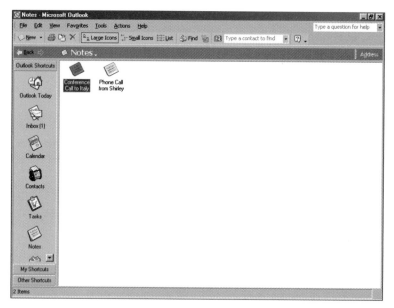

6 Double-click the note you created.

The Note form appears.

7 Edit the contents of the note by clicking at the end of the second line, pressing [Enter], and typing **Sent payment date and check number by e-mail**.

Your note looks like this:

8 To save the note, click the **Close** button.

The updated note is saved in the Notes folder.

9 Now you'll jot down a few notes about an upcoming meeting agenda. On the toolbar, click the **New Note** button, type **Meeting Agenda**, press [Enter], and then type **Current project status**, **Roadblocks**, and **Next steps**, pressing [Enter] after each. Finish by clicking the **Close** button.

The updated note is saved in your Notes folder.

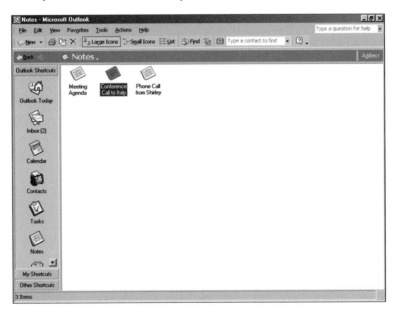

Delete

10 In the Notes folder, click the **Conference Call** note, and on the toolbar, click the **Delete** button.

The note is deleted.

Organizing and Managing Notes

OL2002-5-4
OL2002-5-5

It doesn't take long before you accumulate a variety of notes from different days and about different topics. When this happens, it can become increasingly difficult to find that crucial bit of information you jotted down last week. But Outlook makes it easy to view, sort, organize, and manage your notes to help you find the information you need when you need it. You can view notes as large icons, as small icons, or in a list. You can organize notes by date, category, and color. For example, you might view all the notes on a given date to find the notes you took during a conference call, or you might assign all notes related to personal issues to the Personal category and then view only those notes when taking time to handle personal items. You can also forward notes to others and link notes to contacts. For example, after a phone call with a client, you might link a note you created during that call to the contact information for that client. You can also forward that note to a co-worker who is working with the same client.

In this exercise, you will change view options, sort notes, filter notes, forward a note, and link a note to a contact.

Important

Agenda

If you haven't installed and copied the practice files for this book, please do so now. For details about installing and copying the practice files, see "Using the Book's CD-ROM" at the beginning of this book. For this exercise, you will also need the Meeting Agenda note. If you didn't create this note in an earlier exercise, follow the instructions in "Using the Book's CD-ROM" to copy the Agenda practice file from the SBS\Outlook\Notes folder to the **Notes** icon on the **Outlook Bar**.

Notes

1 On the **Outlook Bar**, click the **Notes** icon.

If you have your own notes or the practice files that came with this book installed, you will see them displayed in Large Icons view.

List

2 On the toolbar, click the **List** button.

The notes are displayed as icons in a list.

3 On the **View** menu, point to **Current View**, and click **Notes List**.

The notes are displayed in a list, with the contents of the notes visible. They are sorted by the **Created** column, with the newest at the top.

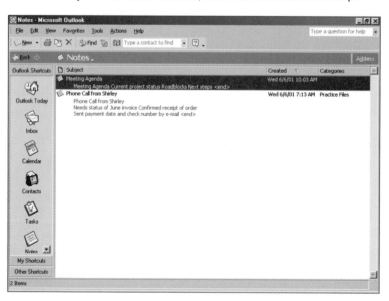

4 Click the **Subject** column heading.

The notes are sorted alphabetically by subject.

5 Double-click the **Meeting Agenda** note.

The Note form appears.

6 In the top left corner, click the **Note** icon, and then click **Categories** on the drop-down menu.

The **Categories** dialog box appears.

7 Click in the **Item(s) belong to these categories** box, type **To Do**, and click the **Add to List** button.

The category is added to the **Available categories** list.

8 In the **Available categories** list, scroll down to see the new category.

The **To Do** check box is selected.

9 Click **OK**.

The **Categories** dialog box closes. The **To Do** category is added to the Meeting Agenda note, although the appearance of the note in this view does not change.

Close

10 Close the note by clicking its **Close** button.

11 Double-click the **Phone Call from Shirley** note.

The Note form appears.

12 In the top left corner, click the **Note** icon, and click **Categories** on the drop-down list.

The **Categories** dialog box appears.

13 In the **Available categories** list, select the **Business** check box, and click **OK**.

The **Categories** dialog box closes. The **Business** category is added to the Phone Call from Shirley note, although the appearance of the note in this view does not change.

14 Close the note by clicking its **Close** button.

The categories are now visible, as shown on the next page.

Categories column

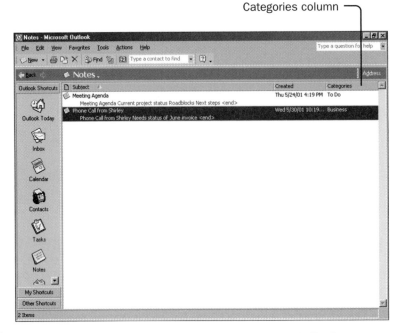

15 On the **View** menu, point to **Current View**, and click **By Category**.

The notes are grouped by category.

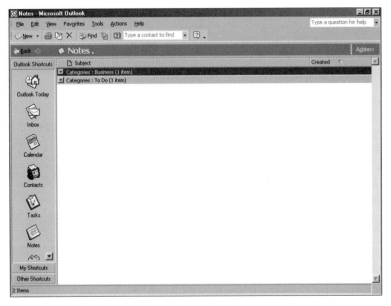

16 Click the plus (+) sign to the left of the **To Do** category.

The contents of the **To Do** category (the Meeting Agenda note) are displayed.

17 On the **View** menu, point to **Current View**, and click **Notes List**.

The notes are displayed in a list, with the content of the notes visible.

18 Double-click the **Phone Call from Shirley** note.

The Note form appears.

19 In the top left corner, click the **Note** icon, and click **Forward** in the drop-down list.

A new Message form appears, with the Phone Call from Shirley note attached.

20 In the **To** box, type **kimy@gardenco.msn.com**.

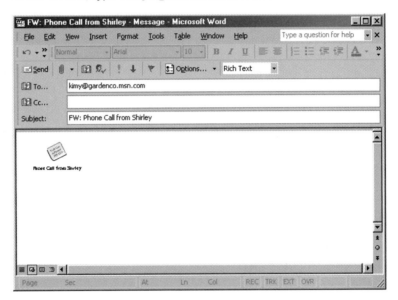

Tip

Microsoft Word is used as the default editor throughout this book. If Word is not your default editor, your screen will look slightly different from this one.

📧 Send

21 Click in the message body to the right of the Note icon, type **For your information**, and click the **Send** button.

The message is sent.

Important

The e-mail addresses used in these exercises are not valid, so any messages you send to them will be returned as undeliverable. You can delete the returned messages at any time.

22 In the top left corner of the Phone Call from Shirley note, click the **Note** icon, and click **Contacts** in the drop-down list.

The **Contacts for Note** dialog box appears.

23 Click the **Contacts** button.

The **Select Contacts** dialog box appears.

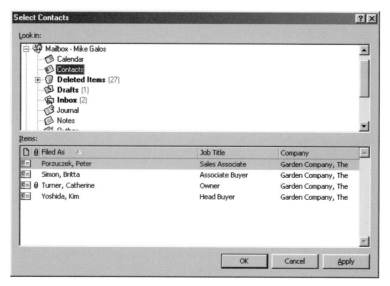

24 In the **Items** list, click the **Kim Yoshida** contact, and click **OK**. If your Contacts folder does not contain a contact for Kim Yoshida, click any other contact, and then click **OK**.

The **Select Contacts** dialog box closes. The contact's name appears in the **Contacts for Note** dialog box.

25 Click the **Close** button.

The **Contacts for Note** dialog box closes.

26 On the Note form, click the **Close** button.

The updated note is saved.

Contacts

27 On the **Outlook Bar**, click the **Contacts** icon.

The contents of the Contacts folder are displayed.

28 Double-click **Kim Yoshida** or whichever contact you linked to the Phone Call from Shirley note.

The Contact form appears.

29 Click the **Activities** tab.

The Phone Call from Shirley note appears in the **Activities** list.

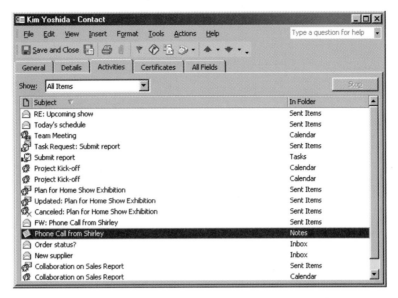

30 Click the **Phone Call from Shirley** note, and press the Del key on your keyboard.

The **Activities** list indicates that the note is now in the Deleted Items folder. When the Deleted Items folder is emptied, the note will no longer appear in **Activities** list for this contact.

31 Click the **Save and Close** button.

The Contact form closes.

32 On the **Outlook Bar**, click the **Notes** icon.

The contents of the Notes folder are displayed. The Phone Call from Shirley note no longer appears here.

Inbox

33 Close any open notes, appointments, or messages. Then on the **Outlook Bar**, click the **Inbox** icon, and on the **File** menu, click **Exit** to quit Outlook.

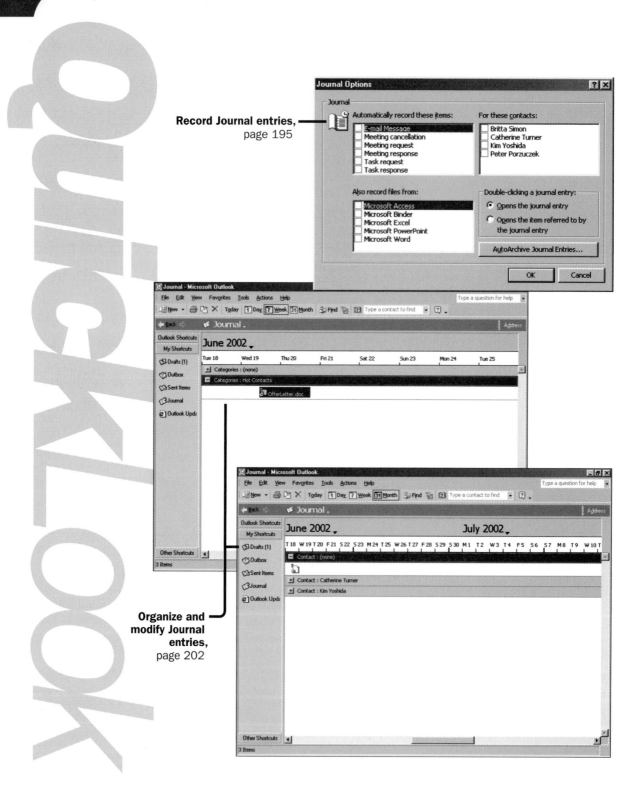

Record Journal entries,
page 195

Organize and modify Journal entries,
page 202

Chapter 9
Using the Journal

After completing this chapter, you will be able to:

✔ **Record Journal entries**

✔ **Organize and modify Journal entries**

With Microsoft Outlook's Journal, you can keep a record of any kind of interaction or activity, even if it is not associated with an item on your computer. You can log phone conversations and meetings with contacts, as well as hard-copy letters you've mailed or received. For example, you might track all interactions with a client to support the hours you bill to that client at the end of the month. Or, you might use the Journal to record meeting minutes and document phone conversations related to a particular project so that you can reference them as you work. In addition to tracking items such as e-mail messages and Microsoft Office documents, you can choose which Outlook items will be automatically tracked for the contacts you specify.

This chapter uses the practice files that you installed from this book's CD-ROM onto your hard disk and copied into Outlook. For details about installing and copying the practice files, see "Using the Book's CD-ROM" at the beginning of this book.

Recording Journal Entries

OL2002e-4-4

A **Journal entry** is a shortcut to an activity, such as a task, meeting, or e-mail message, that has been registered, typically in relation to a contact. You can choose to record Journal entries automatically for the items and contacts you specify, or you can record individual items manually.

To automatically record items in the Journal, first you specify which items you want to record. Then you select the contacts for which these items should be recorded. No items are recorded in the Journal by default. You can automatically record e-mail messages, meeting requests and updates, meeting responses, task requests, and task responses, as well as the receipt or delivery of Microsoft Office documents.

You can record all of these items manually, too, in addition to a host of other common interactions, such as conversations, phone calls, faxes, and letters. You can also track the amount of time devoted to any item recorded as a Journal entry. This time is entered as the duration for the entry.

In this exercise, you will configure Outlook to automatically record Journal entries for a contact, manually record a Journal entry for an individual Outlook item, and manually record a Journal entry for a Word document.

Important

CatherineT
KimY
OfferLetter.doc

If you haven't installed the practice files for this book, please do so now. For details about installing the practice files, see "Using the Book's CD-ROM" at the beginning of this book. In this exercise, you will use the Word document OfferLetter located in the SBS\Outlook\Journal folder, which is probably on drive C. You will also need to have contact information for Catherine Turner and Kim Yoshida in your **Contacts** list. If you didn't add this information to your **Contacts** list in an earlier chapter, follow the instructions in "Using the Book's CD-ROM" to copy the CatherineT and KimY practice files from the SBS\Outlook\Journal folder to the **Contacts** icon on the **Outlook Bar.**

1 If it is not already open, start Outlook, and then maximize its window.

Inbox

2 On the **Outlook Bar**, click the **Inbox** icon.

The contents of the Inbox are displayed.

3 On the **Tools** menu, click **Options**.

The **Options** dialog box appears.

4 In the **Contacts** area, click the **Journal Options** button.

The **Journal Options** dialog box appears.

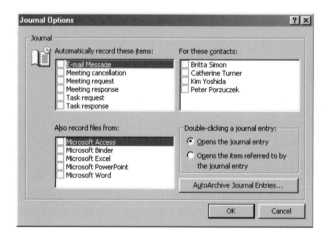

5 In the **Automatically record these items** list, select the **E-mail Message**, **Meeting cancellation**, **Meeting request**, and **Meeting response** check boxes.

6 In the **For these contacts** list, select the **Catherine Turner** check box, and click **OK**.

The **Journal Options** dialog box closes.

7 In the **Options** dialog box, click **OK**.

The **Options** dialog box closes. The Journal options are saved.

Important

You can view all items associated with a contact without using the Journal or setting Journal options. Items associated with a contact appear on the **Activities** tab of the Contact form. However, the items on the **Activities** tab are not displayed in a timeline.

New Mail
Message

New

8 On the toolbar, click the **New Mail Message** button.

A blank Message form appears.

9 Click the **To** button.

The **Select Names** dialog box appears.

10 Click the down arrow to the right of the **Show Names from the** box, and click **Contacts** in the drop-down list.

11 In the **Name** list, click **Catherine Turner**, click the **To** button, and click **OK**.

Catherine Turner is added to the **To** box.

12 Click in the **Subject** box, type Journal Test, press the ⌧ key, and in the body of the message, type This message will be recorded as a Journal entry for this contact.

Tip

Microsoft Word is used as the default editor throughout this book. If Word is not your default editor, you screen will look slightly different from the ones shown in this book.

13 On the toolbar, click the **Send** button.

The message is sent.

Journal

14 On the **Outlook Bar**, click **My Shortcuts**, and then click the **Journal** icon.

The Journal is displayed. By default, the Journal shows eight days of entries, grouped by type.

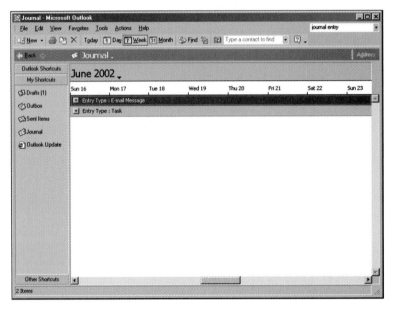

15 Click the plus (+) sign to the left of the **E-mail Message** type.

The Journal entries for e-mail messages are displayed. The entry for the message you sent to Catherine Turner appears for today.

New Journal Entry

16 Now you'll manually create a Journal entry. On the toolbar, click the **New Journal Entry** button.

The Journal Entry form appears.

17 In the **Subject** box, type Request Status Report, click the down arrow to the right of the **Entry type** box, and click **Task** in the drop-down list.

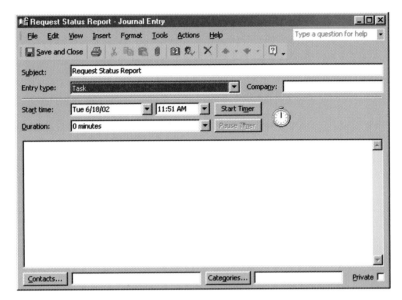

18 In the bottom left corner, click the **Contacts** button.

The **Select Contacts** dialog box appears.

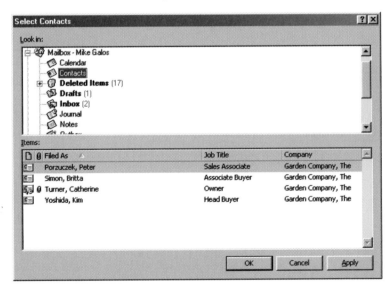

19 In the **Items** list, click **Yoshida, Kim**, and then click **OK**.

The name is added to the **Contacts** box on the Journal Entry form.

20 On the Journal Entry form's toolbar, click the **Save and Close** button.

The Journal entry is saved, as shown on the next page.

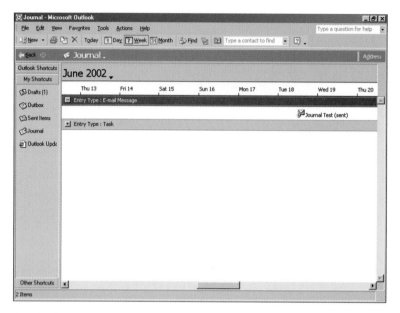

21 On the **Start** menu, point to **Programs** and then click **Windows Explorer** to start Windows Explorer. If necessary, drag the Windows Explorer window to the side so that the Journal icon on the **Outlook Bar** is visible. Then browse to the **SBS/Outlook/Journal** folder, which is probably on drive C, and click it.

The contents of the folder are displayed.

22 Drag the **OfferLetter** document from the SBS/Outlook/Journal folder to the **Journal** icon in the **Outlook Bar**.

The OfferLetter.doc – Journal Entry form appears. The entry is a shortcut to the document. The type, Document, is selected for you automatically.

23 Click the down arrow to the right of the **Duration** box, and then click **2 hours** in the drop-down list.

You are recording that you spent two hours working on this document. Your screen looks similar to this one:

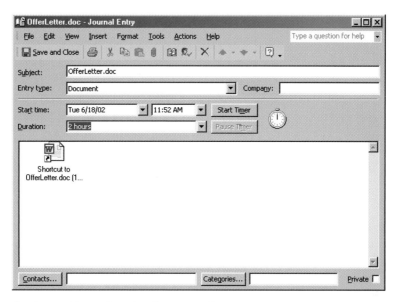

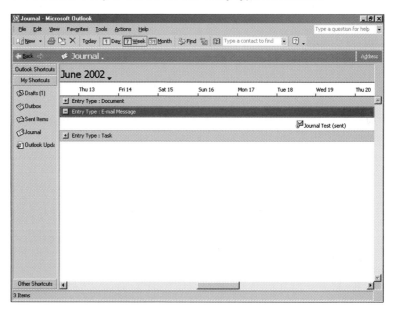

Save and Close

24 On the toolbar, click the **Save and Close** button.

The Journal entry is saved as the entry type *Document*.

Organizing and Modifying Journal Entries

OL2002e-4-4

Journal entries are recorded based on when the interaction occurs and are displayed on a timeline. You can organize the entries by type, category, or contact by using views. As with your Calendar, you can view your Journal entries for a day, a week, or a month at a time. To take full advantage of the Journal, you can associate your entries with contacts to help you track your work for and interactions with clients and others. For example, you might create a Journal entry each time you talk to a client on the phone to record your notes about what was discussed, what was agreed upon, and the time spent on the call. You can easily see which contacts are associated with which Journal entries, and vice versa, either by viewing the Journal by contact, or by clicking the **Activities** tab on the Contact form.

You can modify the date and time associated with a Journal entry, although changing the date and time does not change the date and time of the associated Outlook item, document, or contact.

In this exercise, you will explore the options for viewing Journal entries, assign a Journal entry to a category, associate Journal entries with a contact, view the Journal entries associated with a contact, move a Journal entry to another date, and change the type of a Journal entry.

Important

CatherineT
KimY
JournalTest
RequestStatus
OfferLetter

For this exercise, you will need contact information for Catherine Turner and Kim Yoshida in your **Contacts** list. You will also need the Journal Test, Request Status Report, and Offer Letter entries in your Journal. If you didn't create these contacts or add these entries in an earlier exercise, follow the instructions in "Using the Book's CD-ROM" at the beginning of the book to copy the CatherineT and KimY practice files from the SBS\Outlook\Organize folder to the **Contacts** icon on the **Outlook Bar**, and copy the JournalTest, RequestStatus, and OfferLetter files from the SBS\Outlook\Organize folder to the **Journal** icon on the **Outlook Bar**.

Journal

1 On the **Outlook Bar**, click **My Shortcuts**, and then click the **Journal** icon.

The Journal is displayed, showing entries for the current week, grouped by type.

2 If you are using Journal entries you created in the first exercise in this chapter, skip ahead to step 5.

3 If you are using the practice files for this exercise (rather than entries you created in the first exercise), on the **View** menu, point to **Go To**, and then click **Go to Date**.

The **Go To Date** dialog box appears.

4 In the **Date** box, type **6/18/02**, and click **OK**.

The Journal entries for the week of June 18, 2002, are displayed, grouped by type.

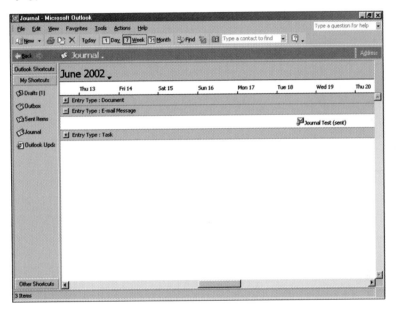

5 On the **View** menu, point to **Current View**, and click **By Contact**.

The entries are now grouped by contact.

6 On the toolbar, click the **Month** button.

The Journal displays a month-long timeline.

7 If you are using Journal entries you created in the first exercise in this chapter, skip ahead to step 10.

8 If you are using the practice files for this exercise, on the **View** menu, point to **Go To**, and then click **Go to Date**.

The **Go To Date** dialog box appears.

9 In the **Date** box, type 6/18/02, and click **OK**.

The Journal entries for the week of June 18, 2002, are displayed.

10 Click the plus (+) sign to the left of the **Contact : (none)** group.

The OfferLetter.doc entry—the only entry not associated with a contact—appears.

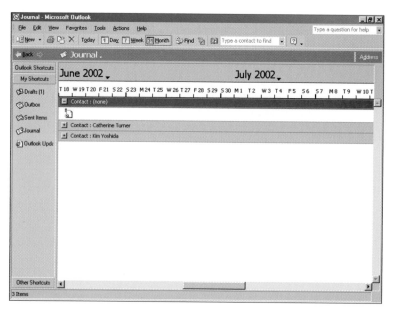

11 Double-click the **OfferLetter.doc** entry.

The OfferLetter.doc – Journal Entry form appears.

12 In the bottom left corner, click the **Contacts** button.

The **Select Contacts** dialog box appears.

13 In the **Items** list, click **Turner, Catherine**, and click **OK**.

Catherine Turner is added to the **Contacts** box.

14 To the right of the **Contacts** box, click the **Categories** button.

The **Categories** dialog box appears.

15 In the **Available categories** list, select the **Hot Contacts** check box, and click **OK**.

The selected category is added to the **Categories** box on the Journal Entry form.

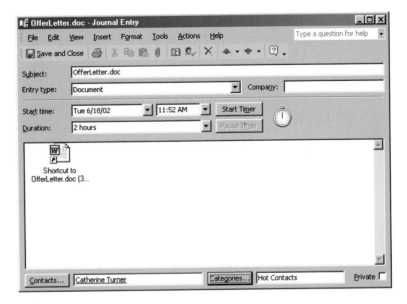

Save and Close **16** On the toolbar, click the **Save and Close** button.

The Journal Entry form closes, and the updated entry is saved.

7 Week **17** On the toolbar, click the **Week** button.

The Journal shows the entries for either the current week or the week of June 18, 2002, depending on whether or not you are using the practice files.

18 Click the plus (+) sign to left of the **Contact: Catherine Turner** group.

The OfferLetter.doc entry now appears in the group for Catherine Turner. (You might have to scroll to the left to see the entry.)

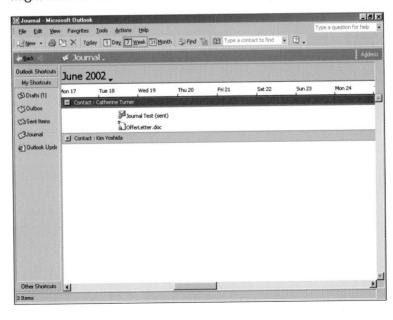

19 On the **View** menu, point to **Current View**, and click **By Category**.

20 If you are using Journal entries you created in the first exercise in this chapter, skip ahead to step 23.

21 If you are using the practice files for this exercise, on the **View** menu, point to **Go To**, and then click **Go to Date**.

The **Go To Date** dialog box appears.

22 In the **Date** box, type **6/18/02**, and click **OK**.

The Journal entries for the week of June 18, 2002, are displayed, grouped by category.

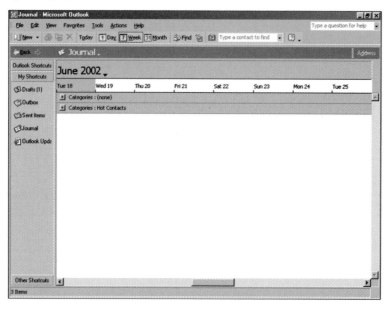

Contacts

23 On the **Outlook Bar**, click **Outlook Shortcuts**, and click the **Contacts** icon.

The contents of the Contacts folder are displayed.

24 Double-click the contact for Catherine Turner.

The Catherine Turner – Contact form appears.

25 Click the **Activities** tab.

All items associated with this contact appear.

26 Click the down arrow to the right of the **Show** box, and then click **Journal** in the drop-down list.

The list includes only the Journal entries associated with this contact.

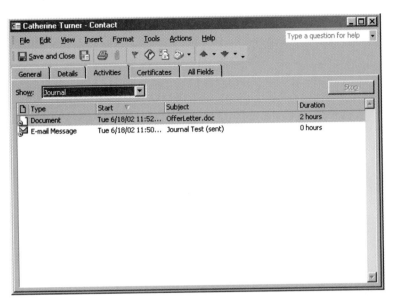

27 On the toolbar, click the **Save and Close** button.

The Catherine Turner – Contact form closes.

28 On the **Outlook Bar**, click **My Shortcuts**, and then click the **Journal** icon.

29 If you are using Journal entries you created in the first exercise in this chapter, skip ahead to step 32.

30 If you are using the practice files for this exercise, on the **View** menu, point to **Go To**, and then click **Go to Date**.

The **Go To Date** dialog box appears.

31 In the **Date** box, type **6/18/02**, and click **OK**.

The Journal entries for the week of June 18, 2002, are displayed, grouped by category.

32 Click the plus (+) sign to the left of the **Categories: Hot Contacts** group, and double-click the **OfferLetter.doc** entry.

The OfferLetter.doc – Journal Entry form appears.

33 Click the down arrow to the right of the **Entry type** box, and click **Letter** in the drop-down list. Then click the down arrow to the right of the **Start time** box, and click tomorrow's date. (Click **6/19/02** if you are using the practice files.)

Your form now looks similar to this one:

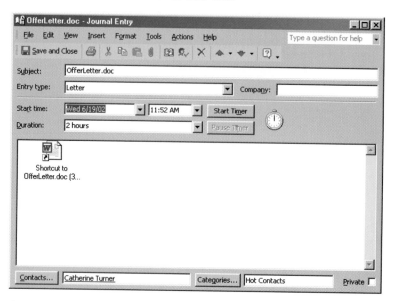

34 On the toolbar, click the **Save and Close** button.

The updated entry is saved.

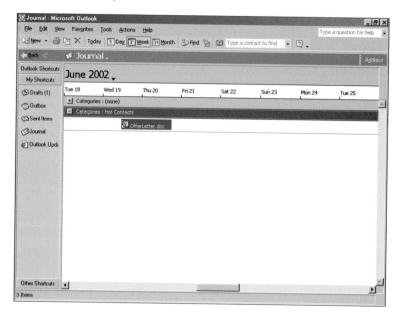

Tip

By default, when you double-click a Journal entry, the entry itself, rather than the item or file it represents, is opened. You can choose to open the item associated with the entry instead. On the **Tools** menu, click **Options**, and in the **Contacts** area, click the **Journal Options** button. In the **Journal Options** dialog box, select the **Opens the item referred to by the journal entry** option, and click **OK**. Click **OK** again to close the **Options** dialog box.

35 If you are not continuing on to the next chapter, close any Journal entries, contacts, or messages. On the **Outlook Bar**, click **Outlook Shortcuts**, and then click the **Inbox** icon. Then on the **File** menu, click **Exit** to quit Outlook.

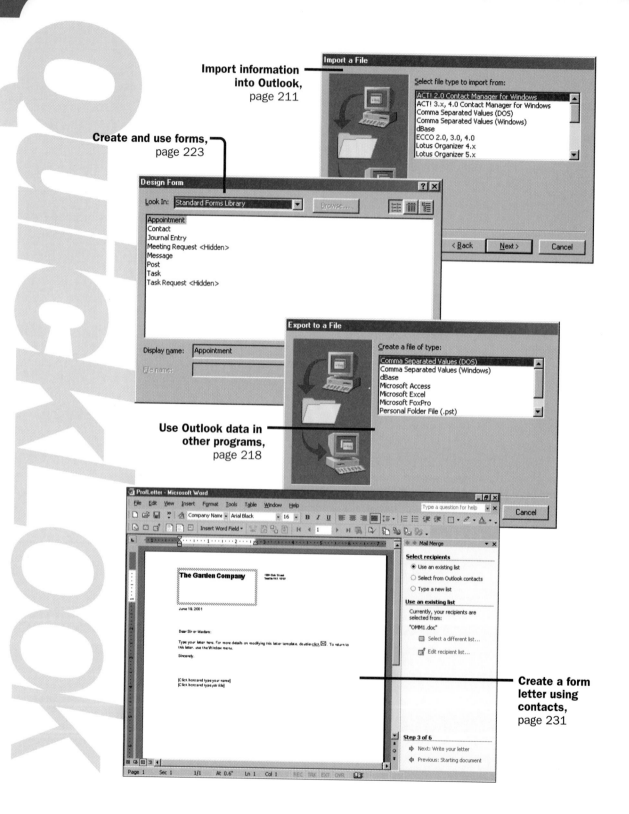

Import information into Outlook, page 211

Create and use forms, page 223

Use Outlook data in other programs, page 218

Create a form letter using contacts, page 231

Chapter 10
Using Outlook
with Other Programs

After completing this chapter, you will be able to:

✔ **Import information into Outlook**
✔ **Use Outlook data in other programs**
✔ **Create and use forms**
✔ **Create a form letter using contacts**

Consolidating your contacts, calendar, e-mail messages, and other information involved in electronic communication is the key to staying organized. Because you can import and export data into and out of Microsoft Outlook 2002, you don't have to retype important information every time you want to use it in conjunction with another program. For example, you might have received an existing list of contacts in a Microsoft Excel file. Rather than retyping the names, phone numbers, addresses, and e-mail addresses for those contacts, you can import the information to your Outlook Contacts folder. The **Import/Export Wizard** guides you through the process.

Standardizing your electronic communication can save time and improve quality and efficiency. With Outlook, you can create forms to control the way information is distributed and collected. For example, you might create a form for employees to use when submitting expenses to the company for reimbursement.

This chapter uses the practice files that you installed from this book's CD-ROM onto your hard disk and copied into Outlook. For details about installing and copying the practice files, see "Using the Book's CD-ROM" at the beginning of this book.

Importing Information into Outlook

OL2002e-4-1

You can copy, or import, data from a variety of other programs for use in Outlook. For example, if you were to take over a collection of sales accounts, you might be given an Outlook Personal Address Book containing key contact information. You can import those contacts into your Contacts folder to begin work on the accounts. Or, if a project is postponed, you might move all related e-mail to a separate **Personal Folders file** for storage. When the project is reactivated, you can import those messages back into your Outlook folders and continue your work.

You can import information from the following sources:

■ Calendar information from a **Schedule+** or a **vCalendar** file.

Tip

Microsoft Schedule+ is a calendar program that was available before the first version of Microsoft Outlook was released. vCalendar is a standard, text-based format for storing calendar information. vCard is a standard, text-based format for storing contact information.

■ Contact information from an Outlook Personal Address Book, an **ACT! For Windows** file, or a **vCard** file.

■ E-mail messages from an Outlook Personal Folders file, a **Eudora** file, or a **Netscape** file.

■ Calendar or contact information from a Microsoft Access, Microsoft Excel, **Microsoft FoxPro**, or **dBASE** file.

Tip

To import a file from an Access, FoxPro, or dBASE database, or from an Excel spreadsheet, the fields in the file you are importing must correspond to the fields Outlook uses to store the items you are importing. For example, contact information you import must have fields or columns that correspond to the name, address, telephone, e-mail address, and other fields in Outlook's Contact form. During the import process, Outlook will interpret how the fields in your file correspond to the fields for the item you are importing. However, you can specify exactly how the fields correspond before starting the import.

To import data, you indicate the type of file to import, select the file containing the data, and choose the Outlook folder where the data should be stored. The **Import/ Export Wizard** guides you through the process.

In this exercise, you will import a contact from a vCard file, import contacts from a Personal Folders file, and import appointments from an Excel file.

Important

SeanC
Contacts
Calendar

If you haven't installed and copied the practice files for this book, please do so now. For details about installing and copying the practice files, see "Using the Book's CD-ROM" at the beginning of this book. For this exercise, you will also need the files listed above the CD icon in the margin, which are located in the SBS\Outlook \Import folder.

1 If it is not already open, start Outlook, and then maximize its window.

Contacts

2 On the **Outlook Bar**, click the **Contacts** icon.

The contents of the Contacts folder are displayed.

3 On the **File** menu, click **Import and Export**.

The **Import and Export Wizard** appears.

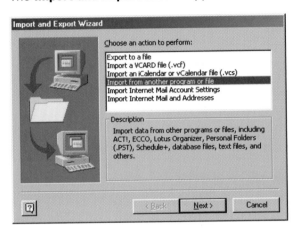

4 In the **Choose an action to perform** list, click **Import a VCARD file (.vcf)**, and then click **Next**.

The **VCARD File** dialog box appears.

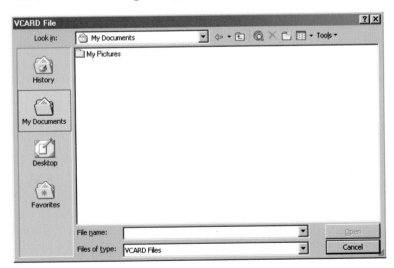

5 In the **VCARD File** dialog box, browse to the SBS\Outlook\Import folder, which is probably on drive C. Then click **SeanC**, and click the **Open** button.

Sean Chai is added to your Contacts folder, as shown on the next page.

213

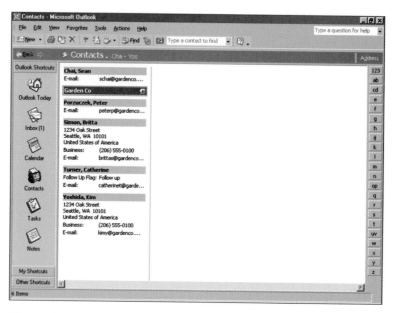

6   Now you'll import a Personal Folders file. On the **File** menu, click **Import and Export**.

The **Import and Export Wizard** appears.

7   In the **Choose an action to perform** list, click **Import from another program or file**, and then click **Next**.

The **Import a File** page of the **Import and Export Wizard** appears.

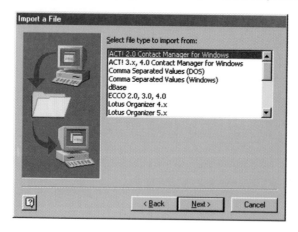

8 In the **Select file type to import from** list, scroll down, click **Personal Folder File (.pst)**, and then click the **Next** button.

The **Import Personal Folders** page of the **Import and Export Wizard**, appears.

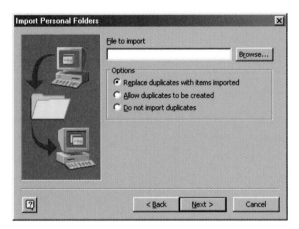

9 Click the **Browse** button.

The **Open Personal Folders** dialog box appears.

10 Browse to the SBS\Outlook\Import folder, click **Contacts**, and then click the **Open** button.

The **Open Personal Folders** dialog box closes, and the path to and name of the Contacts.pst file is added to the **File to import** box on the **Import Personal Folders** page.

11 In the **Options** area, select the **Allow duplicates to be created** option, and then click **Next**.

The next page of the **Import and Export Wizard** appears. If the Contacts file contains any entries with the same full name as an entry in the Contacts folder, Outlook will create a second, duplicate entry for the imported contact rather than replace the existing entry with the imported one.

12 In the **Select the folder to import from** list, click the second **Contacts** folder.

13 Select the **Import items into the current folder** option, and then click the **Finish** button.

Contact information for Mike Galos is added to your Contacts folder, as shown on the next page.

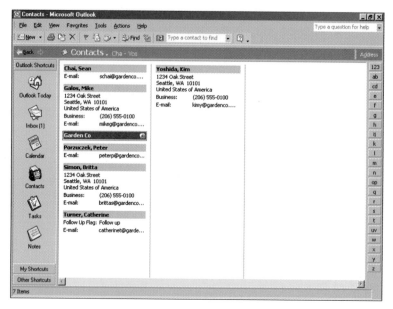

14 Now you'll import schedule information from an Excel file. On the **File** menu, click **Import and Export**.

The **Import and Export Wizard** appears.

15 In the **Choose an action to perform** list, click **Import from another program or file**, and then click **Next**.

The **Import a File** page of the **Import and Export Wizard** appears.

16 In the **Select file type to import from** list, click **Microsoft Excel**, and then click the **Next** button. If prompted to install a translator, click **Yes**.

When installation is complete, the next page of the **Import and Export Wizard** appears.

17 Click the **Browse** button.

The **Browse** dialog box appears.

18 Browse to the SBS\Outlook\Import folder, click **Calendar**, and then click **OK**.

The **Browse** dialog box closes, and the path to and name of the Calendar.xls file is added to the **File to import** box on the **Import a File** page.

19 In the **Options** area, select the **Replace duplicates with items imported** option, and click **Next**.

The next page of the **Import and Export Wizard** appears.

20 In the **Select destination folder** list, click **Calendar**, and then click **Next**.

The next page of the **Import and Export Wizard** appears, showing you that the contents of the Calendar file will be imported into your Calendar folder. To review how the columns in the Excel file will be mapped to the fields for an Outlook contact, click the **Map Custom Fields** button.

The screen indicates that this process may take a few minutes and cannot be canceled.

21 Click the **Finish** button.

The appointments in the Calendar.xls file are added to your Calendar.

Calendar

22 To verify that the appointments have been added, on the **Outlook Bar**, click the **Calendar** icon.

The Calendar is displayed.

23 On the **View** menu, point to **Go To**, and click **Go to Date**.

The **Go To Date** dialog box appears.

24 In the **Date** box, type **6/20/02**, and click **OK**.

The Calendar displays the schedule for June 20, 2002, which contains the imported appointments, including Project Kick-off, Plan for Home Show Exhibition, and Day Care Visit.

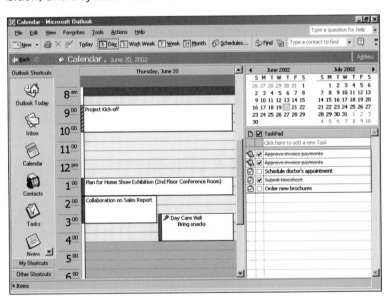

Today

25 On the toolbar, click the **Today** button.

The Calendar displays your schedule for today.

Using Outlook Data in Other Programs

OL2002e-4-2

You can send, or **export**, your Outlook data to a variety of other programs, including Access, Excel, FoxPro, and dBase, or to a standard generic file format. For example, you might export your Contacts folder to Access to be used in a custom database for your business so that you don't have to retype your contact list.

Tip

You can also create a Personal Folders file (with a .pst extension) to store messages, appointments, tasks, and journal entries at any location on your local computer or a network server.

In this exercise, you will export contact information to a vCard file, export appointments to an Excel file, and export messages to a Personal Folders file.

Tip

To complete this exercise, you must have Microsoft Excel installed on your computer.

Important

KimY

If you haven't installed and copied the practice files for this book, please do so now. For details about installing and copying the practice files, see "Using the Book's CD-ROM" at the beginning of this book. For this exercise, you will also need contact information for Kim Yoshida in your **Contacts** list. If you didn't add this information to your **Contacts** list in an earlier chapter, follow the instructions in "Using the Book's CD-ROM" at the beginning of the book to copy the KimY file from the SBS\Outlook \OutlookData folder to the **Contacts** icon on the **Outlook Bar**.

Contacts

1   On the **Outlook Bar**, click the **Contacts** icon.

The contents of the Contacts folder are displayed.

2   Double-click the contact entry for **Kim Yoshida**.

The Kim Yoshida – Contact form opens.

3   On the **File** menu, click **Export to vCard file**.

The **VCARD File** dialog box appears.

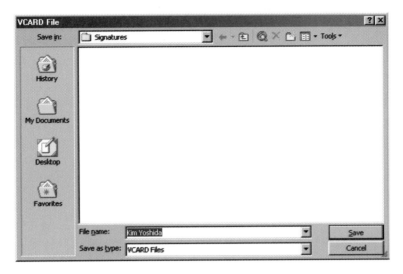

Desktop

4 Click the **Desktop** icon on the left side of the **VCARD File** dialog box, and then click the **Save** button.

vCard

The vCard file is saved on your desktop with the name Kim Yoshida and an icon that looks similar to a business card. This file can be copied to any location or sent as an attachment to an e-mail message. However, you will not need it for any further exercises so you can delete this file at any time.

Close

X

5 In the top right corner of the Contact form, click the **Close** button.

The Contact form closes.

Calendar

6 Now you'll export your schedule as an Excel file. On the **Outlook Bar**, click the **Calendar** icon.

The Calendar is displayed.

7 On the **File** menu, click **Import and Export**.

The **Import and Export Wizard** appears.

8 In the **Choose an action to perform** list, click **Export to a file**, and then click **Next**.

The **Export to a File** page of the **Import and Export Wizard** appears, as shown on the next page.

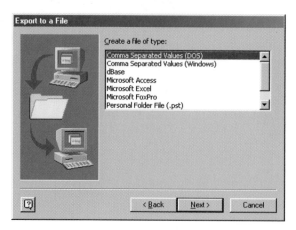

9   In the **Create a file of type** list, click **Microsoft Excel**, and then click **Next**.

     The next page of the **Import and Export Wizard** appears.

10   In the **Select folder to export from** list, click **Calendar**, and click **Next**.

     The next page of the **Import and Export Wizard** appears.

11   Click the **Browse** button.

     The **Browse** dialog box appears.

12   Click the **Desktop** icon on the left side of the **Browse** dialog box, type **Calendar** in the **File name** box, and click **OK**.

     The **Browse** dialog box closes, and the path and file name are inserted into the **Save exported file as** box.

13   Click the **Next** button.

     The next page of the **Import and Export Wizard** appears, indicating that appointments will be exported from your Calendar folder.

14   Click the **Finish** button.

     The **Set Date Range** dialog box appears.

15   Now you'll set the range of dates to be exported to the Excel file. In the first box, type **6/1/02**, press the ⌨Tab key, and in the second box, type **6/30/02**.

16   Click **OK**.

     Outlook exports the appointments for the selected dates to the Calendar.xls file. If the operation takes a while, Outlook might display a status box.

Show Desktop

17 Click the **Show Desktop** button on the Quick Launch toolbar at the left end of the Windows taskbar. Then on the desktop, double-click **Calendar**.

The Calendar file opens as an Excel spreadsheet so that you can review the contents of the file. Note that the fields of your appointments and meetings appear as columns in the spreadsheet.

	A	B	C	D	E	F
1	Subject	StartDate	StartTime	EndDate	EndTime	Alldayeve Re
2	Budget Meeting	6/18/2002	10:00:00 AM	6/18/2002	10:30:00 AM	FALSE F.
3	Team Meeting	6/4/2002	1:00:00 PM	6/4/2002	1:30:00 PM	FALSE F.
4	Team Meeting	6/11/2002	1:00:00 PM	6/11/2002	1:30:00 PM	FALSE F.
5	Team Meeting	6/18/2002	1:00:00 PM	6/18/2002	1:30:00 PM	FALSE F.
6	Team Meeting	6/25/2002	1:00:00 PM	6/25/2002	1:30:00 PM	FALSE F.
7	Project Kick-off	6/20/2002	8:00:00 AM	6/20/2002	9:30:00 AM	FALSE F.
8	Status Report	6/19/2002	10:00:00 AM	6/19/2002	10:30:00 AM	FALSE F.
9	Day Care Visit	6/27/2002	3:00:00 PM	6/27/2002	4:30:00 PM	FALSE F.
10	Day Care Visit	6/25/2002	3:00:00 PM	6/25/2002	4:30:00 PM	FALSE F.
11	Day Care Visit	6/20/2002	3:00:00 PM	6/20/2002	4:30:00 PM	FALSE F.
12	Day Care Visit	6/18/2002	3:00:00 PM	6/18/2002	4:30:00 PM	FALSE F.
13	Day Care Visit	6/13/2002	3:00:00 PM	6/13/2002	4:30:00 PM	FALSE F.
14	Day Care Visit	6/11/2002	3:00:00 PM	6/11/2002	4:30:00 PM	FALSE F.
15	Day Care Visit	6/6/2002	3:00:00 PM	6/6/2002	4:30:00 PM	FALSE F.
16	Day Care Visit	6/4/2002	3:00:00 PM	6/4/2002	4:30:00 PM	FALSE F.
17	Plan for Home Show Exhibition	6/18/2002	1:00:00 PM	6/18/2002	2:00:00 PM	FALSE F.
18	Collaboration on Sales Report	6/20/2002	2:00:00 PM	6/20/2002	3:30:00 PM	FALSE F.
19	Quarterly Status	6/17/2002	9:00:00 AM	6/17/2002	10:00:00 AM	FALSE F.
20	Project Kick-off	6/18/2002	9:00:00 AM	6/18/2002	10:30:00 AM	FALSE F.
21	Status Report	6/15/2002	8:00:00 AM	6/15/2002	9:30:00 AM	FALSE F.
22	Status Report	6/15/2002	10:00:00 AM	6/15/2002	10:30:00 AM	FALSE F.

18 Click the program's **Close** button.

Excel closes. You can delete the Calendar file from your desktop at any time.

19 Click the **Outlook** button on the Windows taskbar to restore the Outlook window.

Inbox

20 Now you'll export your Inbox as a Personal Folders file. On the **Outlook Bar**, click the **Inbox** icon.

The contents of the Inbox are displayed.

21 Now, you will export e-mail messages to share with another Outlook user. On the **File** menu, click **Import and Export**.

The **Import and Export Wizard** appears.

22 In the **Choose an action to perform** list, click **Export to a file**, and then click **Next**.

The **Export to a File** page of the **Import and Export Wizard** appears.

23 In the **Create a file of type** list, click **Personal Folder File (.pst)**, and then click the **Next** button.

The **Export Personal Folders** page of the **Import and Export Wizard** appears.

24 In the **Select the folder to export from** box, click **Inbox**, and then click the **Next** button.

Tip

If you would rather not export the contents of your Inbox (perhaps your Inbox contains many messages), feel free to use another folder containing e-mail messages.

The next page of the **Import and Export Wizard** appears.

25 Click the **Browse** button.

The **Open Personal Folders** dialog box appears.

26 Click the **Desktop** icon on the left side of the **Open Personal Folders** dialog box, and into the **File name** box, type **KimYoshida**, and then click **OK**.

The **Open Personal Folders** dialog box closes, and the path and file name are inserted into the **Save exported file as** box.

27 Click the **Finish** button.

The **Create Microsoft Personal Folders** dialog box appears.

28 In the **Name** box, type **Messages for Kim Y**, and then click **OK**.

The Personal Folders file is saved on your desktop. You can now copy this file to any location on your local computer or a network server. For example, you might place this file on a network server where Kim can access it. You can delete this file at any time.

Creating and Using Forms

OL2002e-4-3
OL2002e-7-1

You can use **forms** to simplify and expedite business communication. Forms are particularly useful for routine requests or communications in which a specific set of information is required. For example, you might create a form for employees in your organization to use to submit their timesheet in a standardized way each week. Then employees could submit their timesheet via e-mail simply by entering the date and hours into a message that is automatically addressed and formatted appropriately. You can create forms by customizing a built-in form, such as the Message or Appointment forms, from Outlook or from another Office file. You can save a form as a file for use as a template or in another program, or publish it to a forms library to make the form available to others.

Important

If you are using Microsoft Word as your default e-mail editor, you must disable it in order to open the Forms design environment. On the **Tools** menu, click **Options**. Click the **Mail Format** tab, and clear the **Use Microsoft Word to edit e-mail messages** check box. Click **OK** to save the change.

In this exercise, you will design a new form for submitting a timesheet to the payroll department, and then you will open and use that form. You don't need any practice files for this exercise.

Inbox

1 On the **Outlook Bar**, click the **Inbox** icon.

The contents of the Inbox are displayed.

2 On the **Tools** menu, point to **Forms**, and click **Design a Form**.

The **Design Form** dialog box appears.

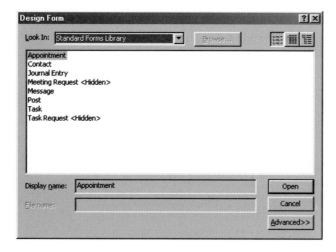

3 In the list of forms, click **Message**, and then click the **Open** button.

The Forms design environment opens, displaying the standard Message form and the **Field Chooser** dialog box. Note that the Message form is displayed as editable, meaning that you can change the elements of the form itself. For example, you can add elements to the form, resize the **To** box, or delete the **Subject** box.

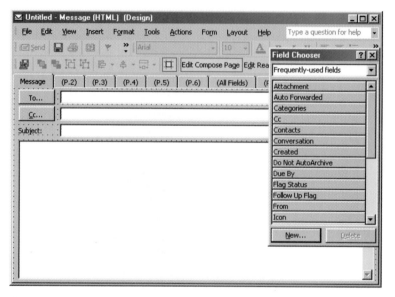

4 Click the **To** box once to select it, and click it again to place the insertion point there.

Be sure not to click too quickly in succession. It might take a moment for the insertion point to appear in the box.

5 In the **To** box, type **payroll@gardenco.msn.com**.

6 Click the **Cc** box once to select it, and click it again to place the insertion point there.

7 In the **Cc** box, type **<<Type your manager's name here>>**.

8 Click the **Subject** box once to select it, and click it again to place the insertion point there.

9 In the **Subject** box, type Timesheet for Period ending **<<Type date here>>**.

10 Now, you'll create a new field for entering the number of hours worked. In the **Field Chooser** dialog box, click the **New** button.

The **New Field** dialog box appears.

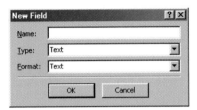

11 In the **Name** box, type Hours, click the down arrow to the right of the **Type** box, and then click **Number** in the drop-down list.

The **Hours** field will accept numbers only.

12 Click the down arrow to the right of the **Format** box, click **2 Decimal** in the drop-down list, and then click **OK**.

The number will be formatted with two decimal places. The **New Field** dialog box closes. The **Field Chooser** now shows the **Hours** field in the **User-defined fields in Inbox** list.

13 In the **Field Chooser** dialog box, drag the **Hours** field into the Message form's header to the right of the **Subject** box.

The **Hours** field is placed in the Message form, like this:

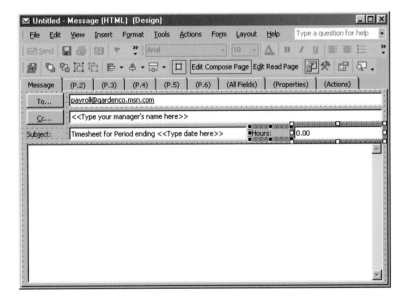

14 On the Formatting toolbar, click the **Edit Read Page** button. (If this button is not visible on the toolbar, click the **Toolbar Options** button, and then click the **Edit Read Page** button in the button palette that appears.)

The form's layout appears as it will when the form is completed and sent to a recipient. The fields in the header of the message appear as read-only.

15 In the **Field Chooser** dialog box, drag the **Hours** field into the Message form's header to the right of the **Subject** box.

The **Hours** field is placed in the Read Page of the Message form.

16 Right-click the **Hours** box, and then click **Properties** in the shortcut menu.

The **Properties** dialog box appears.

17 In the **Settings** area, select the **Read only** check box, clear the **Sunken** check box, and then click **OK**.

The **Hours** box will now appear without 3-D formatting, and users will not be able to modify it. Your screen now looks like this:

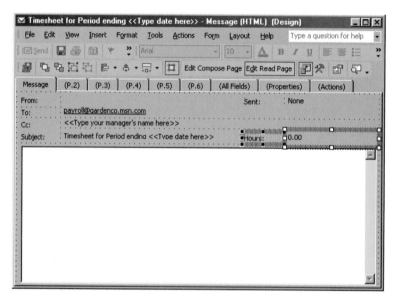

18 On the **Tools** menu, point to **Forms**, and then click **Publish Form**.

The **Publish Form As** dialog box appears.

19 Click the down arrow to the right of the **Look In** box, click **Inbox**, click in the **Display name** box, and type **Timesheet**.

The contents of the **Display name** box are copied to the **Form name** box.

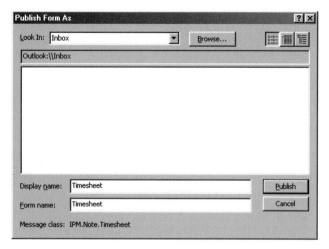

20 Click the **Publish** button, and when prompted to select the **Save Form Definition with Item** check box, click **Yes**.

The Timesheet form is published so that you will be able to use it to create a new item when viewing the Inbox.

Close

21 Click the **Close** button, and when prompted to save your changes, click **No**.

The Forms design environment closes.

22 Now you'll use the form that you just created. On the Outlook Bar, click the **Inbox** icon.

The contents of the Inbox are displayed.

23 On the **Actions** menu, click **New Timesheet**.

Outlook opens your Timesheet form.

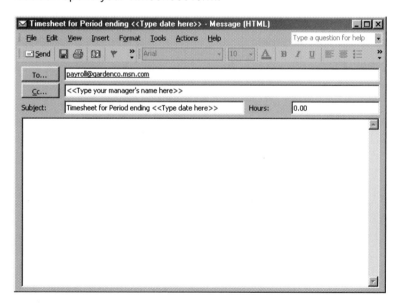

24 Click in the **Cc** box, delete the existing text, and type your own e-mail address.

25 Click in the **Subject** box, delete **<<Type date here>>**, and type **6/21/02**.

26 Click in the **Hours** box, delete the existing text, type **40**, and on the toolbar, click the **Send** button.

The Timesheet form closes, and the message is sent.

27 On the toolbar, click the **Send/Receive** button.

Outlook checks for new messages.

28 Double-click the new message with the subject beginning with **Timesheet**.

The message opens in its own window.

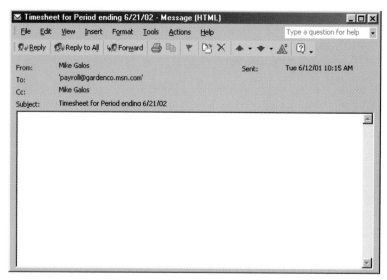

29 Close the Message window by clicking its **Close** button.

Distributing Forms for Others to Use

To share a form with others, you can save it as a file and send it to others via e-mail or save it in a **public folder**, **Organizational Forms Library**, or **Personal Forms Library**. To use a public folder or Organizational Forms Library, you need to be working on a network that uses Microsoft Exchange Server.

Public folders are a separate location outside of your own mailbox where you can create and view Outlook items. Typically, public folders are used by project teams or user groups to share information on a common area of interest. If your administrator enables public folders, you'll see folders labeled *Public Folders* in the **Folder List**. If you have permission, you can open individual public folders to view and add content, and you can set up your own public folders and give other people permission to use them. Items that you open in a public folder look like the items in your own mailbox.

The Organizational Forms Library is a feature of Microsoft Exchange Server. If your administrator has granted you access, you can publish forms to this library to make them available to everyone in your organization. When you publish a form to this library, you can access it by clicking **Choose a Form** on the **Tools** menu.

Forms stored in the Personal Forms Library are stored as hidden items in your mailbox or Personal Folders. You would typically save a form to this library when you create a form for your own personal use, but you want to make it available from all folders. You use forms in this library by clicking **Choose a Form** on the **Tools** menu.

In this exercise, you will save a form as a file and send it via e-mail, open a form that someone has sent to you, save the form in a forms library, delete a form saved in an Outlook folder, and delete a form saved in your Personal Forms Library. You don't need any practice files for this exercise.

1   If the Timesheet form is not already open, open it by clicking **New Timesheet** on the **Actions** menu.

2   On the **File** menu, click **Save As**.

The **Save As** dialog box appears.

3   Click the **My Documents** icon on the left side of the dialog box to specify the My Documents folder as the location in which you want to save the form.

4   In the **File name** box, type Timesheet Copy.

5   Click the down arrow to the right of the **Save as type** box, click **Outlook Template**, and then click the **Save** button.

The Timesheet form is saved in the My Documents folder.

Close

6   Close the Timesheet form by clicking its **Close** button. If prompted to save your changes, click **No**.

New Mail Message

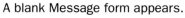

7   On the toolbar, click the **New Mail Message** button.

A blank Message form appears.

8   In the **To** box, type your own e-mail address. Press the Tab key twice, and type Timesheet Copy in the **Subject** box.

Insert File

9   On the toolbar, click the **Insert File** button.

10   On the left side of the **Insert File** dialog box, click the **My Documents** icon, click the **Timesheet Copy** file, and then click the **Insert** button.

The Timesheet Copy file name appears in the **Attach** box in the message header.

11 Click the **Send** button.

The message and attachment are sent.

12 Now you'll open a form that someone else has sent to you. Double-click the **Timesheet Copy** e-mail message.

The Timesheet Copy message opens.

13 In the **Attachments** line, double-click **Timesheet Copy**. When the **Opening Mail Attachment** dialog box appears, click the **Open it** option, and then click **OK**.

The Timesheet form opens.

14 Close the Timesheet Copy, and the message.

15 Now you'll save a form in the forms library, Click **New Timesheet** on the **Actions** menu.

16 On the **Tools** menu, point to **Forms**, and then click **Publish Form As**.

17 Click the down arrow to the right of the **Look In** box, and then click **Personal Forms Library**.

18 Click in the **Display name** box, delete any existing text, and type My Timesheet.

19 Click the **Publish** button.

20 Close the Message form by clicking its **Close** button. If prompted to save your changes, click **No**.

21 If the **Folder List** is not visible, on the **View** menu, click **Folder List**.

22 In the **Folder List**, right-click **Inbox**, and then click **Properties** on the shortcut menu.

23 In the **Inbox Properties** dialog box, click the **Forms** tab.

24 On the **Forms** tab, click the **Manage** button.

25 In the list of forms for the Inbox, click **Timesheet**, click the **Delete** button, and then click **Yes** when asked to confirm the deletion.

26 In the **Forms Manager** dialog box, click the **Close** button, and in the **Inbox Properties** dialog box, click **OK**.

27 Close the **Folder List** by clicking its **Close** button.

28 On the **Tools** menu, click **Options**.

29 Click the **Other** tab, and in the **General** area, click the **Advanced Options** button.

30 In the **Advanced Options** dialog box, click the **Custom Forms** button, and then click the **Manage Forms** button.

31 In the **Personal Forms** list, click **My Timesheet**, click the **Delete** button, and then click **Yes** when asked to confirm the deletion.

32 Click the **Close** button, and then click **OK** to close each of the three open dialog boxes.

Sending Form Letters to Contacts

With the Outlook Contacts folder and Word's Mail Merge feature, you can create and address form letters quickly and easily. Perhaps your company is offering a new product or service and you want to send a letter about it to all existing customers. With Mail Merge, you can create as many letters as you need and address them automatically using the entries in your Contacts folder. You can send a form letter to some or all of your contacts, and you can create a letter based on an existing document or a new one.

Tip

To complete this exercise, you will need Microsoft Word.

In this exercise, you will create a form letter using your Outlook contact entries.

Important

CatherineT
KimY
ProfLetter

For this exercise, you will need contact information for Catherine Turner and Kim Yoshida in your **Contacts** list. If you didn't add this information to your **Contacts** list in an earlier chapter, follow the instructions in "Using the Book's CD-ROM" at the beginning of the book to copy the CatherineT and KimY files from the SBS\Outlook \FormLetter folder to the **Contacts** icon on the **Outlook Bar**. You will also use the ProfLetter document located in the same folder.

Contacts

1   On the **Outlook Bar**, click the **Contacts** icon.

The contents of the Contacts folder are displayed.

2   On the **Tools** menu, click **Mail Merge**.

The **Mail Merge Contacts** dialog box appears.

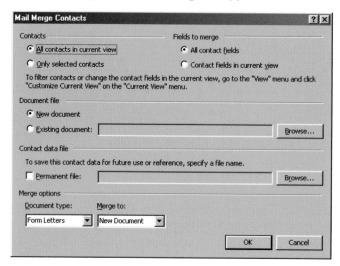

3   In the **Document file** area, click the **Existing document** option, and then click the **Browse** button.

The **Open** dialog box appears.

4   Browse to the SBS\Outlook\FormLetter folder, click **ProfLetter**, and then click **OK**.

The **Open** dialog box closes, and the path to and name of the file appear in the **Existing document** box in the **Mail Merge Contacts** dialog box.

5   Click **OK**. If a message appears, warning you that distribution lists will not be merged, click **OK**.

The Professional Letter document opens in Word.

6   Maximize Word's window, and then on the **Tools** menu, point to **Letters and Mailings**, and click **Mail Merge Wizard**.

The **Mail Merge Wizard** appears on the right side of the Word window.

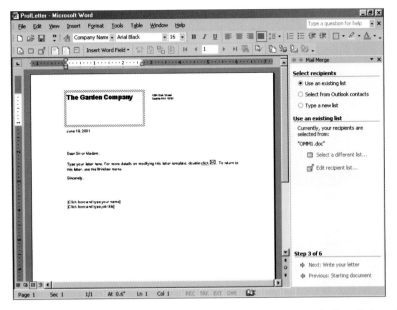

7   In the **Select recipients** list, make sure the **Use an existing list** option is selected, and then click **Next: Write your letter**.

8   In the letter, click the line after the date to place the insertion point there, and in the **Mail Merge Wizard**, click **Address block**.

The **Insert Address Block** dialog box appears.

9   Review the options for the address block, and click **OK**.

A placeholder for the address is inserted into the document.

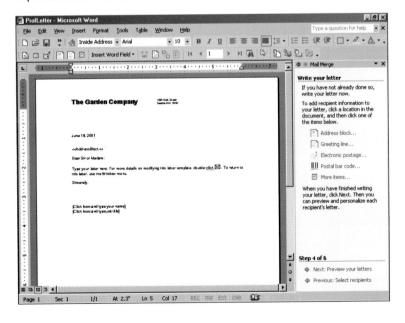

10 In the **Mail Merge Wizard**, click **Next: Preview your letters**.

The letter now includes the contact information for your first contact.

11 Click the **Next Recipient** button

The letter now includes the contact information for your second contact. Note that you may see other recipients if you have entries in your Contacts folder in addition to the practice contacts provided.

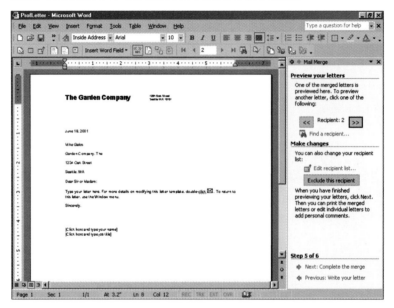

12 In the **Mail Merge Wizard**, click **Next: Complete the merge**.

The next page of the wizard appears.

13 Click **Edit individual letters**. Then in the **Merge to New Document** dialog box, make sure the **All** option is selected, and click **OK**.

Word completes the mail merge process and presents the letters in a new document.

Note that this process may take a few minutes to complete, and might result in a large document if you have many entries in your Contacts folder in addition to the practice contacts provided.

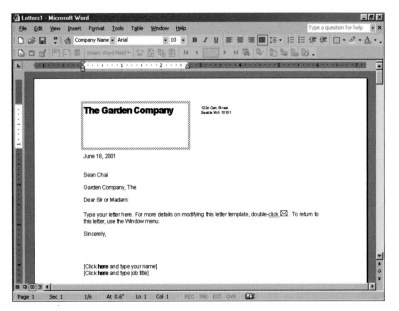

14 Scroll through the document to review the letters.

The document contains a letter for each contact, separated by page breaks and ready to be printed.

Close

15 Click the **Close** button in the top right corner of the merged document, and when prompted to save the document, click **No**.

The merged document closes.

16 In the ProfLetter window, click the **Close** button, and when prompted to save the document, click **No**.

Word closes.

17 Close any contacts, documents, or other files. Then on the **Outlook Bar**, click the **Inbox** icon, and on the **File** menu, click **Exit** to quit Outlook.

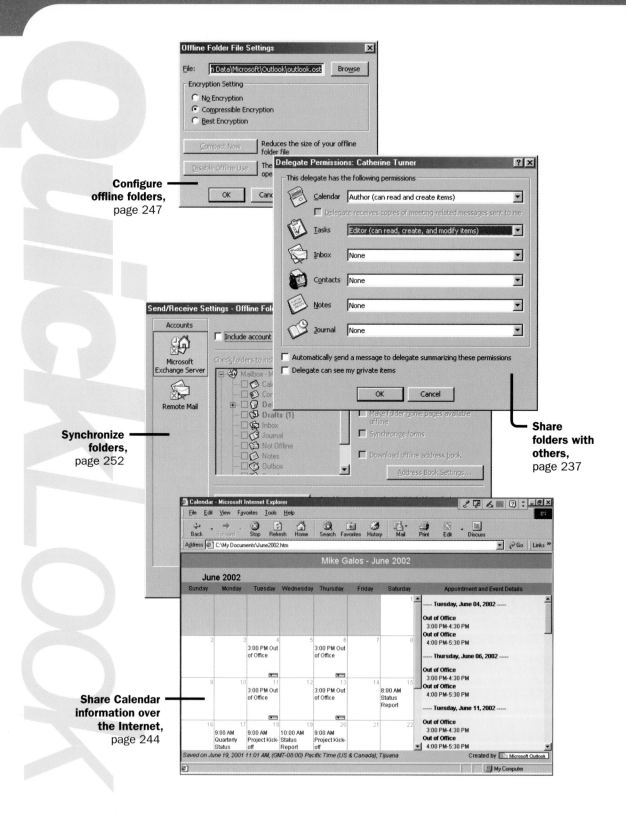

Configure offline folders, page 247

Synchronize folders, page 252

Share folders with others, page 237

Share Calendar information over the Internet, page 244

Chapter 11
Sharing Information and Working Offline

After completing this chapter, you will be able to:

✔ **Share folders with others**

✔ **Share Calendar information over the Internet**

✔ **Configure offline folders**

✔ **Synchronize folders**

In today's workplace, communication, collaboration, and flexibility are crucial. Microsoft Outlook can help you with each of these. You can share Outlook folders to facilitate better communication and collaboration with your co-workers. To the same end, you can share your calendar information with your co-workers and others over the Internet. Offline folders allow you to access your e-mail and other Outlook information even when you're not connected to your e-mail server.

This chapter uses the practice files that you installed from this book's CD-ROM and copied into Outlook. For details about installing the practice files, see "Using the Book's CD-ROM" at the beginning of this book.

Sharing Folders with Others

OL2002e-4-5

When you use Microsoft Outlook 2002, your messages, contacts, appointments, and other items are stored in folders. By default, the standard Outlook folders (Inbox, Calendar, Contacts, Tasks, Notes, Journal, Drafts, Sent Items, Deleted Items, and Outbox) and the folders you create are private, meaning that only you can access them. However, if you are working on a network that uses Microsoft Exchange Server, you can choose to share private folders, allowing others to access them.

You can share folders with others in two ways. First, you can give someone permission to access a folder. For example, you might have a collection of messages you want to share with a partner on a project. You can store those messages in a folder and give your partner access to that folder. You can select from a number of permission levels ranging from Owner (full access) to Reviewer (read-only access). When you select a permission level, Outlook indicates which actions will be allowed. For example, you might grant Author access to your assistant who will help you manage incoming e-mail. As an author, your assistant can read items, create items, and edit and delete items that he or she creates, but those with Author permission level cannot create subfolders. Because permissions are defined as properties of an individual folder, you can grant someone Owner access to one folder and Reviewer access to another. You can also give more than one person permission to access a folder and select a different permission level for each person.

The second option for sharing folders is granting Delegate access. When you define someone as a **delegate**, you specify his or her access level to the Calendar, Tasks, Inbox, Contacts, Notes, or Journal as that of Editor, Author, or Reviewer. An editor can read, create, and modify items in the folder. An author can read and create items in the folder. A reviewer can read items in the folder. A delegate can be an editor in one folder and a reviewer in another. As an author or editor, a delegate can also send messages on your behalf. Recipients of messages sent by a delegate see both the manager's and the delegate's names on the message. Regardless of access level, a delegate cannot create subfolders. To allow someone to create subfolders, you must share the folder using permissions.

Important

This exercise requires that you be connected to a network that includes a Microsoft Exchange Server.

In this exercise, you will create a folder, share the folder by setting permissions, and then share a folder by granting delegate access to it.

Important

If you haven't installed and copied the practice files for this book, please do so now. For details about installing and copying the practice files, see "Using the Book's CD-ROM" at the beginning of this book.

Inbox

1 On the **Outlook Bar**, click the **Inbox** icon.

The contents of the Inbox are displayed.

2 If the **Folder List** is not already open, on the **View** menu, click **Folder List**.

The **Folder List** appears.

3 On the **File** menu, point to **Folder**, and then click **New Folder**.

The **Create New Folder** dialog box appears.

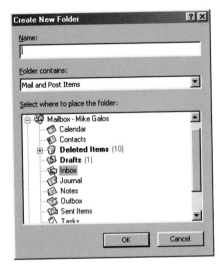

4   In the **Name** box, type **To Do**, and in the **Select where to place the folder** box, click your mailbox, and then click **OK**. If a message appears asking you to add a shortcut to the **Outlook Bar**, click **No**.

The To Do folder is added to the **Folder List**.

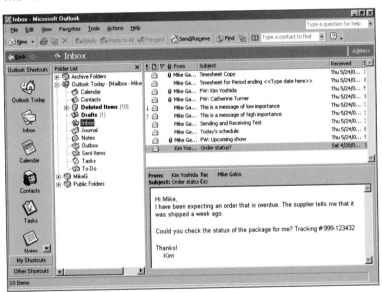

5   On the **Start** menu, point to **Programs** and then click **Windows Explorer**. If necessary, drag the Windows Explorer window to the side so that the To Do folder in the **Folder List** is visible.

6   In the left Windows Explorer pane, browse to the SBS\Outlook\Sharing folder, which contains the practice files for this exercise, and double-click the folder to display its contents in the right pane.

7   Drag the practice files NewSupplier, OrderStatus, Schedule, and NextShow to the To Do folder in the **Folder List**.

The messages are added to the To Do folder.

Close

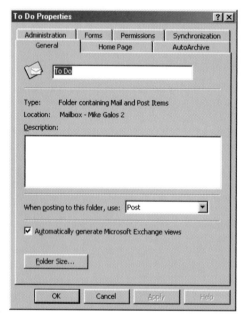

8   Close the Windows Explorer window by clicking its **Close** button.

9   In the **Folder List**, click the **To Do** folder.

The contents of the To Do folder are displayed.

10 On the **File** menu, point to **Folder**, and click **Properties for "To Do"**.

The **To Do Properties** dialog box appears.

11 Click the **Permissions** tab, and click the **Add** button.

The **Add Users** dialog box is displayed.

12 In the **Type Name or Select from List** box, type the name of a co-worker (or another person whose name appears in the **Name** list).

The **Name** list jumps to the entry for the person whose name you typed. The name is selected.

13 Click the **Add** button.

Your co-worker's name appears in the **Add Users** list.

14 Click **OK**.

The **Add Users** dialog box closes, revealing the **To Do Properties** dialog box. Your co-worker's name appears in the list.

15 In the **Name** box, click the name of your co-worker.

16 In the **Permissions** area, click the down arrow to the right of the **Permission Level** box, and then click **Editor**.

The **Create items**, **Read items**, and **Folder visible** check boxes are selected, and the **All** option is selected in both the **Edit items** and **Delete items** areas.

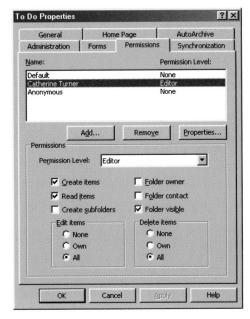

Your co-worker can now view your To Do folder by opening your folder from within Outlook on his or her computer and can create, edit, and delete items within it.

Tip

To open another person's folder, point to **Open** in the **File** menu, and then click **Other User's Folder**. In the **Name** box, type the name of the person sharing the folder with you, and in the **Folder List**, click the folder you want to open.

17 Click **OK**.

The new permission settings are applied to the To Do folder. If your co-worker is available, ask him or her to open your To Do folder to verify that the folder is shared as expected.

18 On the **Tools** menu, click **Options**.

The **Options** dialog box appears.

19 Click the **Delegates** tab, and click the **Add** button.

The **Add Users** dialog box is displayed.

20 In the **Type Name or Select from List** box, type the name of a co-worker (or another person whose name appears in the **Name** list).

The **Name** list jumps to the entry for the person whose name you typed. The name is selected.

21 Click the **Add** button.

Your co-worker's name appears in the **Add Users** list.

22 Click **OK**.

The **Add Users** dialog box closes, and the **Delegate Permissions: Catherine Turner** dialog box appears.

23 In the **Calendar** list, click **Author**, and in the **Tasks** list, click **Editor**. Be sure that **None** is selected in the remaining lists.

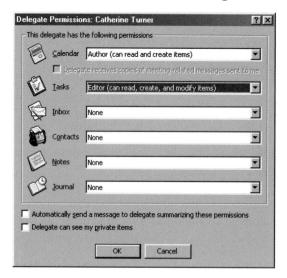

Your co-worker will be allowed to read and create items on your Calendar and to read, create, and modify in your **Tasks** list.

Tip

By default, delegates cannot see private items. To change this, select the **Delegate can see my private items** check box in the **Delegate Permissions** dialog box.

24 Click **OK**.

The **Delegate Permissions** dialog box closes, revealing the **Delegates** tab of the **Options** dialog box. Your co-worker's name appears in the list of delegates.

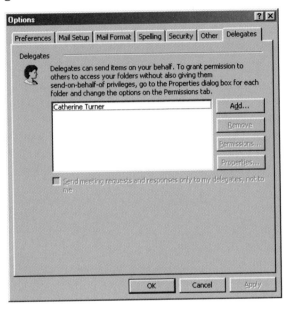

25 Click **OK**.

The delegate settings are saved. If your co-worker is available, ask him or her to open your Calendar or **Tasks** list to verify that the folders are shared as expected. You open another person's Calendar or **Tasks** list just as you would any other folder.

26 When you are finished, on the **Outlook Bar**, click the **Inbox** icon.

The contents of the Inbox are displayed.

Delete

27 In the **Folder List**, click the **To Do** folder, and on the toolbar, click the **Delete** button.

The To Do folder is deleted from your **Folder List**.

28 On the **View** menu, click **Folder List**.

The **Folder List** closes.

Sharing Calendar Information over the Internet

OL2002e-1-2

Outlook
free/busy
sharing
new for
OfficeXP

To help you coordinate your plans with others, you can share your schedule over an intranet or the Internet. Your co-workers and clients can view your schedule even if they aren't using Microsoft Outlook. You can also share your schedule by saving your Calendar as a Web page or by publishing your free and busy times for others to see.

For example, you might post a calendar with important project dates on your company intranet, or you might publish to an Internet location, for your clients to view, the times that you are busy and the times when you are available.

Tip

When you save your Calendar as a Web page, you can save it to your local computer or a network location. You might have to take additional steps to make that Web page available to others. Your administrator can provide the information you need.

Important

To complete this exercise, you will need a server location where you can post a Web page. Your administrator can provide the information you need.

In this exercise, you will save your Calendar as a Web page and publish your free and busy times.

Important

If you haven't installed and copied the practice files for this book, please do so now. For details about installing and copying the practice files, see "Using the Book's CD-ROM" at the beginning of this book.

Calendar

1   On the **Outlook Bar**, click the **Calendar** icon.

     The Calendar is displayed.

2   On the **File** menu, click **Save as Web Page**.

     The **Save as Web Page** dialog box appears.

3   In the **Start date** box, type **6/1/02**, press the ⟨Tab⟩ key, and in the **End date** box, type **6/30/02**.

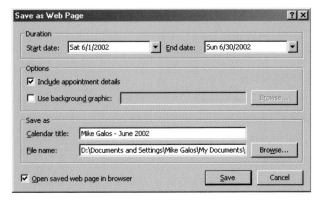

4 Click in the **Calendar title** box, delete any existing text, type your name followed by June 2002, and click the **Browse** button.

The **Calendar File Name** dialog box appears.

5 In the **File name** box, type June2002, and click the **Select** button.

The **Calendar File Name** dialog box closes, and the name of the file (June2002.htm) and the path to it are inserted into the **File name** box in the **Save as Web Page** dialog box. (By default, Outlook saves files in your My Documents folder.)

6 Be sure the **Open saved web page in browser** check box is selected, and click the **Save** button.

The **Save as Web Page** dialog box closes, and the schedule is displayed in your Web browser. (The browser is loading the file from your computer, not the Internet—you haven't published the schedule to the Internet yet.)

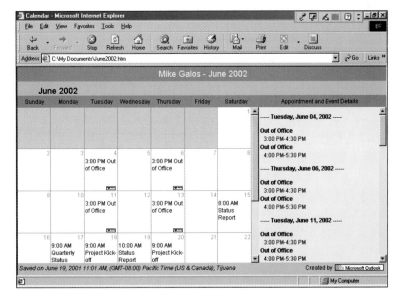

Close

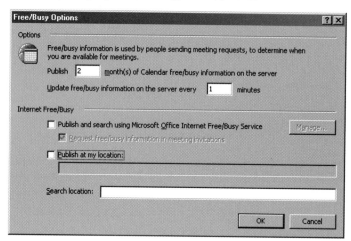

7 Review the Calendar, and click the browser's **Close** button.

The Web browser window closes.

8 In Outlook, on the **Tools** menu, click **Options**.

The **Options** dialog box appears.

9 In the **Calendar** area, click the **Calendar Options** button.

The **Calendar Options** dialog box appears.

10 In the **Advanced options** area, click the **Free/Busy Options** button.

The **Free/Busy Options** dialog box appears.

11 In the **Internet Free/Busy** area, select the **Publish at my location** check box, click in the **Publish at my location** box, and type the server location provided by your administrator, followed by the file name you want.

Tip

The contents of the **Publish at my location** box will typically be something like this: \\server\share\username\June2002.vfb. Be sure to include the full path and file name.

12 In the **Free/Busy Options** dialog box, click **OK**, and then click **OK** in the **Calendar Options** and the **Options** dialog boxes.

Your free/busy information will be published to the location you provided.

13 On the **Tools** menu, point to **Send/Receive**, and click **Free/Busy Information** to publish your free/busy information to your server.

14 To view your free/busy information as it is published, open your Web browser, and in the **Address** box, type the URL of the file on the server.

Your free/busy information appears in your browser window.

The URL might not be the same as the path you entered in the **Publish at my location** box. Your administrator can provide you with the URL.

15 Review the information, and click the browser's **Close** button.

The Web browser window closes.

Configuring Offline Folders

OL2002e-1-1
OL2002e-1-2
OL2002e-1-4

Synchronization improvements
new for
OfficeXP

With **offline folders**, you can access your Outlook information even when you are not connected to your e-mail server. For example, if you are going out of town and want to be able to catch up on messages related to an important project during a cross-country plane trip, you might configure a folder containing the relevant messages so that they are available offline on your laptop. Note that offline folders contain only messages that you received before you started working offline.

If you created any items, deleted any messages, or made any other changes to the contents of an offline folder while you were not connected to your e-mail server, you can connect to your e-mail server and update the corresponding folder on the server to make the contents of the two folders identical. This process is called synchronizing offline folders. Be sure to synchronize your offline folders whenever you make changes to the folder—whether working offline or online. Otherwise, you could be working with obsolete items or missing items that were added while you were offline. Offline folders are stored in the Offline Folder.ost file on your computer's hard disk.

This exercise requires that you be connected to a network that includes a Microsoft Exchange Server.

ToDo

If you haven't installed and copied the practice files for this book, please do so now. For details about installing and copying the practice files, see "Using the Book's CD-ROM" at the beginning of this book. You will also need the ToDo file located in the SBS\Outlook\Offline folder, which is probably on drive C.

In this exercise, you will import some folders to be used offline, create an offline folder file, configure a folder for offline use, and switch between online and offline use.

1 On the **File** menu, click **Import and Export**.

The **Import and Export Wizard** appears.

2 In the **Choose an action to perform** list, click **Import from another program or file**, and click **Next**.

The next page of the **Import and Export Wizard** appears.

3 In the **Select file type to import from** list, click **Personal Folder File (.pst)**, and click **Next**.

The next page of the **Import and Export Wizard** appears.

4 Click the **Browse** button.

The **Open Personal Folders** dialog box appears.

5 Click the down arrow to the right of the **Look in** box, browse to the SBS \Outlook\Offline folder, click **ToDo**, and click the **Open** button.

The **Open Personal Folders** dialog box closes, and the path to the folder you selected appears in the **File to import** box.

6 In the **Import and Export Wizard**, make sure the **Replace duplicates with items imported** option is selected, and click **Next**.

The next page of the **Import and Export Wizard** appears.

7 In the **Select the folder to import from** list, click the **To Do** folder, and click **Finish**.

The To Do and the Not Offline folders are added to your **Folder List**. If the **Folder List** is not visible, display it by clicking **Folder List** on the **View** menu.

8 On the **Tools** menu, click **E-mail Accounts**.

The first page of the **E-mail Accounts Wizard** appears.

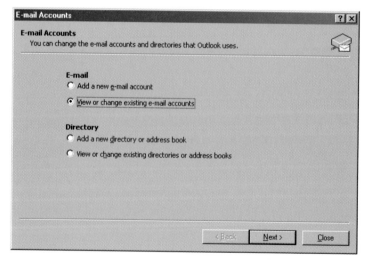

9 Select the **View or change existing e-mail accounts** option, and then click **Next**.

The second page of the **E-mail Accounts Wizard** appears.

10 In the **Outlook processes e-mail for these accounts in the following order** list, click **Microsoft Exchange Server**, and then click the **Change** button.

The next page of the **E-mail Accounts Wizard** appears.

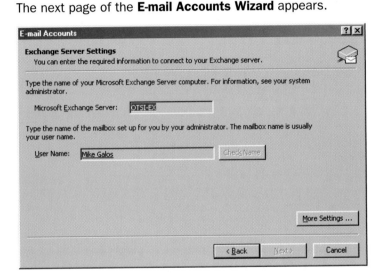

11 Click the **More Settings** button.

The **Microsoft Exchange Server** dialog box appears.

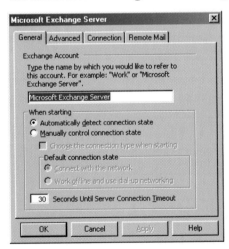

12 Click the **Advanced** tab, and then click the **Offline Folder File Settings** button.

The **Offline Folder File Settings** dialog box appears.

13   Click the **Browse** button.

The **New Offline Folder File** dialog box appears.

14   Click the down arrow to the right of the **Look in** box, and then navigate to the My Documents folder.

15   Make sure **outlook** appears in the **File name** box and **OST Files** appears in the **Files of type** box, and then click the **Open** button.

In the **Offline Folder File Settings** dialog box, the path to the .ost file appears in the **File** box.

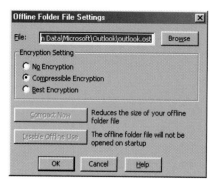

16   Click **OK**. If Outlook asks whether to create the outlook.ost file, click **Yes**.

The **Microsoft Exchange Server** dialog box is displayed.

17   In the **Microsoft Exchange Server** dialog box, click the **General** tab, and in the **When starting** area, select the **Manually control connection state** option. Then select the **Choose the connection type when starting** check box.

18 Click **OK**.

The **Microsoft Exchange Server** dialog box closes.

19 In the **E-mail Accounts Wizard**, click **Next**, and then click the **Finish** button.

The **E-mail Accounts Wizard** closes.

20 On the **Tools** menu, point to **Send/Receive**, and then click **This Folder**.

Outlook synchronizes the To Do folder for offline use.

21 On the **File** menu, click **Exit**.

Outlook closes.

Microsoft
Outlook

22 On your desktop, double-click the **Microsoft Outlook** icon.

Outlook opens, prompting you to choose to connect or work offline.

23 Click the **Work Offline** button.

Outlook opens.

24 In the **Folder List**, click **To Do**.

The contents of the To Do folder are displayed, because the folder is available while you are working offline.

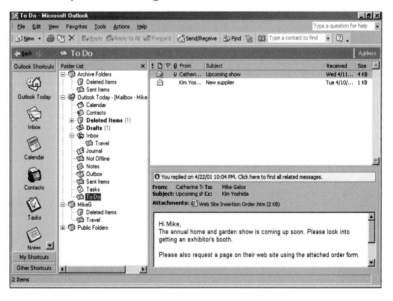

25 In the **Folder List**, click **Not Offline**.

There are no items in this folder because the folder is not available while you are working offline.

26 In the **Folder List**, click **Inbox**, and on the **File** menu, click **Exit**.

Outlook closes.

27 On your desktop, double-click the **Microsoft Outlook** icon.

Outlook opens, prompting you to choose to connect or work offline.

28 Click the **Connect** button, and click **OK**.

Outlook opens, with all folders available.

Synchronizing Folders

After working with an offline folder, you must synchronize it with the corresponding folder on the server to make the contents identical. Be sure to synchronize your offline folders whenever you make changes to the folder—whether working offline or online. Otherwise, you could be working with obsolete items or be missing items that were added while you were offline.

You can synchronize folders manually, or you can synchronize them automatically at a specified time or time interval.

Important

This exercise requires that you be connected to a network that includes a Microsoft Exchange Server. To complete this exercise, you must have completed the preceding topic, "Configuring Offline Folders," which ensures that you will have an .ost file on your computer that is configured for offline use.

In this exercise, you will synchronize an offline folder manually, create a group of folders to be synchronized together, and configure Outlook to synchronize offline folders automatically. You don't need any practice files for this exercise.

Inbox

1 On the **Outlook Bar**, click the **Inbox** icon.

The contents of the Inbox are displayed.

2 If the **Folder List** is not visible, on the **View** menu, click **Folder List**.

3 In the **Folder List**, click **To Do**.

The contents of the To Do folder are displayed. This folder was configured for offline use in the previous exercise.

4 On the **Tools** menu, point to **Send/Receive Settings**, and click **Define Send/Receive Groups** to open the **Send/Receive Groups** dialog box.

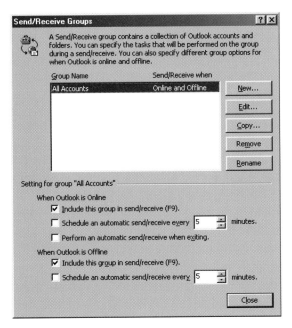

5 Click the **New** button.

The **Send/Receive Group Name** dialog box appears.

6 In the **Send/Receive Group Name** box, type Offline Folders, and click **OK**.

The **Send/Receive Settings – Offline Folders** dialog box appears.

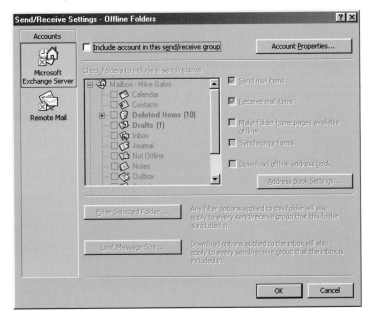

7 Select the **Include account in this send/receive group** check box.

8 In the **Check folders to include in send/receive** list, select the check box next to the To Do folder to select that folder.

9 Make sure the **Send mail items** and **Receive mail items** check boxes are selected, and click **OK**.

The **Send/Receive Settings – Offline Folders** dialog box closes, and the **Send/Receive Groups** dialog box is displayed.

10 In the **Group Name** list, be sure that **Offline Folders** is selected.

11 In the **Setting for group "Offline Folders"** area, under **When Outlook is Online**, clear the **Include this group in send/receive (F9)** check box, and select the **Perform an automatic send/receive when exiting** check box.

12 Under **When Outlook is Offline**, clear the **Include this group in send/receive (F9)** check box, and click the **Close** button.

The **Send/Receive Groups** dialog box closes, and the Offline Folders group is created. Your Offline Folders group will be synchronized automatically when you close Outlook, or when you choose to synchronize manually.

13 On the **Tools** menu, point to **Send/Receive**, and click **Offline Folders**.

Outlook synchronizes the contents of your To Do folder with the corresponding folder on your e-mail server.

14 On the **Tools** menu, point to **Send/Receive Settings**, and click **Define Send/Receive Groups**.

The **Send/Receive Groups** dialog box appears.

15 In the **Group Name** list, click **Offline Folders**.

The Offline Folders group is selected.

16 In the **Settings for group "Offline Folders"** area, under **When Outlook is Online**, select the **Schedule an automatic send/receive every** check box, click in the **minutes** box, delete the existing text, and type **15**.

17 Click the **Close** button.

The **Send/Receive Groups** dialog box closes. When you are working online, your Offline Folders group will be automatically synchronized every 15 minutes.

18 On the **File** menu, click **Exit**.

Outlook closes.

Microsoft
Outlook

19 On your desktop, double-click the **Microsoft Outlook** icon.

Outlook opens, prompting you to choose to connect or work offline.

20 Click the **Work Offline** button.

Outlook opens.

21 In the **Folder List**, click **To Do**.

The contents of the To Do folder are displayed.

Delete

22 Click the **Upcoming show** message, and on the toolbar, click the **Delete** button.

The message is deleted from the To Do folder.

23 On the **File** menu, click **Exit**.

Outlook closes.

24 On your desktop, double-click the **Microsoft Outlook** icon.

Outlook opens, prompting you to choose to connect or work offline.

25 Click the **Connect** button.

Outlook opens.

26 In the **Folder List**, click the **To Do** folder.

The Upcoming show message still appears because the offline folder has not been synchronized with the online folder.

27 On the **Tools** menu, point to **Send/Receive**, and click **Offline Folders**.

Outlook synchronizes your offline folders. The Upcoming show message is deleted from the To Do folder.

28 In the **Folder List**, click the **To Do** folder, and on the toolbar, click the **Delete** button.

29 When asked to confirm that you want to delete the folder and its contents, click **Yes**.

30 In the **Folder List**, click the **Not Offline** folder, and on the toolbar, click the **Delete** button.

31 When asked to confirm that you want to delete the folder and its contents, click **Yes**.

32 In the **Folder List**, click the **Inbox** folder, and on the **View** menu, click **Folder List**.

The contents of the Inbox are displayed, and the **Folder List** closes.

33 If you are not continuing on to the next chapter, close any open messages, and on the **File** menu, click **Exit** to quit Outlook.

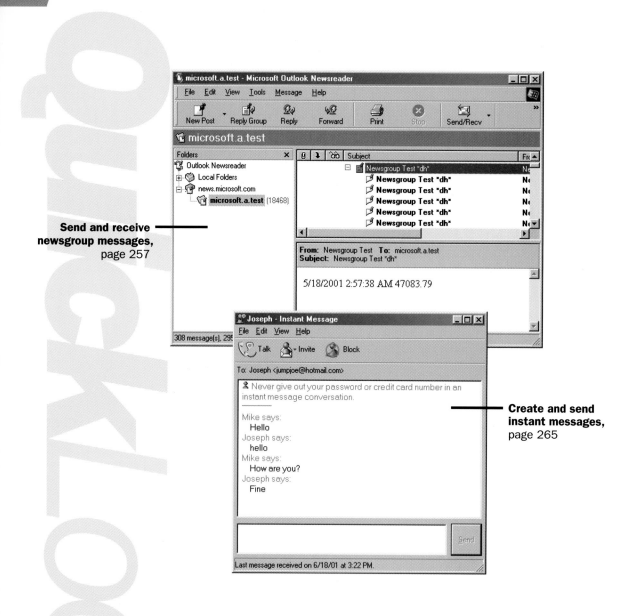

Send and receive newsgroup messages, page 257

Create and send instant messages, page 265

Chapter 12
Sending Newsgroup and Instant Messages

After completing this chapter, you will be able to:

✔ **Send and receive newsgroup messages**
✔ **Create and send instant messages**

Microsoft Outlook offers some alternatives to communicating via e-mail. With instant messages, you can connect with a client who is also using instant messaging to ask a simple question and get the answer immediately. On the other hand, Newsgroups allow you to communicate with a larger audience. When considering the purchase of a new graphics program, for example, you can solicit advice and recommendations by posting a message to a newsgroup for people interested in graphics.

You don't need any practice files to work through the exercises in this chapter.

Sending and Receiving Newsgroup Messages

OL2002e-6-2

A **newsgroup** is a collection of messages related to a particular topic that are posted by individuals to a **news server**. Newsgroups are generally focused on discussion of a particular topic, like a sports team, a hobby, or a type of software. Anyone with access to the group can post to the group and read all posted messages. Some newsgroups have a moderator who monitors their use, but most newsgroups are not overseen in this way. A newsgroup can be private, such as an internal company newsgroup, but there are newsgroups open to the public for practically every topic. You gain access to newsgroups through a news server maintained either on your organization's network or by your Internet service provider (ISP).

You use a **newsreader** program to download, read, and reply to news messages. These programs generally allow you to reply to the person who originally posted a newsgroup message, post your reply to the entire newsgroup, or forward the message to someone else. By default, Microsoft Outlook automatically sets up the Microsoft Outlook Newsreader. Whether you use the Outlook Newsreader or you have a different newsreader already installed, you can start it from within Outlook by pointing to **Go To** on the **View** menu, and then clicking **News**.

After you have started your newsreader, you download a list of the newsgroups available from your news server and **subscribe** to the newsgroups that interest you. After you've subscribed to a newsgroup, you can read and post messages in that group.

Important

This exercise assumes you use the Outlook Newsreader.

In this exercise, you subscribe to a newsgroup, view a newsgroup and its messages, and send newsgroup messages. You don't need any practice files for this exercise.

1 If it is not already open, start Outlook, and then maximize its window.

2 On the **View** menu, point to **Go To**, and click **News**.

Outlook starts the Outlook Newsreader.

3 If you are prompted to make Outlook Express your default mail client, click **No**.

4 If the **Internet Connection Wizard** prompts you to set up Internet mail, click the **Cancel** button, and when asked if you are sure you want to exit the wizard, click **Yes**.

5 If prompted to import your Outlook messages and address book, select the **Do not import at this time** option, click the **Next** button, and then click the **Finish** button.

The Microsoft Outlook Newsreader appears.

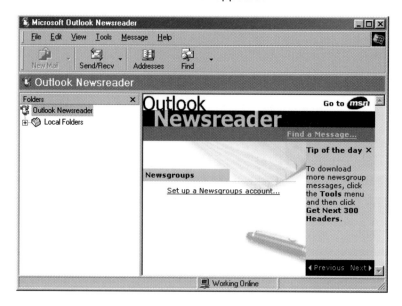

6 On the **Tools** menu, click **Accounts**.

The **Internet Accounts** dialog box appears.

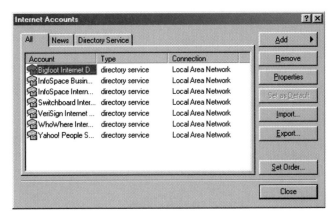

7 Click the **Add** button, and then click **News**.

The **Internet Connection Wizard** starts.

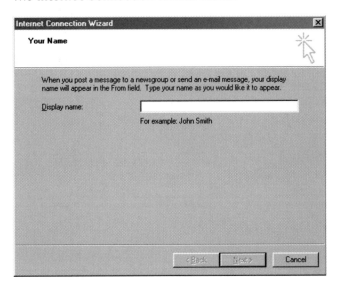

8 In the **Display name** box, type the name you want to appear on your messages (typically your full name), and click the **Next** button.

The next page of the **Internet Connection Wizard** appears.

Tip

When you post messages to a newsgroup, the **From** line on your messages will show the name you entered in the **Display name** box in the **Internet Connection Wizard**.

9 In the **E-mail address** box, type your e-mail address, and click the **Next** button.

The next page of the **Internet Connection Wizard** appears.

10 In the **News (NNTP) server** box, type news.microsoft.com, and click the **Next** button.

The final page of the **Internet Connection Wizard** appears.

Tip

Microsoft maintains this news server (*news.microsoft.com*) to provide access to newsgroups related to Microsoft's products. Your network administrator or ISP can provide you with the names of the news servers that allow access to other public newsgroups.

11 Click the **Finish** button.

The **Internet Connection Wizard** closes. Your news account is saved.

12 In the **Internet Accounts** dialog box, click the **News** tab.

The **News** tab is displayed, listing your news account.

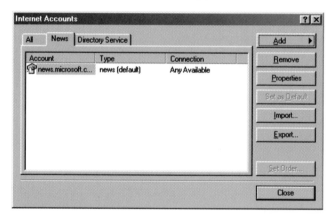

13 Click the **Close** button.

The **Internet Accounts** dialog box closes.

14 When prompted to download newsgroups, click **Yes**.

Downloading the newsgroups might take a few minutes. When the process is complete, the **Newsgroup Subscriptions** dialog box appears.

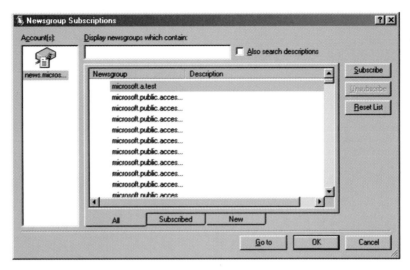

15 In the **Newsgroup** list, click **microsoft.a.test**, and then click the **Subscribe** button.

You have now subscribed to the test newsgroup. After you have subscribed, the newsgroup will appear in your **Folders** list for easy access. The **Folders** list appears on the left side of the Outlook Newsreader window.

16 Click the **Subscribed** tab.

The microsoft.a.test newsgroup appears in the **Newsgroup** list.

17 Click **OK**.

The news account and newsgroup are added to the **Folders** list in the Outlook Newsreader.

18 In the **Folders** list, click **microsoft.a.test**.

The contents of the microsoft.a.test newsgroup are displayed.

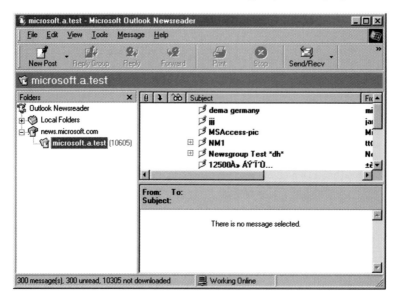

Tip

Because new messages are constantly posted to the newsgroup, you will see a different set of messages than those shown here. Odd characters in the **Subject** or **From** columns indicate that the message was posted in a language that uses an alphabet that is different from English.

19 Double-click the first message.

The message opens. Note the subject of the message so that you can find it later.

Reply Group   **20** Click the **Reply Group** button.

The reply is addressed to the newsgroup, microsoft.a.test.

21   In the message body, type **This is a test message.**

Close

22   If you were going to send the message, you would click the **Send** button. Instead, click the **Close** button to close the message without sending it. If asked to save your changes, click **No**.

Tip

Many senders of junk e-mail use computer programs to collect e-mail addresses from newsgroup posts. If you do not want to receive junk e-mail, it is a good idea to slightly alter your return address so that it is invalid. For example, Catherine Turner might alter her e-mail address, *catherinet@gardenco.msn.com*, to something like *catherinet@nojunk.gardenco.msn.com*. E-mail sent to that address will bounce back to the sender as undeliverable. You can include information at the bottom of your newsgroup posts instructing those who want to e-mail you to take the extra word out of your e-mail address. That way, people who genuinely want to send you valid e-mail can do so, whereas junk e-mailers who use computer programs to collect addresses cannot.

23   Double-click the next message.

The message opens.

24 Click the **Reply** button.

The reply is addressed to the person who posted the message to the newsgroup.

25 If a message appears warning you that a program is attempting to access your Outlook address book, click **No** to prevent it from doing so.

This is one of Outlook's security functions, designed to prevent malicious viruses from sending copies of themselves to the contacts in your address book. When you click **No** in this message, you will prevent Outlook from automatically addressing the reply, so you will have to type in the person's e-mail address yourself. You can typically find the address in the body of the message, following the person's name.

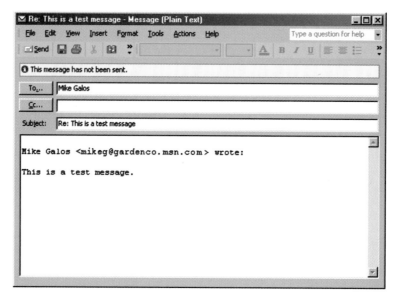

26 Click the **Close** button, and if prompted to save the changes, click **No**.

The reply is discarded.

27 Close the open message window by clicking its **Close** button.

The message closes.

28 On the **Tools** menu, click **Synchronize Newsgroup**.

The **Synchronize Newsgroup** dialog box appears.

29 Select the **Get the following items** check box, make sure the **New messages only** option is selected, and then click **OK**.

Any new messages are downloaded.

30 Find a message with a plus (+) sign to the left of it, and click the plus sign.

The replies to the original message appear associated with the original message.

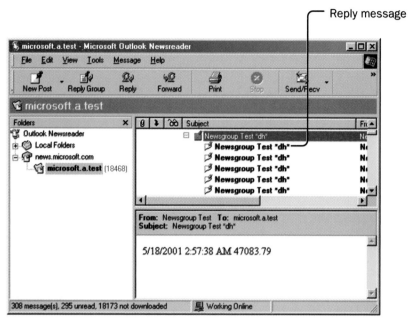

Reply message

31 On the **File** menu, click **Exit**.

The Outlook Newsreader closes.

Creating and Sending Instant Messages

OL2002e-6-3

You can communicate with your contacts in real time with **instant messages**. Instant messaging is a private online chat. After you establish a connection with another person who is online and using instant messaging, messages you send to that person appear on his or her screen instantly. Likewise, you see responses from that person instantly on your screen. Instant messaging is especially useful for brief exchanges and can be much more immediate than e-mail. By default, Outlook supports instant messaging using Microsoft MSN Messenger Service or Microsoft Exchange Instant Messaging Service. When Outlook starts, you are automatically logged on to the service you installed.

Tip

If you want to use MSN Messenger, you can download it by clicking **Options** on the **Tools** menu, clicking the **Other** tab, and in the **Instant Messenging** area, clicking the **Options** button. This will take you to the download Web page for MSN Messenger.

Before you can use instant messaging, you must obtain the instant messaging addresses of the people you want to communicate with in this way and add those addresses to the Outlook Contact forms of those people. Then they have to tell their instant messaging programs to accept messages from your address.

MSN messenger integration new for **Office**XP

Once this setup work is done, when you log on to your instant messaging service, you can see whether a contact is online. A contact's online status is displayed in the InfoBar on the Contact form and on any e-mail address associated with the contact. You can choose how your status appears to others. For example, if you need to step away from your desk, you can set your status to *Be Right Back* so that any contacts who are online can see that you are temporarily unavailable.

Important

For this exercise, you will need the assistance of a co-worker or friend who is using MSN Messenger or Exchange Instant Messaging Service. You must have already added that person to your MSN Messenger contacts, and that person must have accepted your request to add him or her. For help with any of these tasks, refer to the MSN Messenger online Help.

In this exercise, you create and send instant messages. You don't need any practice files for this exercise.

Contacts

1 On the **Outlook Bar**, click the **Contacts** icon.

The contents of the Contacts folder are displayed.

New Contact

New

2 If you already have a contact entry for the person who is assisting you with this exercise, double-click that entry. If you do not have a contact entry for that person, click the **New Contact** button.

The Contact form opens.

3   If you are creating a new contact, in the **Full Name** box, type the person's name.

4   Click in the **IM address** box, and type the e-mail address the person uses for instant messaging.

Note that this address might not be the same address used for e-mail correspondence. You'll need to get this information from the person you want to contact using instant messaging.

Instant messaging address ─┐

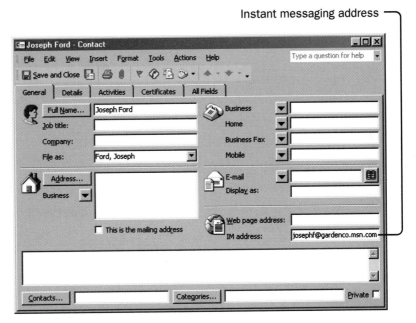

5   Click the **Save and Close** button.

The contact information is saved.

6   Double-click the contact.

The Contact form opens. If your contact is online, the InfoBar displays his or her status, as shown on the next page.

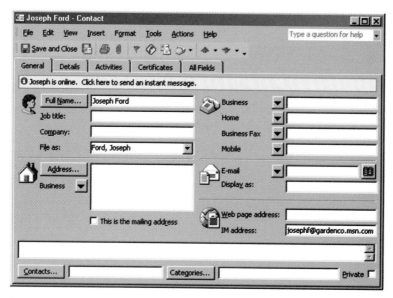

7 Click the InfoBar.

The Instant Message window appears.

8 In the message box, type Hello, and click the **Send** button.

The message is sent. It appears in an Instant Message window on your contact's screen. The status bar indicates when your contact is typing a message. Wait for a reply, and when you receive it, try sending a few more messages.

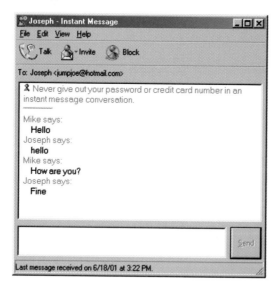

Close

9 When finished, click the **Close** button.

10 If you are not continuing on to the next chapter, on the **File** menu, click **Exit** to quit Outlook.

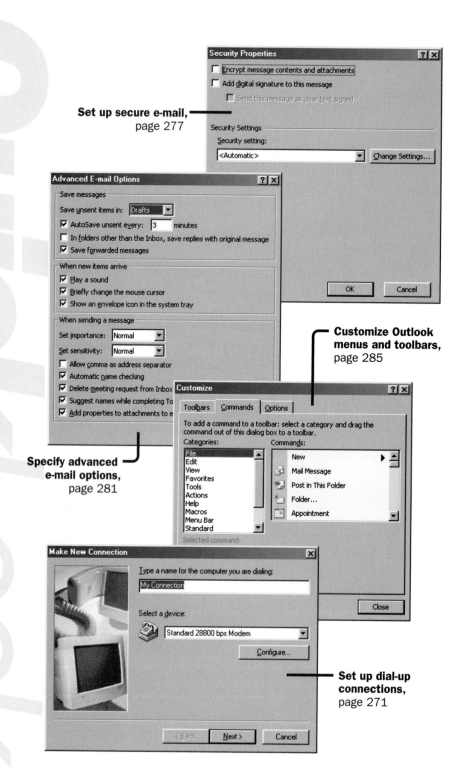

Set up secure e-mail, page 277

Specify advanced e-mail options, page 281

Customize Outlook menus and toolbars, page 285

Set up dial-up connections, page 271

Chapter 13
Configuring and Customizing Outlook

After completing this chapter, you will be able to:

✔ **Set up a dial-up connection**

✔ **Specify advanced e-mail options**

✔ **Set up secure e-mail**

✔ **Customize Outlook**

✔ **Customize menus and toolbars**

A host of configuration and customization options help you make the most of Microsoft Outlook. You can customize the way Outlook starts, the appearance of Outlook Today, and the content of Outlook menus and toolbars. You can use dial-up connections to access your e-mail server when you are away from the office, and the encryption options enable you to send messages securely.

In this chapter, you will work with the practice files that came on this book's CD-ROM. If you have not already installed these files on your hard disk and copied them into Outlook, see "Using the Book's CD-ROM" at the beginning of the book.

Setting Up a Dial-up Connection

OL2002e-7-6
OL2002e-1-4
OL2002e-1-3

Outlook helps you stay connected while you are away from the office. For example, you might need to stay in touch with staff at the office while visiting out-of-state clients, or you might need access to your e-mail while working from home. With **dial-up networking**, you connect to your e-mail server to download message header information (sender name, subject, date received, size, and so on) before downloading the messages themselves. Then you can choose to download only the messages you need, shortening download time. You might choose to download only High Priority messages or opt not to download a message with a large attachment.

Important

The following exercise instructs you to set up a dial-up connection. If you are already connecting to your e-mail server through a dial-up connection, you completed these steps when you set up Outlook and can skip this exercise.

In this exercise, you set up a dial-up connection and download messages for remote use. You don't need any practice files for this exercise.

Important

To complete this exercise you will need a properly configured modem and the phone number, user name, and password of a valid dial-up account. Your network administrator or ISP can provide the information you need.

1 If it is not already open, start Outlook, and then maximize its window.

Important

This procedure assumes that you are using Microsoft Exchange Server. If you are not using Exchange Server (for example, if you are on a dial-up or other stand-alone machine), your screens and dialog boxes will look significantly different from the ones pictured. However, by following the instructions on your screen, you should easily be able to work through the procedures.

Inbox

2 On the **Outlook Bar**, click the **Inbox** icon.

The contents of the Inbox are displayed.

3 On the **Tools** menu, click **E-mail Accounts**.

The **E-mail Accounts Wizard** appears.

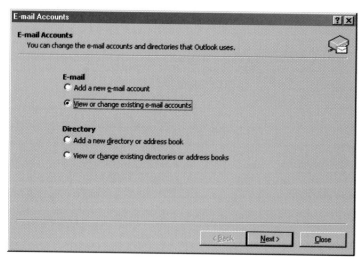

4 Select the **View or change existing e-mail accounts** option, and click **Next**.

The next page of the **E-Mail Accounts Wizard** is displayed, showing the configured e-mail accounts.

5 In the **Outlook processes e-mail for these accounts in the following order** list, click your e-mail account, and then click the **Change** button.

The **Exchange Server Settings** page is displayed, showing the account settings.

6 Click the **More Settings** button.

The **Microsoft Exchange Server** dialog box appears.

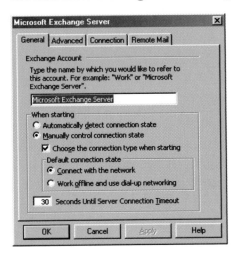

7 Click the **Connection** tab, and select the **Connect using my phone line** option.

8 In the **Modem** area, click the **Add** button.

The **Make New Connection Wizard** appears.

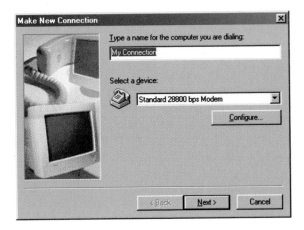

9   In the **Type a name for the computer you are dialing** box, type a meaningful name for the connection you are creating. (For example, Mike Galos might enter *Garden Company Remote Access* here.) In the **Select a device** box, click the name of your modem, and click **Next**.

The next page of the **Make New Connection Wizard** appears.

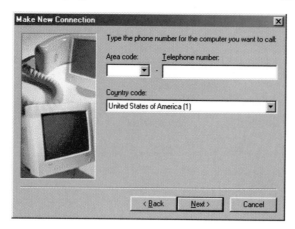

10 In the **Area code** box, type the area code, press the [Tab] key, and in the **Telephone number** box, type the telephone number that you dial to access your e-mail server. If you need to specify a country code, select the country code in the **Country code** list.

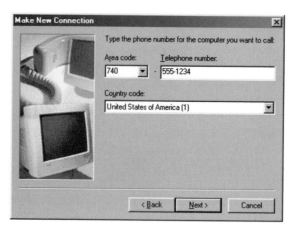

11 Click the **Next** button.

The final page of the **Make New Connection Wizard** is displayed.

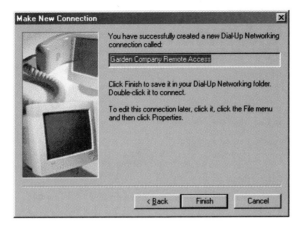

12 Click the **Finish** button.

The **Network Connection Wizard** closes.

13 In the **Use the following Dial-up Networking connection** list, click **Garden Company Remote Access**.

14 In the **Microsoft Exchange Server** dialog box, click **OK**, and in the **E-mail Accounts Wizard**, click **Next**.

The next page of the **E-mail Accounts Wizard** is displayed.

15 Click the **Finish** button.

The **E-mail Accounts Wizard** closes, saving the new account settings.

  16 On the toolbar, click the **Send/Receive** button.

Outlook begins checking for new messages using the new dial-up connection. The **Connect Garden Company Remote Access** dialog box appears.

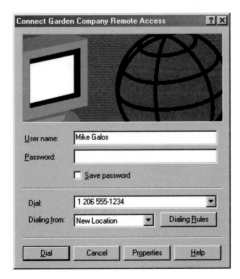

17 Type your user name and password, and then click the **Dial** button.

Tip

If you want Outlook to store your user name and password (so you don't have to enter them each time you use this dial-up connection), select the **Save password** check box.

Outlook connects to your e-mail server using your modem and sends and receives messages.

18 To continue with the exercise, Outlook needs to be configured to use offline folders. On the **Tools** menu, point to **Send/Receive**, point to **Work with Headers**, and then click **Download Headers**.

Outlook connects to your e-mail server to download the headers of any new messages.

Tip

If you have no new messages on your e-mail server, there may be no headers to download. Consider asking a friend or co-worker to send a few messages to you for use in this exercise.

19 Click a message header.

The header is selected.

20 On the **Tools** menu, point to **Send/Receive**, point to **Work with Headers**, point to **Mark/Unmark Messages**, and then click **Mark to Download Message(s)**.

The message is marked to be downloaded.

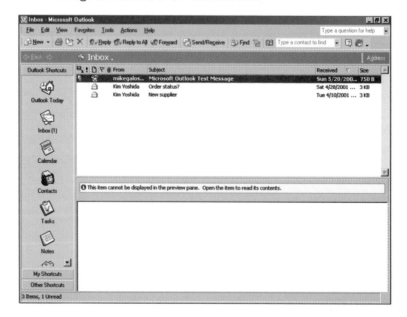

21 On the **Tools** menu, point to **Send/Receive**, point to **Work with Headers**, point to **Mark/Unmark Messages**, and then click **Process Marked Headers**.

Outlook downloads the full message.

22 On the **Tools** menu, click **E-mail Accounts**, click the **View or change existing e-mail accounts** option, and then click the **Next** button.

The **E-mail Accounts** dialog box appears.

23 In the **Outlook processes e-mail for these accounts in the following order** list, click your e-mail account, and click the **Change** button.

The **E-mail Accounts Wizard** shows the settings for your account.

24 Click the **More Settings** button, and click the **Connection** tab.

In the account settings dialog box, the **Connection** tab appears.

25 In the **Connection** area, select the connection method you normally use, and click **OK**.

The account settings dialog box closes.

26 In the **E-mail Accounts Wizard**, click the **Next** button, and then click the **Finish** button.

The wizard closes, restoring your original connection settings.

Setting Up Secure E-mail

OL2002e-7-5

As your e-mail messages travel from server to server en route to you or your recipients, they are vulnerable to interception by hackers and others intent on viewing your messages. You can use Outlook to send e-mail securely by **encrypting** and **digitally signing** your messages. Encryption ensures that only your intended recipients can read the messages you send, and a digital signature provides your recipients with proof that a message is really from you.

To send encrypted mail over the Internet, your intended recipient must first send you a digitally signed message—that is, a message to which he or she has attached his or her **digital ID**. You can then save the recipient's ID with his or her contact information for use when encrypting messages. To receive encrypted messages, you must send a message to which you have attached your digital ID to anyone from whom you want to receive encrypted messages. If you are connected to Microsoft Exchange Server, you can send encrypted messages without first sending or receiving digital ID.

For additional security, you can use **security zones** to control whether **scripts** (a list of commands executed without user interaction) or other active content can be run in HTML messages you send and receive. Microsoft Internet Explorer uses security zones to categorize Web sites so that you can set a suitable security level for them. When visiting a Web site, you can tell which zone it is in by looking at the right end of the Internet Explorer status bar. There are four zones—Internet, Local intranet, Trusted sites, and Restricted sites. You can select from four pre-defined security levels—High, Medium, Medium-Low, and Low—for each security zone. Each level is described in the **Security** dialog box. You can also customize security levels for any zone.

Obtaining a Digital ID

If you want to digitally sign messages, you must obtain a digital ID. To send digitally signed messages using Microsoft Exchange Server, you obtain the ID from the server itself. Your system administrator can provide the information you need.

To send digitally signed messages over the Internet, you must obtain the digital ID from an external company that provides certification services, such as VeriSign, Inc., GlobalSign, or British Telecommunications. On the **Security** tab of the **Options** dialog box, click the **Get a Digital ID** button. Your Web browser will start, displaying a Web page from the Microsoft Office Web site. Click the name of one of the available providers. If a message appears, warning you about viewing pages over a secure connection, click **OK**. Follow the instructions on the Web page to register for a digital ID. Most authorities charge a small fee for IDs, but a free trial period might be available.

You can have more than one digital ID on your computer, and you can select which one to use for each message. For example, you might have one ID for business use and one for personal use. You can also copy digital IDs from one computer to another by importing and exporting ID files. In the **Options** dialog box, click the **Import/Export** button in the **Digital IDs** area.

In this exercise, you encrypt an individual message, configure Outlook to secure all outgoing messages, and change security zone settings. You don't need any practice files for this exercise.

Inbox

1   On the **Outlook Bar**, click the **Inbox** icon.

The contents of the Inbox are displayed.

New Mail
Message

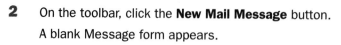

2   On the toolbar, click the **New Mail Message** button.

A blank Message form appears.

3   On the Message form's toolbar, click the **Options** button.

The **Message Options** dialog box appears.

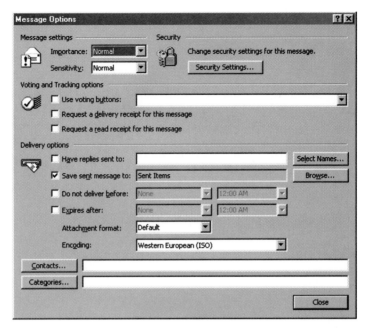

4   In the **Security** area, click the **Security Settings** button.

The **Security Properties** dialog box appears.

5   Select the **Encrypt message contents and attachments** check box, and click **OK**.

The **Security Properties** dialog box closes.

6 In the **Message Options** dialog box, click the **Close** button. If the **Secure E-mail** dialog box appears, click **OK**.

The **Message Options** dialog box closes. When sent, the message will be encrypted, assuring that it can be read only by the intended recipient.

Close

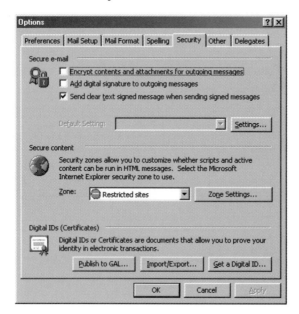

7 In the top right corner of the Message form, click the **Close** button. If prompted to save the message, click **No**.

The message is discarded without being sent or saved.

8 On the **Tools** menu, click **Options**.

The **Options** dialog box appears.

9 Click the **Security** tab.

10 In the **Secure e-mail** area, select the **Encrypt contents and attachments for outgoing messages** and the **Add digital signature to outgoing messages** check boxes.

By default, outgoing messages will be encrypted and digitally signed.

11 In the **Secure content** area, click the **Zone Settings** button.

A message box appears, warning that you are about to change security settings that will affect the way scripts and active content run in other programs.

12 Click **OK**.

The **Security** dialog box appears.

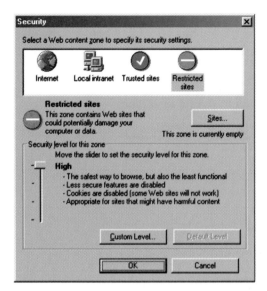

13 In the **Security level for this zone** area, move the slider to **Medium**. If a message appears, warning you about the recommended security level, click **Yes**. In the **Security** dialog box, click **OK**.

The **Security** dialog box closes. At the Medium security level, programs prompt you before downloading potentially unsafe content, and **cookies** (text files created by Web servers to identify users) are enabled.

Tip

To set the security level for individual settings (to specify whether or not a particular type of script or control is allowed to run), click the **Custom Level** button in the **Security** dialog box.

14 In the **Options** dialog box, click **OK**.

Your changes are saved.

Specifying Advanced E-mail Options

OL2002e-7-2

Outlook offers a selection of advanced options for helping you use your e-mail effectively. To avoid losing your work, you can choose to have Outlook automatically save messages you have created but not yet sent. When new messages arrive, you can choose to have Outlook play a sound, briefly change the mouse cursor to an envelope icon, show an envelope icon in the system tray, or any combination of these. You can also set default options for sending a message. For example, if you are concerned about privacy, you might choose to set the sensitivity of all new messages to Private.

In this exercise, you specify how Outlook saves messages, what happens when new messages arrive, and which options are used when sending messages. You don't need any practice files for this exercise.

Inbox

1 On the **Outlook Bar**, click the **Inbox** icon.

The contents of the Inbox are displayed.

2 On the **Tools** menu, click **Options**.

The **Options** dialog box appears.

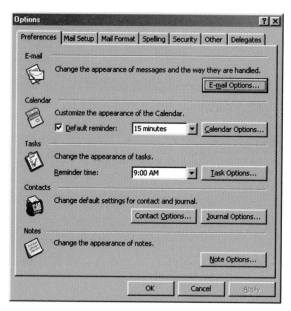

3 Click the **E-mail Options** button.

The **E-mail Options** dialog box appears. From this dialog box, you can open several other dialog boxes that control the settings and appearance of Outlook's features, including E-mail, Tasks, Contacts, Notes, and the Calendar.

4 Click the **Advanced E-mail Options** button.

The **Advanced E-mail Options** dialog box appears.

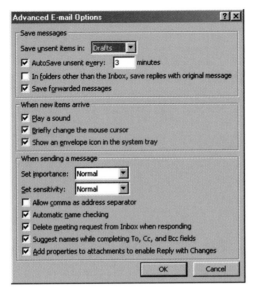

5   In the **Save messages** area, be sure the **AutoSave unsent every** check box is selected, and in the **minutes** box, type **1**.

Outlook will save any messages that you are composing, but have not yet sent, in your Drafts folder after one minute.

6   Clear the **Save forwarded messages** check box.

Outlook will not save a copy of messages that you forward to others.

7   In the **When new items arrive** area, clear the **Briefly change the mouse cursor** check box.

Outlook will play a sound and display an envelope icon in the system tray when new messages arrive, but the cursor will not change.

8   In the **Set importance** list in the **When sending a message** area, click **High**.

By default, all new messages will be set to High priority.

9   Clear the **Allow comma as address separator** and the **Suggest names while completing the To, Cc, and Bcc fields** check boxes.

Outlook will not recognize commas in the **To**, **Cc**, or **Bcc** boxes as separators between names or addresses. You'll need to use semi-colons instead. Outlook will not suggest the names of contacts that match what you type in the **To**, **Cc**, or **Bcc** boxes. The **Advanced E-Mail Options** dialog box now looks like the one shown on the next page.

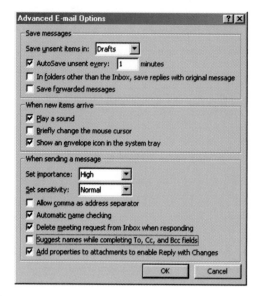

10 In the **Advanced E-mail Options** dialog box, click **OK**.

The **Advanced E-mail Options** dialog box closes.

11 In the **E-mail Options** and the **Options** dialog boxes, click **OK**.

The dialog boxes close, saving your preferences.

New Mail
Message

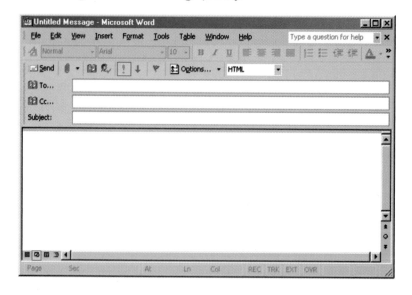

12 On the Standard toolbar, click the **New Mail Message** button.

A new message appears. In the Message form, the toolbar indicates that the message is marked as High priority.

13   Close the message, and if prompted to save the message, click **No**.

14   On the **Tools** menu, click **Options**, click the **E-mail Options** button, and then click the **Advanced E-mail Options** button.

The **Advanced E-mail Options** dialog box appears.

15   In the **Set importance** list in the **When sending a message** area, click **Normal**.

By default, all new messages will be set to Normal priority.

16   Reset or select any other options, and click **OK** in the **Advanced E-mail Options** dialog box, the **E-mail Options** dialog box, and the **Options** dialog box.

Customizing Outlook

OL2002e-7-1
OL2002e-7-4

As you work with Outlook, you will find that certain configurations are more useful to you. For example, you might find that you need to review your schedule and work with your calendar at the beginning of each day. So, you might configure Outlook to start with your Calendar folder displayed. Or, you might find Outlook Today very useful but want to fine-tune the appearance to meet your needs. You can also change the contents of your **Outlook Bar** to add items that you use frequently, and remove those that you don't.

In this exercise, you customize the way Outlook starts, how Outlook Today appears, and the contents of the Outlook Bar. You don't need any practice files for this exercise.

1   You'll start this exercise with Outlook closed, so if necessary, on the **File** menu, click **Exit**.

Outlook closes.

2   Using Windows Explorer, locate the Outlook program file, which is usually located in the C:\Program Files\Microsoft Office\Office10 folder. (If your computer is set to display filename extensions, the Outlook program file will appear as Outlook.exe.)

3   Right-click the Outlook program file, and click **Create Shortcut** on the shortcut menu.

The shortcut appears in the folder.

Close

4   Drag the shortcut to the desktop, and in the Windows Explorer window, click the **Close** button.

The Explorer window closes, and the shortcut appears on your desktop.

5 Right-click the shortcut you just created, and click **Properties** on the short-cut menu.

The **Shortcut** tab of the **Shortcut to Outlook Properties** dialog box appears.

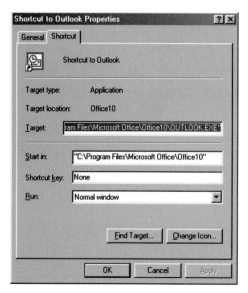

6 To tell Outlook to display the Calendar when it opens, in the **Target** box, type a space after the path, and then type **/select outlook:calendar**, and click **OK**.

The shortcut is saved with your changes.

7 On the desktop, double-click the shortcut you created.

Outlook starts, showing the Calendar.

8 On the **File** menu, click **Exit**.

Outlook closes.

Microsoft
Outlook

9 On the desktop, double-click the **Microsoft Outlook** icon (not the shortcut you created).

Outlook starts, with your default options.

10 On the **Outlook Bar**, click **Outlook Today**.

The **Outlook Today** page is displayed.

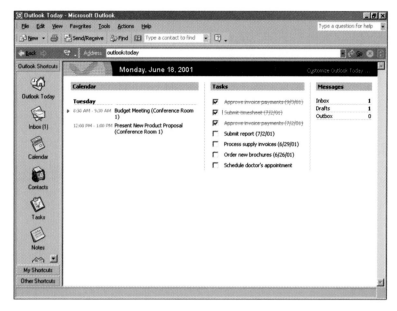

11 Click **Customize Outlook Today**.

The **Customize Outlook Today** page is displayed.

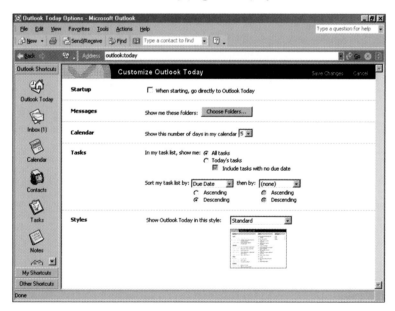

12 In the **Startup** area, select the **When starting, go directly to Outlook Today** check box.

13 Review the options in the **Messages**, **Calendar**, and **Tasks** areas. Feel free to change any options you want.

14 In the **Styles** area, in the **Show Outlook Today in this style** list, click **Standard (two column)**.

A preview of the selected style is shown.

15 In the top right corner, click **Save Changes**.

Outlook Today is displayed in the selected style.

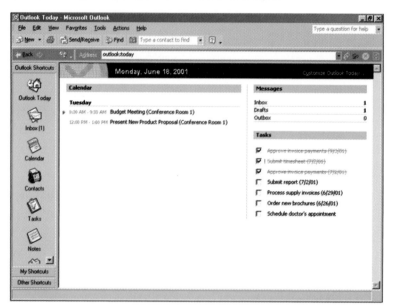

16 On the **File** menu, click **Exit**.

Outlook closes.

17 On the desktop, double-click the **Microsoft Outlook** icon.

Outlook starts, showing Outlook Today.

18 On the **Outlook Bar**, click **My Shortcuts**.

The contents of the My Shortcuts group are displayed.

19 Right-click the background of the **Outlook Bar**, and then click **Outlook Bar Shortcut** on the shortcut menu.

The **Add to Outlook Bar** dialog box appears.

20 Click the plus (+) sign to the left of **Mailbox** to expand its list of folders.

21 In the list of folders, click **Deleted Items**, and click **OK**.

A shortcut to the Deleted Items folder is added to the **Outlook Bar**, in the My Shortcuts group.

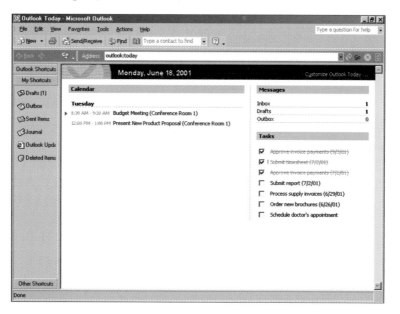

22 On the **Outlook Bar**, click **Deleted Items** to display the Deleted Items folder.

23 On the **Outlook Bar**, right-click the **Deleted Items** shortcut, and click **Remove from Outlook Bar** on the shortcut menu.

A message box appears, asking you to confirm that you want to remove the shortcut from the **Outlook Bar** and explaining how to add the shortcut back later.

24 In the message box, click **Yes**.

The Deleted Items shortcut is removed from the **Outlook Bar**.

25 On the **Outlook Bar**, click **Outlook Shortcuts**.

The icons in the Outlook Shortcuts group are displayed.

Customizing Menus and Toolbars

OL2002-e-7-7

You will most likely find that you use certain menus and toolbar buttons quite frequently and that you never use others. To make Outlook more effective, you can customize your menus and toolbars to contain the items you use and display them in the way that you use them. You can add and remove items from both menus and toolbars, hide or display toolbars, move toolbars, and create your own toolbars. For example, if you use dial-up networking frequently, you might create a toolbar containing commands you use to mark message headers. Or, if you don't use custom forms, you might remove the **Forms** command from the **Tools** menu.

In this exercise, you select which toolbars are displayed, set options for how menus appear, add and remove items from menus, and add and remove items from toolbars. You don't need any practice files for this exercise.

Inbox

1 On the **Outlook Bar**, click the **Inbox** icon.

The Inbox is displayed.

2 On the **View** menu, point to **Toolbars**, and click **Advanced**.

The Advanced toolbar appears near the top of the Outlook window.

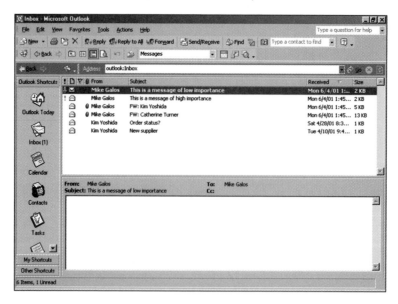

3   On the **Tools** menu, click **Customize**.

The **Customize** dialog box appears.

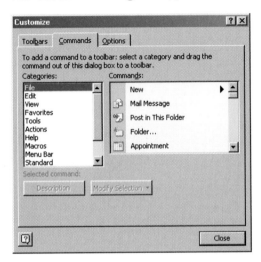

4   Click the **Options** tab.

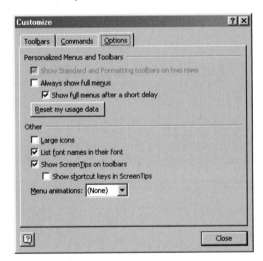

5   In the **Personalized Menus and Toolbars** area, select the **Always show full menus** check box.

6   In the **Other** area, click the down arrow to the right of the **Menu animations** box, click **Slide** in the drop-down list, and then click **Close**.

Your selections are saved.

7   Click the **Tools** menu.

The menu opens, showing all its commands.

8   On the **Tools** menu, click **Customize** to display the **Customize** dialog box.

9 Click the **Commands** tab.

10 In the **Categories** list, click **View**.

The list of commands in the **View** category is displayed in the **Commands** list.

11 In the **Commands** list, click **My Computer**, drag it to the **View** menu, drag it to **Go To**, and drop it just above **News**.

The command is added to the **View** menu.

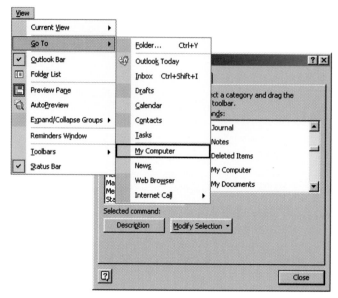

12 In the **Customize** dialog box, click the **Close** button.

The **Customize** dialog box closes, saving your changes.

13 On the **View** menu, point to **Go To**, and click **My Computer**.

The contents of the My Computer folder are displayed in the Outlook window.

14 On the **Outlook Bar**, click the **Inbox** icon.

The Inbox is displayed.

15 On the **Tools** menu, click **Customize**.

The **Customize** dialog box appears. When this dialog box is open, you can add and remove items from visible menus and toolbars, using the menus and toolbars themselves.

16 On the **View** menu, click **Go To**, and then drag **My Computer** off the menu.

The **command** is removed from the menu.

17 In the **Customize** dialog box, click the **Commands** tab.

18 In the **Categories** list, click **View**.

The list of commands for the **View** category is displayed.

19 In the **Commands** list, click **Go To**, and drag it to the toolbar.

The **Go To** button is added to the toolbar.

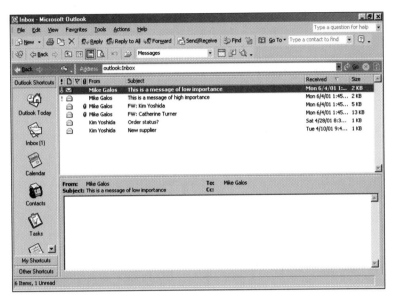

20 In the **Customize** dialog box, click the **Close** button.

The **Customize** dialog box closes.

Go To ▼

21 On the toolbar, click the **Go To** button, and then click **Outlook Today**.

Outlook Today is displayed.

22 On the **Tools** menu, click **Customize**.

The **Customize** dialog box appears.

23 Drag the **Go To** button off the toolbar, releasing the mouse button when the pointer is not on a menu or another toolbar.

The button is removed from the toolbar.

24 In the **Customize** dialog box, click the **Close** button.

The **Customize** dialog box closes.

Tip

You can reset any toolbar to its default settings. In the **Customize** dialog box, click the **Toolbars** tab, select the toolbar you want to reset, and click the **Reset** button.

25 On the **Outlook Bar**, click the **Inbox** icon. Then on the **File** menu, click **Exit** to quit Outlook.

Quick Reference

10   To forward a message

Forward

1   Open the message you want to forward.

2   On the message form's toolbar, click the **Forward** button.

11   To create a new message

New Mail
Message

New

1   Make sure the Inbox is displayed.

2   On the toolbar, click the **New Mail Message** button.

12   To show and hide the Folder List

●   On the **View** menu, click **Folder List**.

12   To address a message

●   Type the recipient's e-mail address in the **To** box, or click the **To** button to select a name from the Address Book.

13   To send a message

Send

1   Open the e-mail message you want to send.

2   On the message form's toolbar, click the **Send** button.

14   To add an entry to the Address Book

New Entry

1   On the **Tools** menu, click **Address Book**.

2   Select the address book you want, and then click the **New Entry** button.

16   To create a distribution list

New Entry

1   On the **Tools** menu, click **Address Book**.

2   Select the address book you want, click the **New Entry** button, and then select **Distribution List**.

19   To attach a file to a message

Insert File

1   Create a new message, and on the toolbar, click the **Insert File** button.

2   In the **Insert File** dialog box, browse to the file that you want to attach, click that file, and then click the **Insert** button.

20 **To create a message signature**

1 On the **Tools** menu, click **Options**.

2 In the **Options** dialog box, click the **Mail Format** tab, click the **Signatures** button, and then click the **New** button.

3 In the **Create New Signature** dialog box, type the name of your signature, and then click the **Next** button.

4 In the **Signature Text** box, type and style your signature, and then click **Finish**.

25 **To check for new messages**

● On the toolbar, click the **Send/Receive** button.

27 **To print a message**

Print

1 Select the message you want to print.

2 On the toolbar, click the **Print** button.

Chapter 2 **Managing E-mail Messages**

Page 30 **To sort messages**

● Click the heading of the column by which you'd like to sort messages.

30 **To group messages**

1 Right-click the heading of the column by which you'd like to group messages.

2 Click **Group by This Field** in the shortcut menu.

31 **To change the message view**

● On the **View** menu, click **Current View**, and then click the view you want.

32 **To customize the message view**

● On the **View** menu, click **Current View**, and then click **Customize Current View**.

36 **To create a folder**

1 On the **File** menu, click **New**, and then click **New Folder**.

2 In the **Create New Folder** dialog box, type the name of the folder, and in the **Folder contains** list, click the kind of items you want to store in the folder.

3 In the **Select where to place the folder** list, click a location for the folder.

38 **To move a message to a folder**

Move to Folder

1   Select the message.

2   On the toolbar, click the **Move to Folder** button.

38 **To move a folder**

●   In the **Folder List**, drag the folder to the location you want.

38 **To rename a folder**

●   In the **Folder List**, right-click the folder, and click **Rename**.

38 **To delete a folder**

Delete

1   In the **Folder List**, click the folder you want to delete.

2   On the toolbar, click the **Delete** button.

39 **To color-code messages**

1   On the **Tools** menu, click **Organize**.

2   In the **Ways to Organize Inbox** pane, click **Using Colors**.

3   Select what type of messages you want color-coded and what color you want them to be, and then click the **Apply Color** button.

42 **To find messages**

1   On the toolbar, click the **Find** button.

2   In the **Look for** box in the **Find** pane, type a word that you know is in the message you are looking for.

3   Click the **Find Now** button.

42 **To assign a message to a category**

1   Select the message, and on the **Edit** menu, click **Categories**.

2   In the **Item(s) belong to these categories** box, type the name of a new category, or, in the **Available Categories** list, select the appropriate category for the message.

3   Click **OK**.

46 **To save a message as an HTML file**

1   Select the message, and on the **File** menu, click **Save As**.

2   In the **Save As** dialog box, make sure HTML is selected in the **Save as type** drop-down list, and then click the **Save** button.

298

46 **To save a message as a text file**

1 Select the message, and on the **File** menu, click **Save As**.

2 In the **Save As** dialog box, select **Text Only** in the **Save as type** drop-down list, and then click the **Save** button.

49 **To specify archive settings for a folder**

1 In the **Folder List**, click the folder you want to archive.

2 On the **File** menu, point to **Folder,** and then click **Properties**.

3 In the **Properties** dialog box, click the **AutoArchive** tab.

4 Select the settings with which you want to archive the folder, and click **OK**.

49 **To archive messages manually**

1 On the **File** menu, click **Archive**.

2 In the **Archive** dialog box, select the setting you want to use and click **OK**.

50 **To specify global archive settings**

1 On the **Tools** menu, click **Options**. Click the **Other** tab, and then click the **AutoArchive** button.

2 In the **AutoArchive** dialog box, choose the global archive settings you want, and click **OK** twice to close the dialog boxes.

Chapter 3 Customizing and Organizing E-mail Messages

Page 56 **To select the message format**

● On the Message form's toolbar, click the down arrow to the right of the **Message format** box, and click **HTML**, **Rich Text**, or **Plain Text**.

58 **To use stationery to format messages**

1 On the **Tools** menu, click **Options**, and in the **Options** dialog box, click the **Mail Format** tab.

2 In the **Use this stationery by default** list, select the stationery you want.

58 **To customize message stationery**

1 On the **Tools** menu, click **Options**, and in the **Options** dialog box, click the **Mail Format** tab.

2 Click the **Stationery Picker** button, click the **Edit** button, apply the formatting you want, and click **OK**.

59   To format a message using a theme

1   On the **Format** menu, click **Theme**.

2   In the **Theme** dialog box, click the theme you want from the **Choose a Theme** list, and then click **OK**.

61   To set the importance of a message

1   On the Message form's toolbar, click the **Options** button.

2   In the **Message settings** area of the **Message Options** dialog box, click the down arrow to the right of the **Importance** box, click the level of importance you want, and then click **OK**.

62   To set delivery options for a message

1   On the Message form's toolbar, click the **Options** button.

2   In the **Delivery options** area of the **Message Options** dialog box, select the options you want.

64   To recall a message

1   In the **Folder List**, click **Sent Items**.

2   Open the message you want to recall, and on the **Actions** menu, click **Recall This Message**.

3   Select what you want to do with the unread copies of the recalled message, and then click **OK**.

65   To create a view to filter messages

●   On the **View** menu, point to **Current View**, and click **Define Views**.

67   To create a rule to filter messages

●   On the **Tools** menu, click **Rules Wizard**, and then follow the wizard's instructions to create the rule.

73   To filter junk or adult content messages

Organize

1   On the toolbar, click the **Organize** button

2   In the **Ways to Organize Inbox** pane, click **Junk E-mail**.

3   Select whether you want to move or color the unwanted messages, select the color or the location to which you want the messages moved, and click the **Turn On** button.

75 **To create a Personal Folders file**

1 On the **Tools** menu, click **Options**.

2 On the **Mail Setup** tab of the **Options** dialog box, click the **Data Files** button, and then click the **Add** button.

3 In the **New Outlook Data File** dialog box, click **OK**.

77 **To add a personal address book**

1 On the **Tools** menu, click **E-mail Accounts**.

2 In the **E-Mail Accounts** dialog box, select the **Add a new directory or address book** option and click **Next**.

3 In the **Directory or Address Book Type** page, select the **Additional Address Books** option, and click **Next**.

4 In the **Additional Address Book Types** list of the **Other Address Book Types** page, click **Personal Address Book** and then click **Next**.

5 In the **Personal Address Book** dialog box, browse to the Outlook personal folder from which you want to create a personal address book, and click **OK** twice.

78 **To create a personal distribution list**

1 On the **Tools** menu, click **Address Book**.

New Entry

2 On the **Address Book** window's toolbar, click the **New Entry** button.

3 In the **New Entry** dialog box, click the down arrow to the right of the **In the** box, and then click **Personal Address Book** in the drop-down list.

4 In the **Select the entry type** list, click **Personal Distribution List**, and then click **OK**.

81 **To specify which address books Outlook checks when addressing messages**

1 On the **Tools** menu, click **Address Book**.

2 On the **Address Book** window's **Tools** menu, click **Options**.

3 In the **Addressing** dialog box, click the **Add** button.

4 In the **Add Address List** dialog box, click **Personal Address Book**, and click the **Add** button.

Chapter 4 Managing Your Calendar

Page 84 **To view your schedule for a specific date**

● In the Date Navigator, scroll to and click the date you want.

85   To schedule an appointment

1   In the Calendar, double-click the time slot in the day you want to schedule the appointment.

🖫 Save and Close   **2**   In the Appointment form, enter the relevant information about the appointment, and click the **Save and Close** button.

86   To schedule a recurring appointment

1   In the Calendar, double-click the time slot in the day you want to schedule the first occurrence of the recurring appointment.

↻ Recurrence...   **2**   In the Appointment form, enter the relevant information about the appointment, and then click the **Recurrence** button.

3   In the **Appointment Recurrence** dialog box, enter the recurrence settings you want and then click **OK**.

🖫 Save and Close   **4**   Click the **Save and Close** button.

88   To schedule an event

1   In the Calendar, double-click the day on which you want to schedule the event.

🖫 Save and Close   **2**   In the Event form, enter the relevant information about the event, and click the **Save and Close** button.

91   To assign a category to an appointment

1   Click the **Categories** button at the bottom of the Appointment form.

2   In the **Categories** dialog box, select the category, and click **OK**.

92   To move an appointment

●   Click the left edge of the appointment and drag it to the new time or date.

92   To copy an appointment

●   Right-click the left edge of the appointment and drag it to the new time or date.

93   To delete an appointment

Delete   **1**   Click the appointment you want to delete.

✕   **2**   On the toolbar, click the **Delete** button.

95 **To view your schedule for the work week**

1 Make sure the Calendar is displayed.

2 On the toolbar, click the **Work Week** button.

5 Work Week

95 **To view your schedule for a full week**

1 Make sure the Calendar is displayed.

2 On the toolbar, click the **Week** button.

7 Week

95 **To view your schedule for a month**

1 Make sure the Calendar is displayed.

2 On the toolbar, click the **Month** button.

31 Month

96 **To select a calendar view**

● On the **View** menu, point to **Current View**, and then click the view you want.

98 **To color-code appointments, meetings, and events**

Organize

1 On the toolbar, click the **Organize** button.

2 On the **Organize** panel, click **Using Colors**.

101 **To change your time zone**

1 On the **Tools** menu, click **Options**.

2 On the **Preferences** tab of the **Options** dialog box, click the **Calendar Options** button, and then click the **Time Zone** button.

103 **To print your calendar**

1 On the **File** menu, click **Print**.

2 In the **Print** dialog box, select a print style, and click the **Print** button.

Chapter 5 **Scheduling and Managing Meetings**
Page 110 **To plan a meeting**

1 On the **Actions** menu, click **Plan a Meeting**.

2 Click the **Add Others** button to add other attendees, and then click the **Make Meeting** button.

113 **To set or remove a reminder**

- On the Meeting form, select or clear the **Reminder** check box. If setting a reminder, select the date and time that you want to be reminded.

117 **To accept a meeting request**

1 Open the meeting request.

2 Click the **Accept** button.

117 **To decline a meeting request**

1 Open the meeting request.

2 Click the **Decline** button.

118 **To propose a new meeting time**

1 Open the request, and click the **Propose New Time** button.

2 In the **Free/Busy** area, click the time you are proposing, and click the **Propose Time** button.

120 **To respond to meeting requests automatically**

1 On the **Tools** menu, click **Options**. On the **Preferences** tab, click the **Calendar Options** button, and then click the **Resource Scheduling** button.

2 Select the automatic response options you want, and then click **OK**.

122 **To reschedule a meeting**

1 Open the meeting, and click the **Scheduling** tab.

2 In the **Free/Busy** area, select new start and end dates and times. Click the **Send Update** button.

123 **To cancel a meeting**

1 Open the meeting, and on the **Actions** menu, click **Cancel Meeting**.

2 Choose whether to send a cancellation notice to the attendees, and then click **OK**.

124 **To schedule an online meeting**

New
Appointment

New

1 On the toolbar, click the down arrow to the right of the **New Appointment** button and then click **Meeting Request**.

2 On the Meeting form, select the **This is an online meeting using** check box.

125   **To invite others to a meeting**

     1   On the Meeting form, click the **Scheduling** tab, and then click the **Add Others** button.

     2   Click the contacts you want to add, click the **Required** or **Optional** button, and then click **OK**.

128   **To create a group schedule**

View Group
Schedules

 Schedules...

     1   With the Calendar displayed, on the toolbar, click the **View Group Schedules** button, and then click the **New** button.

     2   Type a name for the group schedule, and then click **OK**.

     3   Click the **Add Others** button, add the members you want, and then click **OK**.

130   **To open another person's calendar directly**

     1   On the **File** menu, point to **Open**, and click **Other User's Folder**.

     2   Click the **Name** button, click the name of the person whose folder you want to open, and then click **OK**.

     3   Make sure Calendar appears in the **Folder** box, and then click **OK**.

Chapter 6   **Creating and Organizing a List of Contacts**

Page **135**   **To create a contact**

New Contact

⌐≡ **New**

     1   On the **Outlook Bar**, click the **Contacts** icon.

     2   On the toolbar, click the **New Contact** button.

137   **To create multiple contacts from the same company**

     ●   Open a contact from the company, and on the **Actions** menu, click **New Contact from Same Company**.

139   **To delete a contact**

Delete

✕

     1   Click the contact you want to delete.

     2   On the toolbar, click the **Delete** button.

143   **To assign a category to a contact**

     1   Open the contact, and click the **Categories** button.

     2   In the **Available categories** list of the **Categories** dialog box, select the category you want to assign to the contact, and click **OK**.

167 **To change your task view**

● On the **View** menu, point to **Current View**, and click the view you want.

168 **To assign a category to a task**

1 Open the task, and click the **Categories** button.

2 In the **Available categories** list, select the check box for the category you want, and then click **OK**.

171 **To view your tasks in the TaskPad**

Calendar

1 Display the Outlook Bar by clicking **Outlook Bar** on the **View** menu.

2 Click the **Calendar** icon to display the **TaskPad**.

174 **To accept a task request**

1 Open the request.

2 On the toolbar, click the **Accept** button.

174 **To decline a task request**

1 Open the request.

2 On the toolbar, click the **Decline** button.

✕ Decline

175 **To send a status report on a task**

Send Status
Report

1 Double-click the task to open it.

2 On the toolbar, click the **Send Status Report** button.

3 In the Message form, type a message if you wish, and then click the **Send** button.

Send

176 **To mark a task as complete**

● Open the task, and on the toolbar, click the **Mark Complete** button.

178 **To stop a task from recurring**

Recurrence...

1 Open the task, and click the **Recurrence** button.

2 Click the **Remove Recurrence** button.

178 **To delete a task**

To link a note to a contact

1   Open the note, click the **Note** icon in the upper left corner, and click **Contacts** in the drop-down list.

2   Click the **Contacts** button, in the **Items** list, click the contact you want to add to the note, and then click **OK**.

Chapter   9   Using the Journal
Page   196   **To record Journal entries automatically**

1   On the **Tools** menu, click **Options**, and then click the **Journal Options** button.

2   Select the check boxes for the items you want to be recorded as Journal entries, and then click **OK**.

To manually record a Journal entry for an Outlook item

New Journal
Entry

📇 New

1   Display the Journal.

2   On the toolbar, click the **New Journal Entry** button.

To manually record a Journal entry for a Microsoft Office document

1   Drag the Office document to the **Journal** icon on the **Outlook Bar**.

💾 Save and Close

2   Click the **Save and Close** button.

To change your Journal view

●   On the **View** menu, point to **Current View**, and click the view you want.

To assign a category to a Journal entry

1   Open the Journal entry, and click the **Categories** button.

2   Select the check boxes next to the categories you want, and click **OK**.

To associate a Journal entry with a contact

1   Open the Journal entry, and click the **Contacts** button.

2   In the **Items** list, click the name of the contact you want to add, and click **OK**.

To view the Journal entries associated with a contact

●   Open the contact, click the **Activities** tab, and in the **Show** list, click **Journal**.

Chapter 10   Using Outlook with Other Programs

● On the **File** menu, click **Import and Export**, select the type of file to import, and click **Next**. Then follow the rest of the instructions in the **Import and Export Wizard**.

● On the **File** menu, click **Import and Export**, click **Export to a file**, and click **Next**. Then follow the rest of the instructions in the **Import and Export Wizard**.

1   On the **Tools** menu, point to **Forms**, and click **Design a Form**.

2   In the list of forms, click the one you want to create, and then click the **Open** button.

3   Modify the form until it looks the way you want it to.

1   On the **Tools** menu, point to **Forms**, and click **Choose a Form**.

2   Click the form you want, and then click **Open**.

1   Open the form, and on the **Tools** menu, point to **Forms**, and click **Publish Form As**.

2   In the **Look In** box, click the location you want to publish the form in, type a name for the form in the **Display name** box, and then click the **Publish** button.

1   In the **Folder List**, right-click the folder and click **Properties** on the shortcut menu. Click the **Forms** tab, and then click the **Manage** button.

Delete
✕

2   In the list of forms, click the one you want to delete, and then click the **Delete** button.

231   **To delete a form from a forms library**

1   On the **Tools** menu, click **Options**. Click the **Other** tab, and click the **Advanced Options** button.

Delete

✕

2   Click the **Custom Forms** button, and then click the **Manage Forms** button. In the **Personal Forms** list, click the form you want to delete, and then click the **Delete** button.

232   **To send form letters using Outlook contacts**

1   Display the Contacts folder, and on the **Tools** menu, click **Mail Merge**.

2   In the **Document file** area, select the document you want to use, and then click **OK**.

3   On the **Tools** menu, point to **Letters and Mailings**, and then click **Mail Merge Wizard**. Follow the rest of the instructions in the wizard.

Chapter 11   **Sharing Information and Working Offline**

Page   240   **To share a folder**

1   In the **Folder List**, right-click the folder, click **Properties**, and then click the **Permissions** tab.

2   Click the **Add** button, and in the **Type Name or Select from List** box, type the name of the person you want to share your folder with.

3   Click the **Add** button, and then click **OK**.

244   **To save your Calendar as a Web page**

1   Display the Calendar, and on the **File** menu, click **Save as Web Page**.

2   Select the dates that you want to be published, type the title you want, and click the **Save** button.

246   **To publish your free/busy information on the Internet**

1   On the **Tools** menu, click **Options**. Click **Calendar Options** and then click the **Free/Busy Options** button.

2   Select the options you want in the **Internet Free/Busy** area, and then click **OK**.

3   On the **Tools** menu, point to **Send/Receive**, and then click **Free/Busy Information**.

3   Click the **Connection** tab, click the **Connect using my phone line** option, and then click the **Add** button.

4   Type a name for your connection, click the name of your modem in the **Select a device** box, and then click **Next**.

5   Type the telephone number, click **Next**, and then click **Finish**.

276   **To download messages for remote use**

●   On the **Tools** menu, point to **Send/Receive**, point to **Work with Headers**, and click **Download Headers**. Then use the same menu to mark and download the messages you want.

276   **To mark message headers for download**

●   Click the message headers to select them, and on the **Tools** menu, point to **Send/Receive**, point to **Work with Headers**, point to **Mark/Unmark Messages**, and then click **Mark to Download Message(s)**.

277   **To download messages**

●   On the **Tools** menu, point to **Send/Receive**, point to **Work with Headers**, point to **Mark/Unmark Messages**, and then click **Process Marked Headers**.

278   **To obtain a digital ID**

1   On the **Tools** menu, click **Options**, click the **Security** tab, and click the **Get a Digital ID** button.

2   Click the name of one of the available providers, and then click **OK**. Follow the instructions on the Web page to register for a digital ID.

279   **To send a secure message**

1   On the Message form, click the **Options** button.

2   Click the **Security Settings** button, select the **Encrypt message contents and attachment** check box, and then click OK.

280   **To secure all messages automatically**

●   On the **Tools** menu, click **Options**, click the **Security** tab, and select the **Encrypt contents and attachments for outgoing messages** check box.

280   **To digitally sign all messages automatically**

●   On the **Tools** menu, click **Options**, click the **Security** tab, and select the **Add digital signature to outgoing messages** check box.

282 **To specify advanced e-mail options**

1 On the **Tools** menu, click **Options**, click the **E-mail Options** button, and click the **Advanced E-mail Options** button.

2 Choose the settings you want, and then click **OK**.

287 **To customize Outlook Today**

1 Display Outlook Today, and click **Customize Outlook Today**.

2 Choose the settings you want, and then click **Save Changes**.

290 **To customize menus and toolbars**

● On the **Tools** menu, click **Customize**. Modify the menus and toolbars as you like, and then click the **Close** button.

290 **To show or hide toolbars**

● On the **View** menu, point to **Toolbars**, and click the toolbar you want to show or hide.

291 **To specify menu and toolbar options**

1 On the **Tools** menu, click **Customize**, and click the **Options** tab.

2 Select the options you want, and then click the **Close** button.

Glossary

ACT! For Windows   A contact management program.

address book   A collection of names, e-mail addresses, and distribution lists used to address messages. An address book may be provided by Microsoft Outlook, Microsoft Exchange Server, or Internet directory services, depending on how you have set up Outlook.

address card   Contact information displayed in a block that looks like a paper business card.

appointment   An entry in your Outlook Calendar that does not involve inviting other people or resources.

archiving   Moving old or expired items out of your Inbox and other message folders to an alternate location for storage.

attachment   A file that accompanies an e-mail message.

AutoArchive   An Outlook feature that archives messages automatically at scheduled intervals, clearing out old and expired items from folders. AutoArchive is active by default.

Calendar   The scheduling component of Outlook that is fully integrated with e-mail, contacts, and other Outlook features.

category   A keyword or phrase that you assign to Outlook items so that you can easily find, sort, filter, or group them.

contact   A person, inside or outside of your organization, about whom you can save information, such as street and e-mail addresses, telephone and fax numbers, and Web page URLs, in an entry in your Contacts folder in Outlook.

cookies   Text files created by Web servers to identify users and possibly prepare customized Web pages for them.

Date Navigator   The small calendar that appears next to the appointment area in the Outlook Calendar. The Date Navigator provides a quick and easy way to change and view dates.

dBASE   A type of database file.

dial-up networking   A component of Windows that enables you to connect your computer to a network server via a modem.

digital ID A private key that stays on the sender's computer and a certificate that contains a public key. The certificate is sent with digitally signed messages.

digitally signing Proving one's identity by attaching a digital certificate to an e-mail message. The certificate is part of the sender's digital ID.

distribution list A collection of e-mail addresses combined into a single list name. All members of the list receive the e-mail message sent to the list name.

downloading Moving or copying items from a server to a local computer.

draft A message that has not yet been sent.

e-mail Electronic mail.

e-mail address Identifies the e-mail account of a message recipient, including the user name and domain name separated by the @ sign. For example, *some-one@microsoft.com*.

e-mail server A computer, on a network, that routes and stores e-mail messages.

encrypting Encoding data to prevent unauthorized access. An encrypted message is unreadable to all but the recipient, who has a public key that will decrypt it because the key matches the private key that the sender used to encrypt it.

Eudora An e-mail client program.

event An Outlook Calendar entry for an activity that lasts 24 hours or longer.

export To convert a file from one application format to another.

filtering A way to view only those items or files that meet conditions you specify.

Folder banner The area of the Outlook window that displays the name of the current folder and indicates whether the items in the folder are filtered. If the Folder List is not visible, you can click the folder name in the folder banner to temporarily show the Folder List.

Folder List The list that displays the folders available in your mailbox. If the Folder List is not visible, on the View menu, click Folder List.

follow-up flag An icon associated with a message indicating a need to act on the message.

form The feature in Outlook in which the user can define how items will be displayed. For example, the Outlook Message form defines how messages are displayed on the screen.

Forms Design Environment The component of Outlook used to edit or create forms.

global address list   An address book, provided by Microsoft Exchange Server, that contains all user and distribution list e-mail addresses in your organization. The Exchange administrator creates and maintains this address book.

HTML   Hypertext Markup Language, the authoring language used to create Web pages and other documents on the Internet.

HTML format   The default format for Outlook e-mail messages. This format supports text formatting, numbering, bullets, alignment, horizontal lines, pictures (including backgrounds), HTML styles, stationery, signatures, and Web pages.

Inbox   The default message folder in Outlook. Typically, incoming messages are delivered to the Inbox.

importance   Indicates the magnitude of a message. Messages can be of High, Normal, or Low importance.

import   To read and use data produced by a different program.

instant messaging   A method of communication in which you send electronic messages that appear on the recipient's screen immediately.

Internet mail   A type of e-mail account that requires that you connect to the e-mail server over the Internet. POP3, IMAP, and HTTP (for example, Hotmail) are examples of Internet mail accounts.

Internet service provider (ISP)   A business that provides access to the Internet for such things as electronic mail, chat rooms, or use of the World Wide Web.

local area network (LAN)   A network that connects computers in a relatively small area, typically a single building or groups of buildings. Generally, all computers in an organization are connected to a LAN. Organizations may have multiple LANs that are connected to each other.

Journal entry   An item in the Journal folder that acts as a shortcut to an activity that has been recorded. You can distinguish a journal entry from other items by the clock that appears in the lower left corner of the icon.

Mailbox Cleanup   An Outlook feature that helps you manage the size of your mailbox. You can view the total size of your mailbox and of individual folders within it, find items that are larger than a certain size or older than a certain date, and archive items from within Mailbox Cleanup. You can also view the size of your Deleted Items folder and empty it from within Mailbox Cleanup.

meeting   A Calendar entry to which you invite people or for which you reserve resources.

meeting request   An e-mail message inviting its recipients to a meeting.

message header   Summary information that you download to your computer to determine whether to download, copy, or delete the entire message from the server. The header may include the subject, the sender's name, the received date, the importance, the attachment flag, and the size of the message.

Microsoft Exchange Server   An enterprise-level e-mail and collaboration server.

Microsoft FoxPro   A database program.

Microsoft Office Internet Free/Busy Service   A Web-based service that enables you to publish your schedule to a shared Internet location.

NetMeeting   A program that enables groups to teleconference using the Internet.

Netscape   A Web browser program.

newsgroup   A collection of messages related to a particular topic posted to a news server by individuals.

newsreader   A program that enables you to read messages posted to a newsgroup.

news server   A computer, in your organization or at your Internet service provider (ISP), which is set up specifically to host newsgroups.

notes   Outlook items that are the electronic equivalent of paper sticky notes.

offline folder   A folder that enables you to work with the contents of the folder when you are not connected to the network, and then update the folder and its corresponding server folder to make the contents of both identical.

Organizational Forms Library   A feature of Microsoft Exchange Server that enables you to publish forms and make them available to everyone in your organization.

Outlook Rich Text Format (RTF)   One format for Outlook e-mail messages that supports a host of formatting options including text formatting, bullets, numbering, background colors, borders, and shading. Rich Text Format is supported by some Microsoft e-mail clients, including Outlook 97 and Outlook 2000.

Out of Office Assistant   An Outlook feature that helps you manage your Inbox when you're out of the office. The Out of Office Assistant can respond to incoming messages automatically, and it enables you to create rules for managing incoming messages.

personal folders file   A data file in which Microsoft Outlook saves messages, appointments, tasks, and journal entries on your computer.

plain text   A format for Outlook e-mail addresses that does not support any text formatting but is supported by all e-mail programs.

print style   A combination of paper and page settings that determines the way items are printed. For most items, Outlook provides a set of built-in print styles, and you can create your own.

profile   A group of e-mail accounts and address books configured to work together in Outlook.

recurring   Describes items that occur repeatedly. For example, an appointment or task that occurs on a regular basis, such as a weekly status meeting or a monthly haircut, can be designated as recurring.

reminder   A message that appears at a specified interval before an appointment, meeting, or task, announcing when the activity is set to occur. Reminders appear any time Outlook is running, even if it isn't your active program.

Schedule+   A calendar and scheduling program.

script   A list of commands executed without user interaction.

security zone   A feature into which the Internet is divided so that you can assign a Web site to a zone with a suitable security level.

sensitivity   A security setting of an e-mail message that indicates whether a message should be treated as normal, personal, private, or confidential.

signature   Text and/or pictures that are automatically added to the end of an outgoing e-mail message.

stationery   A preset or automatic format for e-mail messages that specifies fonts, bullets, background color, horizontal lines, images, and other design elements.

subscribe   The process of selecting a newsgroup so that you can read and post messages.

task list   A list of tasks that appears in the Tasks folder and in the TaskPad in Calendar.

tasks   Personal or work-related activities that you want to track through completion.

TaskPad   The list of tasks that appears on the right side of the Outlook Calendar window.

theme   A set of unified design elements and color schemes used to automatically format e-mail messages. Themes offer more formatting options than stationery.

Uniform Resource Locator (URL)   Represents the address of Web pages and other resources available on the Internet.

vCard   A standard text-based format for storing contact information.

vCalendar   A standard text-based format for storing calendar appointment information.

view   A way to display messages and other information in a folder by using different arrangements and formats.

work week   The days you are available for work-related appointments and meetings each week. Outlook displays the days outside your selected work week as shaded, to indicate that you are normally not available on those days.

Index

M

About the Author

With more than five years of experience as a technical writer and information architect, Kristen Crupi brings her expertise in user assistance to *Microsoft Outlook Version 2002 Step by Step*. Kristen served as a technical resource on the Windows 95 Resource Kit team and contributed to the *Microsoft Excel 2000 Step by Step* courseware. Her background includes extensive online help and training development, and most recently, information architecture for Web-based applications.

The manuscript for this book was prepared and submitted to Microsoft Press in electronic form. Text files were prepared using Microsoft Word 2000. Pages were composed by Online Training Solutions, Inc. (OTSI) using Adobe FrameMaker+SGML 6.0, with text in Garamond and display type in Franklin Gothic.

Editing, production, and graphic services for this book were provided by OTSI. The hard-working project team included:

Project Editor:	Joyce Cox
Editorial Team:	Jan Bednarczuk
	Nancy Depper
Graphics & Production:	R.J. Cadranell
	Liz Clark

Contact OTSI at:

- E-mail: info@otsiweb.com
- Web site: *www.otsiweb.com*

Self-paced
training
that works
as hard as you do!

Information-packed STEP BY STEP courses are the most effective way to teach yourself how to complete tasks with Microsoft® Office XP. Numbered steps and scenario-based lessons with practice files on CD-ROM make it easy to find your way while learning tasks and procedures. Work through every lesson or choose your own starting point—with STEP BY STEP modular design and straightforward writing style, *you* drive the instruction. And the books are constructed with lay-flat binding so you can follow the text with both hands at the keyboard. Select STEP BY STEP titles also provide complete, cost-effective preparation for the Microsoft Office User Specialist (MOUS) credential. It's an excellent way for you or your organization to take a giant step toward workplace productivity.

- **Microsoft Office XP Step by Step**
  ISBN 0-7356-1294-3

- **Microsoft Word Version 2002 Step by Step**
  ISBN 0-7356-1295-1

- **Microsoft Excel Version 2002 Step by Step**
  ISBN 0-7356-1296-X

- **Microsoft PowerPoint® Version 2002 Step by Step**
  ISBN 0-7356-1297-8

- **Microsoft Outlook® Version 2002 Step by Step**
  ISBN 0-7356-1298-6

- **Microsoft FrontPage® Version 2002 Step by Step**
  ISBN 0-7356-1300-1

- **Microsoft Access Version 2002 Step by Step**
  ISBN 0-7356-1299-4

- **Microsoft Project Version 2002 Step by Step**
  ISBN 0-7356-1301-X

- **Microsoft Visio® Version 2002 Step by Step**
  ISBN 0-7356-1302-8

Microsoft Press® products are available worldwide wherever quality computer books are sold. For more information, contact your book or computer retailer, software reseller, or local Microsoft Sales Office, or visit our Web site at mspress.microsoft.com. To locate your nearest source for Microsoft Press products, or to order directly, call 1-800-MSPRESS in the United States. (in Canada, call 1-800-268-2222).

Prices and availability dates are subject to change.

mspress.microsoft.com

Target your
solution and fix it
yourself—fast!

Get a **Free**
e-mail newsletter, updates,
special offers, links to related books,
and more when you
register on line!

Register your Microsoft Press® title on our Web site and you'll get a FREE subscription to our e-mail newsletter, *Microsoft Press Book Connections.* You'll find out about newly released and upcoming books and learning tools, online events, software downloads, special offers and coupons for Microsoft Press customers, and information about major Microsoft® product releases. You can also read useful additional information about all the titles we publish, such as detailed book descriptions, tables of contents and indexes, sample chapters, links to related books and book series, author biographies, and reviews by other customers.

Registration is easy. Just visit this Web page and fill in your information:

http://mspress.microsoft.com/register

Microsoft®

- -

Proof of Purchase

Use this page as proof of purchase if participating in a promotion or rebate offer on this title. Proof of purchase must be used in conjunction with other proof(s) of payment such as your dated sales receipt—see offer details.

Microsoft® Outlook® Version 2002 Step by Step
0-7356-1298-6

CUSTOMER NAME

Microsoft Press, PO Box 97017, Redmond, WA 98073-9830

MICROSOFT LICENSE AGREEMENT

Book Companion CD

IMPORTANT—READ CAREFULLY: This Microsoft End-User License Agreement ("EULA") is a legal agreement between you (either an individual or an entity) and Microsoft Corporation for the Microsoft product identified above, which includes computer software and may include associated media, printed materials, and "online" or electronic documentation ("SOFTWARE PRODUCT"). Any component included within the SOFTWARE PRODUCT that is accompanied by a separate End-User License Agreement shall be governed by such agreement and not the terms set forth below. By installing, copying, or otherwise using the SOFTWARE PRODUCT, you agree to be bound by the terms of this EULA. If you do not agree to the terms of this EULA, you are not authorized to install, copy, or otherwise use the SOFTWARE PRODUCT; you may, however, return the SOFTWARE PRODUCT, along with all printed materials and other items that form a part of the Microsoft product that includes the SOFTWARE PRODUCT, to the place you obtained them for a full refund.

SOFTWARE PRODUCT LICENSE

The SOFTWARE PRODUCT is protected by United States copyright laws and international copyright treaties, as well as other intellectual property laws and treaties. The SOFTWARE PRODUCT is licensed, not sold.

1. **GRANT OF LICENSE.** This EULA grants you the following rights:

   a. **Software Product.** You may install and use one copy of the SOFTWARE PRODUCT on a single computer. The primary user of the computer on which the SOFTWARE PRODUCT is installed may make a second copy for his or her exclusive use on a portable computer.

   b. **Storage/Network Use.** You may also store or install a copy of the SOFTWARE PRODUCT on a storage device, such as a network server, used only to install or run the SOFTWARE PRODUCT on your other computers over an internal network; however, you must acquire and dedicate a license for each separate computer on which the SOFTWARE PRODUCT is installed or run from the storage device. A license for the SOFTWARE PRODUCT may not be shared or used concurrently on different computers.

   c. **License Pak.** If you have acquired this EULA in a Microsoft License Pak, you may make the number of additional copies of the computer software portion of the SOFTWARE PRODUCT authorized on the printed copy of this EULA, and you may use each copy in the manner specified above. You are also entitled to make a corresponding number of secondary copies for portable computer use as specified above.

   d. **Sample Code.** Solely with respect to portions, if any, of the SOFTWARE PRODUCT that are identified within the SOFTWARE PRODUCT as sample code (the "SAMPLE CODE"):

   i. **Use and Modification.** Microsoft grants you the right to use and modify the source code version of the SAMPLE CODE, *provided* you comply with subsection (d)(iii) below. You may not distribute the SAMPLE CODE, or any modified version of the SAMPLE CODE, in source code form.

   ii. **Redistributable Files.** Provided you comply with subsection (d)(iii) below, Microsoft grants you a nonexclusive, royalty-free right to reproduce and distribute the object code version of the SAMPLE CODE and of any modified SAMPLE CODE, other than SAMPLE CODE, or any modified version thereof, designated as not redistributable in the Readme file that forms a part of the SOFTWARE PRODUCT (the "Non-Redistributable Sample Code"). All SAMPLE CODE other than the Non-Redistributable Sample Code is collectively referred to as the "REDISTRIBUTABLES."

   iii. **Redistribution Requirements.** If you redistribute the REDISTRIBUTABLES, you agree to: (i) distribute the REDISTRIBUTABLES in object code form only in conjunction with and as a part of your software application product; (ii) not use Microsoft's name, logo, or trademarks to market your software application product; (iii) include a valid copyright notice on your software application product; (iv) indemnify, hold harmless, and defend Microsoft from and against any claims or lawsuits, including attorney's fees, that arise or result from the use or distribution of your software application product; and (v) not permit further distribution of the REDISTRIBUTABLES by your end user. Contact Microsoft for the applicable royalties due and other licensing terms for all other uses and/or distribution of the REDISTRIBUTABLES.

2. **DESCRIPTION OF OTHER RIGHTS AND LIMITATIONS.**

   • **Limitations on Reverse Engineering, Decompilation, and Disassembly.** You may not reverse engineer, decompile, or disassemble the SOFTWARE PRODUCT, except and only to the extent that such activity is expressly permitted by applicable law notwithstanding this limitation.

   • **Separation of Components.** The SOFTWARE PRODUCT is licensed as a single product. Its component parts may not be separated for use on more than one computer.

   • **Rental.** You may not rent, lease, or lend the SOFTWARE PRODUCT.

   • **Support Services.** Microsoft may, but is not obligated to, provide you with support services related to the SOFTWARE PRODUCT ("Support Services"). Use of Support Services is governed by the Microsoft policies and programs described in the user manual, in "online" documentation, and/or in other Microsoft-provided materials. Any supplemental software code provided to you as part of the Support Services shall be considered part of the SOFTWARE PRODUCT and subject to the terms and conditions of this EULA. With respect to technical information you provide to Microsoft as part of the Support Services, Microsoft may use such information for its business purposes, including for product support and development. Microsoft will not utilize such technical information in a form that personally identifies you.

- **Software Transfer.** You may permanently transfer all of your rights under this EULA, provided you retain no copies, you transfer all of the SOFTWARE PRODUCT (including all component parts, the media and printed materials, any upgrades, this EULA, and, if applicable, the Certificate of Authenticity), **and** the recipient agrees to the terms of this EULA.

- **Termination.** Without prejudice to any other rights, Microsoft may terminate this EULA if you fail to comply with the terms and conditions of this EULA. In such event, you must destroy all copies of the SOFTWARE PRODUCT and all of its component parts.

3. **COPYRIGHT.** All title and copyrights in and to the SOFTWARE PRODUCT (including but not limited to any images, photographs, animations, video, audio, music, text, SAMPLE CODE, REDISTRIBUTABLES, and "applets" incorporated into the SOFTWARE PRODUCT) and any copies of the SOFTWARE PRODUCT are owned by Microsoft or its suppliers. The SOFTWARE PRODUCT is protected by copyright laws and international treaty provisions. Therefore, you must treat the SOFTWARE PRODUCT like any other copyrighted material **except** that you may install the SOFTWARE PRODUCT on a single computer provided you keep the original solely for backup or archival purposes. You may not copy the printed materials accompanying the SOFTWARE PRODUCT.

4. **U.S. GOVERNMENT RESTRICTED RIGHTS.** The SOFTWARE PRODUCT and documentation are provided with RESTRICTED RIGHTS. Use, duplication, or disclosure by the Government is subject to restrictions as set forth in subparagraph (c)(1)(ii) of the Rights in Technical Data and Computer Software clause at DFARS 252.227-7013 or subparagraphs (c)(1) and (2) of the Commercial Computer Software—Restricted Rights at 48 CFR 52.227-19, as applicable. Manufacturer is Microsoft Corporation/One Microsoft Way/Redmond, WA 98052-6399.

5. **EXPORT RESTRICTIONS.** You agree that you will not export or re-export the SOFTWARE PRODUCT, any part thereof, or any process or service that is the direct product of the SOFTWARE PRODUCT (the foregoing collectively referred to as the "Restricted Components"), to any country, person, entity, or end user subject to U.S. export restrictions. You specifically agree not to export or re-export any of the Restricted Components (i) to any country to which the U.S. has embargoed or restricted the export of goods or services, which currently include, but are not necessarily limited to, Cuba, Iran, Iraq, Libya, North Korea, Sudan, and Syria, or to any national of any such country, wherever located, who intends to transmit or transport the Restricted Components back to such country; (ii) to any end user who you know or have reason to know will utilize the Restricted Components in the design, development, or production of nuclear, chemical, or biological weapons; or (iii) to any end user who has been prohibited from participating in U.S. export transactions by any federal agency of the U.S. government. You warrant and represent that neither the BXA nor any other U.S. federal agency has suspended, revoked, or denied your export privileges.

DISCLAIMER OF WARRANTY

NO WARRANTIES OR CONDITIONS. MICROSOFT EXPRESSLY DISCLAIMS ANY WARRANTY OR CONDITION FOR THE SOFTWARE PRODUCT. THE SOFTWARE PRODUCT AND ANY RELATED DOCUMENTATION ARE PROVIDED "AS IS" WITHOUT WARRANTY OR CONDITION OF ANY KIND, EITHER EXPRESS OR IMPLIED, INCLUDING, WITHOUT LIMITATION, THE IMPLIED WARRANTIES OF MERCHANTABILITY, FITNESS FOR A PARTICULAR PURPOSE, OR NONINFRINGEMENT. THE ENTIRE RISK ARISING OUT OF USE OR PERFORMANCE OF THE SOFTWARE PRODUCT REMAINS WITH YOU.

LIMITATION OF LIABILITY. TO THE MAXIMUM EXTENT PERMITTED BY APPLICABLE LAW, IN NO EVENT SHALL MICROSOFT OR ITS SUPPLIERS BE LIABLE FOR ANY SPECIAL, INCIDENTAL, INDIRECT, OR CONSEQUENTIAL DAMAGES WHATSOEVER (INCLUDING, WITHOUT LIMITATION, DAMAGES FOR LOSS OF BUSINESS PROFITS, BUSINESS INTERRUPTION, LOSS OF BUSINESS INFORMATION, OR ANY OTHER PECUNIARY LOSS) ARISING OUT OF THE USE OF OR INABILITY TO USE THE SOFTWARE PRODUCT OR THE PROVISION OF OR FAILURE TO PROVIDE SUPPORT SERVICES, EVEN IF MICROSOFT HAS BEEN ADVISED OF THE POSSIBILITY OF SUCH DAMAGES. IN ANY CASE, MICROSOFT'S ENTIRE LIABILITY UNDER ANY PROVISION OF THIS EULA SHALL BE LIMITED TO THE GREATER OF THE AMOUNT ACTUALLY PAID BY YOU FOR THE SOFTWARE PRODUCT OR US$5.00; PROVIDED, HOWEVER, IF YOU HAVE ENTERED INTO A MICROSOFT SUPPORT SERVICES AGREEMENT, MICROSOFT'S ENTIRE LIABILITY REGARDING SUPPORT SERVICES SHALL BE GOVERNED BY THE TERMS OF THAT AGREEMENT. BECAUSE SOME STATES AND JURISDICTIONS DO NOT ALLOW THE EXCLUSION OR LIMITATION OF LIABILITY, THE ABOVE LIMITATION MAY NOT APPLY TO YOU.

MISCELLANEOUS

This EULA is governed by the laws of the State of Washington USA, except and only to the extent that applicable law mandates governing law of a different jurisdiction.

Should you have any questions concerning this EULA, or if you desire to contact Microsoft for any reason, please contact the Microsoft subsidiary serving your country, or write: Microsoft Sales Information Center/One Microsoft Way/Redmond, WA 98052-6399.

New Features in Outlook 2002

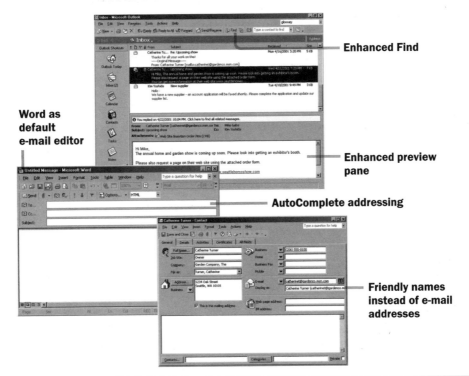

Enhanced Find

Word as default e-mail editor

Enhanced preview pane

AutoComplete addressing

Friendly names instead of e-mail addresses

Common Keyboard Shortcuts

Ctrl + Shift + A	Create a new appointment
Ctrl + Shift + C	Create a new contact
Ctrl + Shift + Q	Create a new meeting request
Ctrl + Shift + M	Create a new message
Ctrl + D	Delete the selected item
Ctrl + P	Print the selected item
Alt + K	Check names with Word as the e-mail editor
Ctrl + K	Check names with Outlook as the e-mail editor
Ctrl + R	Reply to a message
Ctrl + Shift + R	Reply all to a message
Ctrl + M or F5	Check for new messages
Ctrl + Shift + B	Display the Address Book
Ctrl + Q	Mark a message as read
Alt + C	Accept a meeting or task request
Alt + D	Decline a meeting or task request

To add an entry to the Address Book

1 On the **Tools** menu, click **Address Book**.
2 In the **Show Names from the** list, select the address book you want, and then click the **New Entry** button.

To create a distribution list

1 On the **Tools** menu, click **Address Book**.
2 Select the address book you want, click the **New Entry** button, and then select **Distribution List**.

To attach a file to a message

1 Create a new message, and on the toolbar, click the **Insert File** button.
2 In the **Insert File** dialog box, browse to the file that you want to attach, click that file, and then click the **Insert** button.

To filter junk or adult content messages

1 On the toolbar, click the **Organize** button
2 In the **Ways to Organize Inbox** pane, click **Junk E-mail**.
3 Select whether you want to move or color the unwanted messages, select the color or the location to which you want the messages moved, and click the **Turn On** button.

To create a folder

1 On the **File** menu, click **New**, and then click **Folder**.
2 In the **Create New Folder** dialog box, type the name of the folder, and in the **Folder contains** list, click the kind of items you want to store in the folder.
3 In the **Select where to place the folder** list, click a location for the folder, and then click **OK**.

To find messages

1 On the toolbar, click the **Find** button.
2 In the **Look for** box in the **Find** pane, type a word that you know is in the message you are looking for.
3 Click the **Find Now** button.

To schedule an appointment

1 In the Calendar, double-click the time slot in the day you want to schedule the appointment.
2 In the Appointment form, enter the relevant information about the appointment, and click the **Save and Close** button.

To delete an appointment

1 Click the appointment you want to delete.
2 On the toolbar, click the **Delete** button.

To plan a meeting

● On the **Actions** menu, click **Plan a Meeting**. Click the **Add Others** button to add other attendees from your address book, and then click the **Make Meeting** button.

To send form letters using Contacts

1 Display the Contacts folder, and on the **Tools** menu, click **Mail Merge**.
2 In the **Document file** area, select the document you want to use, and then click **OK**.
3 On the **Tools** menu, point to **Letters and Mailings**, and then click **Mail Merge Wizard**. Follow the rest of the instructions in the wizard.

To share a folder

1 In the **Folder List**, right-click the folder, click **Properties**, and then click the **Permissions** tab.
2 Click the **Add** button, and in the **Type Name or Select from List** box, type the name of the person you want to share your folder with.
3 Click the **Add** button, and then click **OK**.

To save your calendar as a Web page

1 Display the Calendar, and on the **File** menu, click **Save as Web Page**.
2 Select the dates that you want to be published, type the title you want, and click the **Save** button.

To set up a dial-up connection

1 On the **Tools** menu, click **E-mail Accounts**. Select the **View or change existing e-mail accounts** option, and click **Next**.
2 Click your e-mail account in the list, click the **Change** button, and then click the **More Settings** button.
3 Click the **Connection** tab, click the **Connect using my phone line** option, and then click the **Add** button.
4 Type a name for your connection, click the name of your modem in the **Select a device** box, and then click **Next**.
5 Type the telephone number, click **Next**, and then click **Finish**.